Alice Walker won the Pulitzer Prize and the American Book Award for her novel *The Color Purple*. Her other bestselling novels include *By the Light of My Father's Smile*, *Possessing the Secret of Joy* and *The Temple of My Familiar*. She is also the author of several collections of short stories, essays and poetry, as well as children's books. Her books have been translated into more than two dozen languages. Born in Eatonton, Georgia, Alice Walker now lives in northern California.

In Search of Our Mothers' Gardens

WOMANIST PROSE

ALICE WALKER

PHOENIX

A PHOENIX PAPERBACK

First published in the United States of America in 1983
by Harcourt Brace Jovanovich, Inc.
First published in Great Britain in 1984
by The Women's Press
This paperback edition published in 2005
by Phoenix,
an imprint of Orion Books Ltd,
Orion House, 5 Upper St Martin's Lane,
London WC2H 9EA

1 3 5 7 9 10 8 6 4 2

A CIP catalogue record for this book
is available from the British Library.

ISBN 0 75381 960 0

Printed and bound in Great Britain
by Clays Ltd, St Ives plc

Womanist 1. From *womanish.* (Opp. of "girlish," i.e., frivolous, irresponsible, not serious.) A black feminist or feminist of color. From the black folk expression of mothers to female children, "You acting womanish," i.e., like a woman. Usually referring to outrageous, audacious, courageous or *willful* behavior. Wanting to know more and in greater depth than is considered "good" for one. Interested in grown-up doings. Acting grown up. Being grown up. Interchangeable with another black folk expression: "You trying to be grown." Responsible. In charge. *Serious.*

. . .

2. *Also:* A woman who loves other women, sexually and/or nonsexually. Appreciates and prefers women's culture, women's emotional flexibility (values tears as natural counterbalance of laughter), and women's strength. Sometimes loves individual men, sexually and/or nonsexually. Committed to survival and wholeness of entire people, male *and* female. Not a separatist, except periodically, for health. Traditionally universalist, as in: "Mama, why are we brown, pink, and yellow, and our cousins are white, beige, and black?" Ans.: "Well, you know the colored race is just like a flower garden, with every color flower represented." Traditionally capable, as in: "Mama, I'm walking to Canada and I'm taking you and a bunch of other slaves with me." Reply: "It wouldn't be the first time."

. . .

3. Loves music. Loves dance. Loves the moon. *Loves* the Spirit. Loves love and food and roundness. Loves struggle. *Loves* the Folk. Loves herself. *Regardless.*

.   .   .

4. Womanist is to feminist as purple to lavender.

CONTENTS

Contents

Contents

.   .   .   .

PART   FOUR

ACKNOWLEDGMENTS

.   .   .   .

The essays, articles, reviews, and statements in this collection were written between 1966 and 1982. For her early reading of some of them and discussing her thoughts about them with me, I thank my friend June Jordan. For gathering them together and insisting I publish them as soon as possible (five years ago), I thank my friend Susan Kirschner. For her help in reading the essays and suggesting an order for them (other than the one in which they now appear), I thank Elizabeth Phillips. For creating the order in which they do appear, I thank my editor, John Ferrone. For his way of making the creation of a writing space for me the first priority wherever we lived, I thank my former husband and friend, Mel Leventhal. And for her help in gluing me to Life, present and future, I thank our daughter, Rebecca Leventhal. For their active pride in me when I was a child (which translated into quarters and dollars and from Miss Bessie an old velvet-covered Victrola), I thank the good "ladies" of the church, to whom I would still turn in looking for justice. And for the three magic gifts I needed to escape the poverty of my hometown, I thank my mother, who gave me a sewing machine, a typewriter, and a suitcase, all on less than twenty dollars a week. My father's gifts, for which I deeply thank him, are daily surprises: my love of naturalness, the tone of my voice, my very face, eyes, and hair. For his expressed pleasure in sharing adventures and making me happy ("hitting the road with just our music and our lunch money"), I thank my much cherished companion, Robert Allen.

In my development as a human being and as a writer I have been, it seems to me, extremely blessed, even while complaining. Wherever I have knocked, a door has opened. Wherever I have wandered, a path has appeared. I have been helped, supported, encouraged, and nurtured by people of all races, creeds, colors, and dreams; and I have, to the best of my ability, returned help, support, encouragement, and nurture. This receiving, returning, or passing on has been one of the most amazing, joyous, and continuous experiences of my life.

PART ONE

I come out of a tradition where those things are valued; where you talk about a woman with big legs and big hips and black skin. I come out of a black community where it was all right to have hips and to be heavy. You didn't feel that people didn't like you. The values that [imply] you must be skinny come from another culture. . . . Those are not the values that I was given by the women who served as my models. I refuse to be judged by the values of another culture. I am a black woman, and I will stand as best I can in that imagery.

—Bernice Reagon,
BLACK WOMEN AND LIBERATION MOVEMENTS

SAVING THE LIFE THAT IS YOUR OWN:

THE IMPORTANCE OF MODELS

IN THE ARTIST'S LIFE

There is a letter Vincent Van Gogh wrote to Emile Bernard that is very meaningful to me. A year before he wrote the letter, Van Gogh had had a fight with his domineering friend Gauguin, left his company, and cut off, in desperation and anguish, his own ear. The letter was written in Saint-Remy, in the South of France, from a mental institution to which Van Gogh had voluntarily committed himself.

I imagine Van Gogh sitting at a rough desk too small for him, looking out at the lovely Southern light, and occasionally glancing critically next to him at his own paintings of the land-scape he loved so much. The date of the letter is December 1889. Van Gogh wrote:

However hateful painting may be, and however cumber-some in the times we are living in, if anyone who has chosen this handicraft pursues it zealously, he is a man of duty, sound and faithful.

Society makes our existence wretchedly difficult at times, hence our impotence and the imperfection of our work.

. . . I myself am suffering under an absolute lack of models.

But on the other hand, there are beautiful spots here. I have just done five size 30 canvasses, olive trees. And the reason I am staying on here is that my health is improving a great deal.

What I am doing is hard, dry, but that is because I am trying to gather new strength by doing some rough work, and I'm afraid abstractions would make me soft.

Six months later, Van Gogh—whose health was "improving a great deal"—committed suicide. He had sold one painting during his lifetime. Three times was his work noticed in the press. But these are just details.

The real Vincent Van Gogh is the man who has "just done five size 30 canvasses, olive trees." To me, in context, one of the most moving and revealing descriptions of how a real artist thinks. And the knowledge that when he spoke of "suffering under an absolute lack of models" he spoke of that lack in terms of both the intensity of his commitment and the quality and singularity of his work, which was frequently ridiculed in his day.

The absence of models, in literature as in life, to say nothing of painting, is an occupational hazard for the artist, simply because models in art, in behavior, in growth of spirit and intellect—even if rejected—enrich and enlarge one's view of existence. Deadlier still, to the artist who lacks models, is the curse of ridicule, the bringing to bear on an artist's best work, especially his or her most original, most strikingly deviant, only a fund of ignorance and the presumption that, as an artist's critic, one's judgment is free of the restrictions imposed by prejudice, and is well informed, indeed, about all the art in the world that really matters.

What is always needed in the appreciation of art, or life, is the larger perspective. Connections made, or at least attempted, where none existed before, the straining to encompass in one's glance at the varied world the common thread, the unifying theme through immense diversity, a fearlessness of growth, of search, of looking, that enlarges the private and the public world. And yet, in our particular society, it is the narrowed and narrowing view of life that often wins.

Recently, I read at a college and was asked by one of the audience what I considered the major difference between the literature written by black and by white Americans. I had not spent a lot of time considering this question, since it is not the difference between them that interests me, but, rather, the way black writers and white writers seem to me to be writing one immense story—the same story, for the most part—with different parts of this immense story coming from a multitude of different perspectives. Until this is generally recognized, literature will always be broken into bits, black and white, and there will always be questions, wanting neat answers, such as this.

Still, I answered that I thought, for the most part, white American writers tended to end their books and their characters' lives as if there were no better existence for which to struggle. The gloom of defeat is thick.

By comparison, black writers seem always involved in a moral and/or physical struggle, the result of which is expected to be some kind of larger freedom. Perhaps this is because our literary tradition is based on the slave narratives, where escape for the body and freedom for the soul went together, or perhaps this is because black people have never felt themselves guilty of global, cosmic sins.

This comparison does not hold up in every case, of course, and perhaps does not really hold up at all. I am not a gatherer of statistics, only a curious reader, and this has been my impression from reading many books by black and white writers.

There are, however, two books by American women that illustrate what I am talking about: *The Awakening*, by Kate Chopin, and *Their Eyes Were Watching God*, by Zora Neale Hurston.

The plight of Mme Pontellier is quite similar to that of Janie Crawford. Each woman is married to a dull, society-conscious husband and living in a dull, propriety-conscious community. Each woman desires a life of her own and a man who loves her and makes her feel alive. Each woman finds such a man.

Mme Pontellier, overcome by the strictures of society and the existence of her children (along with the cowardice of her lover), kills herself rather than defy the one and abandon the other. Janie Crawford, on the other hand, refuses to allow society to dictate behavior to her, enjoys the love of a much younger, freedom-loving man, and lives to tell others of her experience.

When I mentioned these two books to my audience, I was not surprised to learn that only one person, a young black poet in the first row, had ever heard of *Their Eyes Were Watching God* (*The Awakening* they had fortunately read in their "Women in Literature" class), primarily because it was written by a black woman, whose experience—in love and life—was apparently assumed to be unimportant to the students (and the teachers) of a predominantly white school.

Certainly, as a student, I was not directed toward this book, which would have urged me more toward freedom and experience than toward comfort and security, but was directed instead toward a plethora of books by mainly white male writers who thought most women worthless if they didn't enjoy bullfighting or hadn't volunteered for the trenches in World War I.

Loving both these books, knowing each to be indispensable to my own growth, my own life, I choose the model, the example, of Janie Crawford. And yet this book, as necessary to me and to other women as air and water, is again out of print.* But I have distilled as much as I could of its wisdom in this poem about its heroine, Janie Crawford:

> I love the way Janie Crawford
> left her husbands
> the one who wanted to change her
> into a mule
> and the other who tried to interest her
> in being a queen.
> A woman, unless she submits,
> is neither a mule
> nor a queen
> though like a mule she may suffer
> and like a queen pace the floor.

It has been said that someone asked Toni Morrison why she writes the kind of books she writes, and that she replied: Because they are the kind of books I want to read.

This remains my favorite reply to that kind of question. As if anyone reading the magnificent, mysterious *Sula* or the grim, poetic *The Bluest Eye* would require more of a reason for their existence than for the brooding, haunting *Wuthering Heights*, for example, or the melancholy, triumphant *Jane Eyre*. (I am not speaking here of the most famous short line of that book, "Reader, I married him," as the triumph, but, rather, of the triumph of Jane Eyre's control over her own sense of morality

*Reissued by the University of Illinois Press, 1979.

and her own stout will, which are but reflections of her creator's, Charlotte Brontë, who no doubt wished to write the sort of book *she* wished to read.)

Flannery O'Connor has written that more and more the serious novelist will write, not what other people want, and certainly not what other people expect, but whatever interests her or him. And that the direction taken, therefore, will be away from sociology, away from the "writing of explanation," of statistics, and further into mystery, into poetry, and into prophecy. I believe this is true, *fortunately true;* especially for "Third World Writers"; Morrison, Marquez, Ahmadi, Camara Laye make good examples. And not only do I believe it is true for serious writers in general, but I believe, as firmly as did O'Connor, that this is our only hope—in a culture so in love with flash, with trendiness, with superficiality, as ours—of acquiring a sense of essence, of timelessness, and of vision. Therefore, to write the books one wants to read is both to point the direction of vision and, at the same time, to follow it.

When Toni Morrison said she writes the kind of books she wants to read, she was acknowledging the fact that in a society in which "accepted literature" is so often sexist and racist and otherwise irrelevant or offensive to so many lives, she must do the work of two. She must be her own model as well as the artist attending, creating, learning from, realizing the model, which is to say, herself.

(It should be remembered that, as a black person, one cannot completely identify with a Jane Eyre, or with her creator, no matter how much one admires them. And certainly, if one allows history to impinge on one's reading pleasure, one must cringe at the thought of how Heathcliff, in the New World far from Wuthering Heights, amassed his Cathy-dazzling fortune.)

·   ·   ·

I have often been asked why, in my own life and work, I have felt such a desperate need to know and assimilate the experiences of earlier black women writers, most of them unheard of by you and by me, until quite recently; why I felt a need to study them and to teach them.

I don't recall the exact moment I set out to explore the works of black women, mainly those in the past, and certainly, in the beginning, I had no desire to teach them. Teaching being for me, at that time, less rewarding than star-gazing on a frigid night. My discovery of them—most of them out of print, abandoned, discredited, maligned, nearly lost—came about, as many things of value do, almost by accident. As it turned out—and this should not have surprised me—I found I was in need of something that only one of them could provide.

Mindful that throughout my four years at a prestigious black and then a prestigious white college I had heard not one word about early black women writers, one of my first tasks was simply to determine whether they had existed. After this, I could breathe easier, with more assurance about the profession I myself had chosen.

But the incident that started my search began several years ago: I sat down at my desk one day, in a room of my own, with key and lock, and began preparations for a story about voodoo, a subject that had always fascinated me. Many of the elements of this story I had gathered from a story my mother several times told me. She had gone, during the Depression, into town to apply for some government surplus food at the local commissary, and had been turned down, in a particularly humiliating way, by the white woman in charge.

My mother always told this story with a most curious expression on her face. She automatically raised her head higher than ever—it was always high—and there was a look of righteousness, a kind of holy *heat* coming from her eyes. She said she had lived to see this same white woman grow old and senile and so badly crippled she had to get about on *two* sticks.

To her, this was clearly the working of God, who, as in the old spiritual, ". . . may not come when you want him, but he's right on time!" To me, hearing the story for about the fiftieth time, something else was discernible: the possibilities of the story, for fiction.

What, I asked myself, would have happened if, after the crippled old lady died, it was discovered that someone, my mother perhaps (who would have been mortified at the thought, Christian that she is), had voodooed her?

Then, my thoughts sweeping me away into the world of hexes and conjurings of centuries past, I wondered how a larger story could be created out of my mother's story; one that would be true to the magnitude of her humiliation and grief, and to the white woman's lack of sensitivity and compassion.

My third quandary was: How could I find out all I needed to know in order to write a story that used *authentic* black witchcraft?

Which brings me back, almost, to the day I became really interested in black women writers. I say "almost" because one other thing, from my childhood, made the choice of black magic a logical and irresistible one for my story. Aside from my mother's several stories about root doctors she had heard of or known, there was the story I had often heard about my "crazy" Walker aunt.

Many years ago, when my aunt was a meek and obedient girl growing up in a strict, conventionally religious house in the rural South, she had suddenly thrown off her meekness and had run away from home, escorted by a rogue of a man permanently attached elsewhere.

When she was returned home by her father, she was declared quite mad. In the backwoods South at the turn of the century, "madness" of this sort was cured not by psychiatry but by powders and by spells. (One can see Scott Joplin's *Treemonisha* to understand the role voodoo played among black people of that period.) My aunt's madness was treated by the community conjurer, who promised, and delivered, the desired results. His treatment was a bag of white powder, bought for fifty cents, and sprinkled on the ground around her house, with some of it sewed, I believe, into the bodice of her nightgown.

So when I sat down to write my story about voodoo, my crazy Walker aunt was definitely on my mind.

But she had experienced her temporary craziness so long ago that her story had all the excitement of a might-have-been. I needed, instead of family memories, some hard facts about the *craft* of voodoo, as practiced by Southern blacks in the nineteenth century. (It never once, fortunately, occurred to me that voodoo was not worthy of the interest I had in it, or was too ridiculous to study seriously.)

I began reading all I could find on the subject of "The Negro and His Folkways and Superstitions." There were Botkin and Puckett and others, all white, most racist. How was I to believe anything they wrote, since at least one of them, Puckett, was capable of wondering, in his book, if "The Negro" had a large enough brain?

Well, I thought, where are the *black* collectors of folklore? Where is the *black* anthropologist? Where is the *black* person who took the time to travel the back roads of the South and collect the information I need: how to cure heart trouble, treat dropsy, hex somebody to death, lock bowels, cause joints to swell, eyes to fall out, and so on. Where was this black person?

And that is when I first saw, in a *footnote* to the white voices of authority, the name Zora Neale Hurston.

Folklorist, novelist, anthropologist, serious student of voodoo, also all-around black woman, with guts enough to take a slide rule and measure random black heads in Harlem; not to prove their inferiority, but to prove that whatever their size, shape, or present condition of servitude, those heads contained all the intelligence anyone could use to get through this world.

Zora Hurston, who went to Barnard to learn how to study what she really wanted to learn: the ways of her own people, and what ancient rituals, customs, and beliefs had made them unique.

Zora, of the sandy-colored hair and the daredevil eyes, a girl who escaped poverty and parental neglect by hard work and a sharp eye for the main chance.

Zora, who left the South only to return to look at it again. Who went to root doctors from Florida to Louisiana and said, "Here I am. I want to learn your trade."

Zora, who had collected all the black folklore I could ever use.

That Zora.

And having found *that Zora* (like a golden key to a storehouse of varied treasure), I was hooked.

What I had discovered, of course, was a model. A model, who, as it happened, provided more than voodoo for my story, more than one of the greatest novels America had produced—though, being America, it did not realize this. She had provided, as if she knew someday I would come along wandering in the wilderness, a nearly complete record of her life. And though her life sprouted an occasional wart, I am eternally grateful for that life, warts and all.

It is not irrelevant, nor is it bragging (except perhaps to gloat a little on the happy relatedness of Zora, my mother, and me), to mention here that the story I wrote, called "The Revenge of Hannah Kemhuff," based on my mother's experiences during the Depression, and on Zora Hurston's folklore collection of the 1920s, and on my own response to both out of a contemporary existence, was immediately published and was later selected, by a reputable collector of short stories, as one of the *Best Short Stories of 1974.*

I mention it because this story might never have been written, because the very bases of its structure, authentic black folklore, viewed from a black perspective, might have been lost.

Had it been lost, my mother's story would have had no historical underpinning, none I could trust, anyway. I would not have written the story, which I enjoyed writing as much as I've enjoyed writing anything in my life, had I not known that Zora had already done a thorough job of preparing the ground over which I was then moving.

In that story I gathered up the historical and psychological threads of the life my ancestors lived, and in the writing of it I felt joy and strength and my own continuity. I had that wonderful feeling writers get sometimes, not very often, of being *with* a great many people, ancient spirits, all very happy to see me consulting and acknowledging them, and eager to let me know, through the joy of their presence, that, indeed, I am not alone.

To take Toni Morrison's statement further, if that is possible, in my own work I write not only what I want to read—understanding fully and indelibly that if I don't do it no one else is so vitally interested, or capable of doing it to my satisfaction —I write all the things *I should have been able to read.* Consulting, as belatedly discovered models, those writers—most of whom, not surprisingly, are women—who understood that their experience as ordinary human beings was also valuable, and in danger of being misrepresented, distorted, or lost:

Zora Hurston—novelist, essayist, anthropologist, autobiographer;

Jean Toomer—novelist, poet, philosopher, visionary, a man who cared what women felt;

Colette—whose crinkly hair enhances her French, part-black face; novelist, playwright, dancer, essayist, newspaper-woman, lover of women, men, small dogs; fortunate not to have been born in America;

Anaïs Nin—recorder of everything, no matter how minute;

Tillie Olson—a writer of such generosity and honesty, she literally saves lives;

Virginia Woolf—who has saved so many of us.

It is, in the end, the saving of lives that we writers are about. Whether we are "minority" writers or "majority." It is simply in our power to do this.

We do it because we care. We care that Vincent Van Gogh mutilated his ear. We care that behind a pile of manure in the yard he destroyed his life. We care that Scott Joplin's music *lives!* We care because we know this: *the life we save is our own.*

1976

THE BLACK WRITER AND THE
SOUTHERN EXPERIENCE

My mother tells of an incident that happened to her in the thirties during the Depression. She and my father lived in a small Georgia town and had half a dozen children. They were sharecroppers, and food, especially flour, was almost impossible to obtain. To get flour, which was distributed by the Red Cross, one had to submit vouchers signed by a local official. On the day my mother was to go into town for flour she received a large box of clothes from one of my aunts who was living in the North. The clothes were in good condition, though well worn, and my mother needed a dress, so she immediately put on one of those from the box and wore it into town. When she reached the distribution center and presented her voucher she was confronted by a white woman who looked her up and down with marked anger and envy.

"What'd you come up here for?" the woman asked.

"For some flour," said my mother, presenting her voucher.

"Humph," said the woman, looking at her more closely and with unconcealed fury. "Anybody dressed up as good as you don't need to come here *begging* for food."

"I ain't begging," said my mother; "the government is giving away flour to those that need it, and I need it. I wouldn't be here if I didn't. And these clothes I'm wearing was given to me." But the woman had already turned to the next person in line, saying over her shoulder to the white man who was behind the counter with her, "The *gall* of niggers coming in here dressed better than me!" This thought seemed to make her angrier still, and my mother, pulling three of her small children behind her and crying from humiliation, walked sadly back into the street.

"What did you and Daddy do for flour that winter?" I asked my mother.

"Well," she said, "Aunt Mandy Aikens lived down the road from us and she got plenty of flour. We had a good stand of corn so we had plenty of meal. Aunt Mandy would swap me a bucket of flour for a bucket of meal. We got by all right."

Then she added thoughtfully, "And that old woman that turned me off so short got down so bad in the end that she was walking on *two* sticks." And I knew she was thinking, though she never said it: Here I am today, my eight children healthy and grown and three of them in college and me with hardly a sick day for years. Ain't Jesus wonderful?

In this small story is revealed the condition and strength of a people. Outcasts to be used and humiliated by the larger society, the Southern black sharecropper and poor farmer clung to his own kind and to a religion that had been given to pacify him as a slave but which he soon transformed into an antidote against bitterness. Depending on one another, because they had nothing and no one else, the sharecroppers often managed to come through "all right." And when I listen to my mother tell and retell this story I find that the white woman's vindictiveness is less important than Aunt Mandy's resourceful generosity or my mother's ready stand of corn. For their lives were not about that pitiful example of Southern womanhood, but about themselves.

What the black Southern writer inherits as a natural right is a sense of *community*. Something simple but surprisingly hard, especially these days, to come by. My mother, who is a walking history of our community, tells me that when each of her children was born the midwife accepted as payment such home-grown or homemade items as a pig, a quilt, jars of canned fruits and vegetables. But there was never any question that the midwife would come when she was needed, whatever the eventual payment for her services. I consider this each time I hear of a hospital that refuses to admit a woman in labor unless she can hand over a substantial sum of money, cash.

Nor am I nostalgic, as a French philosopher once wrote, for lost poverty. I am nostalgic for the solidarity and sharing a modest existence can sometimes bring. We knew, I suppose, that we were poor. Somebody knew; perhaps the landowner who grudgingly paid my father three hundred dollars a year for twelve months' labor. But we never considered ourselves to be poor, unless, of course, we were deliberately humiliated. And because we never believed we were poor, and therefore worthless, we could depend on one another without shame. And always there were the Burial Societies, the Sick-and-Shut-in Societies, that sprang up out of spontaneous need. And no one seemed terribly upset that black sharecroppers were ignored by white insurance companies. It went without saying, in my mother's day, that birth and death required assistance from the community, and that the magnitude of these events was lost on outsiders.

As a college student I came to reject the Christianity of my parents, and it took me years to realize that though they had been force-fed a white man's palliative, in the form of religion, they had made it into something at once simple and noble. True, even today, they can never successfully picture a God who is not white, and that is a major cruelty, but their lives testify to a greater comprehension of the teachings of Jesus than the lives of people who sincerely believe a God *must* have a color and that there can be such a phenomenon as a "white" church.

The richness of the black writer's experience in the South can be remarkable, though some people might not think so. Once, while in college, I told a white middle-aged Northerner that I hoped to be a poet. In the nicest possible language, which still made me as mad as I've ever been, he suggested that a "farmer's daughter" might not be the stuff of which poets are made. On one level, of course, he had a point. A shack with only a dozen or so books is an unlikely place to discover a young Keats. But it is narrow thinking, indeed, to believe that a Keats is the only kind of poet one would want to grow up to be. One wants to write poetry that is understood by one's people, not by the Queen of England. Of course, should she be able to profit by it too, so much the better, but since that is not likely, catering to her tastes would be a waste of time.

For the black Southern writer, coming straight out of the country, as Wright did—Natchez and Jackson are still not as citified as they like to think they are—there is the world of comparisons; between town and country, between the ugly crowding and griminess of the cities and the spacious cleanliness (which actually seems impossible to dirty) of the country. A country person finds the city confining, like a too tight dress. And always, in one's memory, there remain all the rituals of one's growing up: the warmth and vividness of Sunday worship (never mind that you never quite believed) in a little church hidden from the road, and houses set so far back into the woods that at night it is impossible for strangers to find them. The daily dramas that evolve in such a private world are pure gold. But this view of a strictly private and hidden existence, with its triumphs, failures, grotesqueries, is not nearly as valuable to the socially conscious black Southern writer as his double vision is. For not only is he in a position to see his own world, and its close community ("Homecomings" on First Sundays, barbecues to raise money to send to Africa—one of the smaller ironies—the simplicity and eerie calm of a black funeral, where the beloved one is buried way in the middle of a wood with nothing to mark the spot but perhaps a wooden cross already coming apart), but also he is capable of knowing, with remarkably silent accuracy, the people who make up the larger world that surrounds and suppresses his own.

It is a credit to a writer like Ernest J. Gaines, a black writer who writes mainly about the people he grew up with in rural Louisiana, that he can write about whites and blacks exactly as he sees them and *knows* them, instead of writing of one group as a vast malignant lump and of the other as a conglomerate of perfect virtues.

In large measure, black Southern writers owe their clarity of vision to parents who refused to diminish themselves as human beings by succumbing to racism. Our parents seemed to know that an extreme negative emotion held against other human beings for reasons they do not control can be blinding. Blindness about other human beings, especially for a writer, is equivalent to death. Because of this blindness, which is, above all, racial, the works of many Southern writers have died. Much that we read today is fast expiring.

My own slight attachment to William Faulkner was rudely broken by realizing, after reading statements he made in *Faulkner in the University*, that he believed whites superior morally to blacks; that whites had a duty (which at their convenience they would assume) to "bring blacks along" politically, since blacks, in Faulkner's opinion, were "not ready" yet to function properly in a democratic society. He also thought that a black man's intelligence is directly related to the amount of white blood he has.

For the black person coming of age in the sixties, where Martin Luther King stands against the murderers of Goodman, Chaney, and Schwerner, there appears no basis for such assumptions. Nor was there any in Garvey's day, or in Du Bois's or in Douglass's or in Nat Turner's. Nor at any other period in our history, from the very founding of the country; for it was hardly incumbent upon slaves to be slaves and saints too. Unlike Tolstoy, Faulkner was not prepared to struggle to change the structure of the society he was born in. One might concede that in his fiction he did seek to examine the reasons for its decay, but unfortunately, as I have learned while trying to teach Faulkner to black students, it is not possible, from so short a range, to separate the man from his works.

One reads Faulkner knowing that his "colored" people had to come through "Mr. William's" back door, and one feels uneasy, and finally enraged that Faulkner did not burn the whole house down. When the provincial mind starts out *and continues* on a narrow and unprotesting course, "genius" itself must run on a track.

Flannery O'Connor at least had the conviction that "reality" is at best superficial and that the puzzle of humanity is less easy to solve than that of race. But Miss O'Connor was not so much of Georgia, as in it. The majority of Southern writers have been too confined by prevailing social customs to probe deeply into mysteries that the Citizens Councils insist must never be revealed.

Perhaps my Northern brothers will not believe me when I say there is a great deal of positive material I can draw from my "underprivileged" background. But they have never lived, as I have, at the end of a long road in a house that was faced by the edge of the world on one side and nobody for miles on the other. They have never experienced the magnificent quiet of a summer day when the heat is intense and one is so very thirsty, as one moves across the dusty cotton fields, that one learns forever that water is the essence of all life. In the cities it cannot be so clear to one that he is a creature of the earth, feeling the soil between the toes, smelling the dust thrown up by the rain, loving the earth so much that one longs to taste it and sometimes does.

Nor do I intend to romanticize the Southern black country life. I can recall that I hated it, generally. The hard work in the fields, the shabby houses, the evil greedy men who worked my father to death and almost broke the courage of that strong woman, my mother. No, I am simply saying that Southern black writers, like most writers, have a heritage of love and hate, but that they also have enormous richness and beauty to draw from. And, having been placed, as Camus says, "halfway between misery and the sun," they, too, know that "though all is not well under the sun, history is not everything."

No one could wish for a more advantageous heritage than that bequeathed to the black writer in the South: a compassion for the earth, a trust in humanity beyond our knowledge of evil, and an abiding love of justice. We inherit a great responsibility as well, for we must give voice to centuries not only of silent bitterness and hate but also of neighborly kindness and sustaining love.

1970

. . . .

"BUT YET AND STILL THE COTTON GIN

KEEP ON WORKING . . ."

Dear Kind Friend:

I am writing on this occasion because they tell me you teach the teachers at the new Headstart Friends of the Children of Mississippi and want to know all about us, or as much as we can think to tell. I myself think FCM is a good thing for the Negro children. I have three grandchildren attending myself.

Well, you know all over the state of Mississippi we have had a hard time and it doesn't seem to be getting any better, but, if you all say so, through the Lord, we may conquer later. I am praying to the Lord that it will be better in the future because it seem just like we haven't done any good yet.

I have to say that we are in a mean world down here in Amite County. It makes me say like Jose, the Lord giveth and the Lord taketh, so blesseth be the Lord.

I am B.E.F. When I was seventeen, the white folks was wanted to take me away from my mother because I was a good worker, but she didn't agree to it because my father was dead, and no one there but my mother and I. They wanted me to run off from home and work for them. Because I didn't they arrested me claiming that I stole a cow. But no alterdavis was made out against me. They arrested me May 20, 1910 and kept me in jail until October. They sentenced me October 26, to the prison for five years and then I was back home in 1914 when I got married. I have seen some bad things done in Amite, such as a man whose name was Issac Simond who had gone to Jackson and redeemed his land of taxes and got title for him and his father and the white folks wanted to buy his timber and he wouldn't seel it to them. They went to his home one Sunday morning, six of them. They stuck a knife in his jaw and led him to the car, and put him and his son in the car and they drove down the road toward the church and got out the car to get a switch to whip him but he got out of the car and ran and they shot him down with buckshots. Mr. Wiley S .... was the sheriff, he came out and had an inquest. One of the Negroes asked Mr. Wiley "what are we going to do now." he said, "there he is take him and do anything you want with him." All of them had guns of all kind and we didn't have no protection at all, when we picked him up the blood ran out of him like water through screens.

Another man by the name of Herbert Lee, was shot down at the cotton gin by one of the Representatives of Amite County and he laid there about four hours before any one paid any attention to him. But yet and still the cotton gin kept on working. There were four in the gin, they made three of the Negroes who witness forget what they saw but when they made Louis Allen say he didn't see anything he wouldn't. Later he was killed because he was going to testify against the sheriff. He was shot with buckshots at his gate three times. His brain was piled up under the truck.

So this is most of the histry that I can recall, if you sure you want it, and I hope it will help the little children who are enroll in Headstart.

Yours truly,
B. E. F., Amite County, Miss.

The letter from "B. E. F." was passed on to me by a friend. I never met the writer. Mrs. Winson Hudson, on the other hand, I've come to know well. She is a large handsome woman with bright coppery skin and crisp dark hair. Her eyes are deeply brown and uncommonly alert. When she is speaking to you her eyes hold you; at the same time they seem to be scanning the landscape. Her eyes tell a great deal about Mrs. Hudson, for she is one of the "sleepless ones" found in embattled Mississippi towns whose fight has been not only against unjust laws and verbal harassment, but against guns and fire bombs as well.

The first time I met Mrs. Hudson, having heard much about her from my husband and others who have witnessed personally the Hudson stamina and courage, she handed me twenty pages of writing. We sat down under some trees at the Headstart center where she is director and read parts of her "story" together. She was writing about her life, she said, because, among other reasons, she did not know how long it was going to last. She wanted, she added, to leave some kind of record for her community, setting straight all that had happened, so that the children would know about it, and the role she played. It bothered her very much that often her "own people" seemed to misunderstand her and failed to see that the agitation she caused in the community—for desegregated, quality schooling, for jobs, for Headstart—was not for herself or for any one group, but for everybody in the county.

We worked out a plan, Mrs. Hudson and I. She would mail newly written pages of her autobiography to me as she wrote them; I would be typist and editor, sending the typed pages back to her to be proofread. The interesting thing about Mrs. Hudson and her autobiography is that she wants only enough copies printed so that all the black people in her community will have a chance to read it. (At present we are in the middle of her story. She had to leave Mississippi recently for a long, much needed rest, and I am momentarily stumped as to where and how we will finally get her story out the way she wants it.) Working with Mrs. Hudson has been, for me, humbling, because she is such an eloquent part of a largely silent and unsung force. When people speak of the courage and "honor" of the South they do not mean people like Mrs. Hudson; they do not even know such people exist. They do exist, however, and for all the sons and daughters of the South, their existence is a reason to rejoice. Here is an excerpt from *The Autobiography of Mrs. Winson Hudson, a Black Woman of Mississippi*:

My sister's house was bombed twice, because she used her daughter's name in the integration lawsuit along with Medgar Evers' son and Doctor Mason's son at Biloxi, Mississippi. Our home was meant to be bombed in November 1967, but we heard the truck. I happened to be night watching until twelve on that night. Medgar always warned us to be careful at all times. He said, I must tell you the truth. You have no protection. I believed in Medgar Evers; about three weeks before he was killed we were with him in federal court in Jackson. He seemed so blue. Every now and then we could find something to laugh about. Medgar was a foreseer; many things he told us have come to pass. You will have heartaches, your people will deny you. . . .

The night the Klan was backing into our house to throw off a bomb my only daughter was living with us while her husband was in Vietnam. She was expecting a baby. She was sick that night and she heard the truck also. I told her to get up and rush into the back room. My husband and I started getting out to start shooting. By this time the German shepherd dog had forced the Klan to move on. I ran to the phone to tell my sister to be ready. By this time a bomb went off at my sister's house. I picked up the receiver and I heard my sister's baby girl screaming "Oh, mama!" "Oh, mama!" I started outside. My husband was shooting, emptying every gun. My daughter was swinging to me thinking the Klan might kill me. She said she didn't know where all the shooting and bombing was. I pulled aloose from my daughter and she fell on our concrete porch. When I came to myself I heard my daughter say "Mama, I am hurt." In a day or so we had to rush her to Hinds General Hospital. The baby had to come. The baby was saved but had to stay in the hospital for a long time. But we were so glad to save the baby. . . .

Just a month later we came home one Sunday evening and found my daughter crying. The deputy sheriff had brought her a telegram saying your husband has been injured in Vietnam. My daughter wrote him almost every day but he only got his mail by chances. He was on guard the night that plans were set up to destroy our home and his family here in the U.S.A. He was on guard in Vietnam guarding the Cambodian border.

He came home in November from Vietnam. He was hit three times, once in his leg, once in his knee, and once in his chest. The bullet in his chest will have to stay there forever or as long as he lives. I asked my daughter not to write to tell him of this terrible incidence while he was in Vietnam. But he knows all about it now. And I'll let anyone decide within themselves how he feels about this country that his son will have to grow up in.

Last summer I was offered a job as consultant in black history for Friends of the Children of Mississippi. This is a Headstart program that interested me because for three years it existed without government help or intervention. Its director was a young man from SNCC, the Student Nonviolent Coordinating Committee. My job was to create black history materials for teachers of the children in the Headstart centers, since Friends of the Children realized how impossible it would be for teachers to teach "blackness" to small children if they had no grasp of what black history was themselves. I was to devote two week-long workshop sessions to teaching these teachers, who turned out to be ninety women from various parts of the state. Some of them had been schoolteachers in Mississippi public schools, most had been maids, many had been fieldworkers. Almost all of them had children of their own, though often these were grown-up and away from home. The average educational level was perhaps fifth grade, though all the women were intelligent, industrious, anxious to learn, and deeply concerned about the welfare of the children they were teaching. How did I know this? Because many of them, indeed most, had worked for from one to eighteen months at the Headstart centers for less than ten dollars a week. Many months they worked for nothing.

I came to my job filled with enthusiasm. These were women I identified with, women who'd do anything for the good of black children. They were women Charles White might have drawn, heavy-set women with gold teeth and big fat arms; women who'd worked in the cotton fields for fifty cents a day.

I felt, on my first day before my class, as if the room were full of my mothers. Of course, teaching them black history in two weeks of lecturing, films, pictures was something else again.

It was hard. And I've no reason to believe I was a success.

In the first place, "history," to my students, was a total unknown. Many of them were extremely poor readers, and of course how were they to relate to history that was never written? Q.—"When was the period of slavery?" A.—"Around 1942?" And how could I underestimate the value of that answer, although it did not offer the class perspective, which we very much needed.

How *do* you teach earnest but educationally crippled middle-aged and older women the significance of their past? How do you get them to understand the pathos and beauty of a heritage they have been taught to regard with shame? How do you make them appreciate their own endurance, creativity, incredible loveliness of spirit? It should have been as simple as handing them each a mirror, but it was not. How do you show a connection between present and past when, as eloquent but morally befuddled Faulkner wrote, "the past is not even past"?

Try to tell a sixty-year-old delta woman that black men invented anything, black women wrote sonnets, that black people long ago were every bit the human beings they are today. Try to tell her that kinky hair is delightful. Chances are she will begin to talk "Bible" to you, and you will discover to your dismay that the lady still believes in the curse of Ham.

I thought about the problem, talked about it for hours with anybody who'd listen and offer advice. Since time was so short, the important thing, it seemed to me, was not so much teaching my "students" the *facts* of Africa, slavery and Jim Crow (though I did as much of that as I could); I wanted to give them in addition a knowledge of what history itself *is*. And in order that they see themselves and their parents and grandparents as part of a living, working, creating movement in Time and Place, I drew on my experience with Mrs. Hudson, and asked them to write their autobiographies; which they proceeded, some rather laboriously, to do.

I had noticed during workshop sessions that the very word "black" did not come easily to some of the women. (This was especially true of the six or seven white teachers among the others. I never quite understood why they were even in my classes; they were plainly uncomfortable the whole time. None of them wrote autobiographies and all of them rejected the cruel facts of slavery, lynchings, et cetera, I showed on film. "I just naturally don't believe the whites treated 'em *that* bad," said one, pointing to the black women around her, who merely grunted, folded their arms, and smiled knowingly. Ironically, at this very time four Klansmen were being tried for the lynching, two years before, of Vernon Dehmer, head of his local NAACP, and the trial was in all the news media.) I asked the women to write especially about color prejudice within their own families. Many of them were annoyed by the question, for, they said indignantly, "How can we be prejudiced against our own selves; we are all of one race." They did not say "we are all black."

The excerpts below represent part of the tiny scratch these women made on the surface of their memories, of their history.

I was one of three children, brought up by grandparents. There was a bright child and a black child which I am. I always feared adults and keep to myself. My grandmother love her bright child, seem to had only hate for me.
—Mrs. D. M. T.

They had very dark skin. My grandmother was low and fat, she had long hair and would have it braided all over her head. She wore her dresses very long and a apron as long as her dress. My grandfather was tall with long beards under his chin. His hair was very long. They lived on their own little farm and never had what I called a "hard time," they raised corn, cotton and vegetables, cured their own meat and made syrup from cane. They had eight children, six boys and two girls. My father said they would whip them if they wouldn't mind them, or any grown person.

My grandparents thought white folks knew everything, and everything they did was right. They thought black people never knew what they was talking about, or what they was doing.

My mother raised her family to work for what they wanted, and to be honest, proud of your color, to go to church, and school and do the right things. She taught us a white person wasn't no better than a black person, a man was just a man, no matter what color he is.

My mother said that the reason we are black is this: a curse from God.
—Mrs. G. S.

My parents taught us never to have fear of the white peoples because they were just people like anybody else and wouldn't harm us. As long as we be truthful.
—Mrs. O. R.

In 1957 my sixth child was born and then I had two children to help me chop cotton. They was still paying $3.00 a day for chopping cotton. In 1960 my seven and eight was born, another set of twins, by that time I had three kids chopping cotton. In June, 1961 my husband died on the 5th day of June. That was the most awful day of my life. Robert was not sick, hadn't ever been sick. He began having pains in his chest. The pains began to get so bad until

I told my boy to go get my brother-in-law to go get the doctor, before the doctor got out there he was dead. And I was three months pregnant with my ninth child. My sister come out and move me to town.

I went down and put in for Welfare. So I started working in private homes. I was working by the day. Sometimes I would work for three different white women in a day for $3.50. That what all three of them together would pay me. I was paying a woman $1.00 a day to keep my little children. Feb. 26, 1962 I had my baby. I started to working again in private homes. I just work for one lady. I work 4½ days a week for $11.25 from 8 A.M. to 5 P.M. I work all of 1962 until May 1964. So I ask the lady could she pay me any more. So she gave me a $6.25 raise. I had to pay the baby sitter $5.00 a week out of that $18.00. So I got tired of working for nothing. I began to look for another job that could help me support my kids. In 1966 I began volunteer working for CDGM.* I work over at the center for about 6 weeks then CDGM died in Humphries county. Well, we work on. In 1967 we began to get paid $25.00 a week from Friends of the Children. I was making more then than I ever had in my life. On July 26, 1968 when I receive my $65.00 [a week] that was a happy day for me.
—*Mrs. D. G.*

Before I had a chance to go very far with my workshops and fieldwork follow-up sessions I was fired. Unfortunately, the money for my salary, most of it, had come from OEO† which apparently frowns on black studies courses for Headstart teachers. Actually I suppose I am left with a project that will be a

*Child Development Group of Mississippi, the oldest Headstart program in the state.
†Office of Economic Opportunity.

private one whose success will be largely immeasurable, but since I don't believe success must be measurable I don't mind at all.

Slowly I am putting these stories together. Not for the public but for the women who wrote them. Will seeing each other's lives make any of the past clearer to them? I don't know. I hope so. I hope the contradictions will show but also the faith and grace of a people under continuous pressures. So much of the satisfying work of life begins as an experiment; having learned this, no experiment is ever quite a failure.

1970

A TALK: CONVOCATION 1972

When Charles DeCarlo* asked me to speak to you today I was quick to mention I had no idea what one said at such gatherings. I never had such a formal pregraduation ceremony, but was pushed out into the world from beside Mrs. Raushenbush's fireplace with a few words of good cheer and a *very* small glass of champagne.

"What shall I talk about?" I asked. To which Charles replied, "Oh, let me see: The War, Poverty, The Plight of Women, Your Own Writing, Your Life, or How Things Were When You Were at Sarah Lawrence."

There was a pause. Then he said, "It needn't be anything fancy, *or long.* It won't be published or anything, just speak from the heart."

*President of Sarah Lawrence.

So this talk is called "How to Speak about Practically Everything, Briefly, from the Heart."

The last time I spoke here I was already involved in a study of black women writers that has tremendously enriched the past couple of years. It began, this study, shortly after my husband and I moved to Mississippi to live. By the time we had overcome our anxiety that we might be beaten up, mobbed, or bombed, I had worked up a strong interest in how to teach history to mature women; in this case, fifty- and sixty-year-olds who had an average of five years of grammar school. The approach I finally devised was to have them write their own autobiographies. Reading them, we were often able to piece their years together with political and social movements that they were then better able to understand.

Nor were all these women simply waiting around for me to show up and ask them to write about themselves. Mrs. Winson Hudson, whose house was bombed more than once by the KKK, was already writing her autobiography when I was introduced to her. A remarkable woman, living in Harmony, Mississippi, a half-day's drive from anywhere of note, she is acutely aware of history, of change, and of her function as a revolutionary leader. . . . Her defense against the Klan was a big German shepherd dog who barked loudly when he heard the bombers coming, and two shotguns which she and her husband never hesitated to use. She wanted other people to know what it meant to fight alone against intimidation and murder, so she began to write it all down.

From Mrs. Hudson I learned a new respect for women and began to search out the works of others. Women who were generally abused when they lived and wrote, or were laughed at and belittled, or were simply forgotten as soon as critics found it feasible. I found that, indeed, the majority of black women who tried to express themselves by writing and who tried to make a living doing so, died in obscurity and poverty, usually before their time.

We do not know how Lucy Terry lived or died. We do know that Phillis Wheatley died, along with her three children, of malnutrition, in a cheap boardinghouse where she worked as a drudge. Nella Larsen died in almost complete obscurity after turning her back on her writing in order to become a practical nurse, an occupation that would at least buy food for the table and a place to sleep. And Zora Neale Hurston, who wrote what is perhaps the most authentic and moving black love story ever published, died in poverty in the swamps of Florida, where she was again working as a housemaid. She had written six books and was a noted folklorist and anthropologist, having worked while a student at Barnard with Franz Boas.

It is interesting to note, too, that black critics as well as white, considered Miss Hurston's classic, *Their Eyes Were Watching God*, as *second* to Richard Wright's *Native Son*, written during the same period. A love story about a black man and a black woman who spent only about one-eighteenth of their time worrying about whitefolks seemed to them far less important—probably because such a story should be so entirely *normal* —than a novel whose main character really had whitefolks on the brain.

Wright died in honor, although in a foreign land. Hurston died in her native state a pauper and, to some degree, an outcast.

Still, I refuse to be entirely pessimistic about Hurston *et al.* They did commendable and often brilliant work under distressing conditions. They did live full, useful lives. And today, although many of them are dead, their works are being read with gratitude by younger generations.

However, the young person leaving college today, especially if she is a woman, must consider the possibility that her best offerings will be considered a nuisance to the men who also occupy her field. And then, having considered this, she would do well to make up her mind to fight *whoever* would stifle her growth with as much courage and tenacity as Mrs. Hudson fights the Klan. If she is black and coming out into the world she must be doubly armed, doubly prepared. Because for her there is not simply a new world to be gained, there is an old world that must be reclaimed. There are countless vanished and forgotten women who are nonetheless eager to speak to her—from Frances Harper and Anne Spencer to Dorothy West—but she must work to find them, to free them from their neglect and the oppression of silence forced upon them because they were black and they were women.

But please remember, especially in these times of group-think and the right-on chorus, that no person is your friend (or kin) who demands your silence, or denies your right to grow and be perceived as fully blossomed as you were intended. Or who belittles in any fashion the gifts you labor so to bring into the world. That is why historians are generally enemies of women, certainly of blacks, and so are, all too often, the very people we must sit under in order to learn. Ignorance, arrogance, and racism have bloomed as Superior Knowledge in all too many universities.

I am discouraged when a faculty member at Sarah Lawrence says there is not enough literature by black women and men to make a full year's course. Or that the quantity of genuine black literature is too meager to warrant a full year's investigation. This is incredible. I am disturbed when Eldridge Cleaver is considered the successor to Ralph Ellison, on campuses like this one—this is like saying Kate Millet's book *Sexual Politics* makes her the new Jane Austen. It is shocking to hear that the only black woman writer white and black academicians have heard of is Gwendolyn Brooks.

Fortunately, what Sarah Lawrence teaches is a lesson called "How to Be Shocked and Dismayed but Not Lie Down and Die," and those of you who have learned this lesson will never regret it, because there will be ample time and opportunity to use it.

Your job, when you leave here—as it was the job of educated women before you—is to change the world. Nothing less or easier than that. I hope you have been reading the recent women's liberation literature, even if you don't agree with some of it. For you will find, as women have found through the ages, that changing the world requires a lot of free time. Requires a lot of mobility. Requires money, and, as Virginia Woolf put it so well, "a room of one's own," preferably one with a key and a *lock*. Which means that women must be prepared to think for themselves, which means, undoubtedly, trouble with boyfriends, lovers, and husbands, which means all kinds of heartache and misery, and times when you will wonder if independence, freedom of thought, or your own work is worth it all.

We must believe that it is. For the world is not good enough; we must make it better.

But it is a great time to be a woman. A wonderful time to be a black woman, for the world, I have found, is not simply rich because from day to day our lives are touched with new possibilities, but because the past is studded with sisters who, in their time, shone like gold. They give us hope, they have proved the splendor of our past, which should free us to lay just claim to the fullness of the future.

Having mentioned these subjects briefly, from the heart, I must tell you about one other thing I have learned since becoming an advanced ten-year-old. Any school would be worthless without great teachers. Obviously I have some great teachers in mind.

When I came to Sarah Lawrence my don was Helen Merrell Lynd. She was the first person I met who made philosophy understandable, and the study of it natural. It was she who led me through the works of Camus and showed me, for the first time, how life and suffering are always teachers, or, as with Camus, life and suffering, *and* joy. Like Rilke, I came to understand that even loneliness has a use, and that sadness is positively the wellspring of creativity. Since studying with her, all of life, the sadness as well as the joy, has its magnificence, its meaning, and its *use*. She continues to teach me in her role as Older Woman. I had always thought, before knowing her, that after retirement people did nothing. She works and enjoys herself as she did before. Now, of course, she has more time to devote to writing her newest book. This, younger women need to know, that life does not stop at some arbitrary point. Knowing this we can face the years confidently, full of anticipation and courage.

Another great teacher was Muriel Rukeyser, who could link up Fujiyama with the Spanish Civil War, and poetry to potty training. If you have ever talked with a person of cosmic consciousness, you will understand what I mean. Sometimes I think she taught entirely by innuendo and suggestion. But mostly she taught by the courage of her own life, which to me is the highest form of teaching. Afraid of little, intimidated by none, Muriel Rukeyser the Poet and Muriel Rukeyser the Prophet-person, the Truth-doer (and I must add the Original One-of-a-Kind, which would seem redundant if applied to anyone else), taught me that it *is* possible to live in this world on your own terms. If it had not been for her I might never have found the courage, to leave not just Sarah Lawrence, but later the New York City Welfare Department, on my way to becoming a writer.

And who can express the magic that is Jane Cooper's instruction? Helen Lynd I always think of as a tulip. Red-orange.

Fragile yet sturdy. Strong. Muriel Rukeyser I perceive as an amethyst, rich and deep. Purple. Full of mystical changes, moods and spells. But Jane Cooper was always a pine tree. Quiet, listening, true. Like the tree you adopt as your best friend when you're seven. Only dearer than that for having come through so many storms, and still willing to offer that listening and that peace.

These women were Sarah Lawrence's gift to me. And when I think of them, I understand that each woman is capable of truly bringing another into the world. This we must all do for each other.

My gifts to you today are two poems: "Be Nobody's Darling," a kind of sisterly advice about a dangerous possibility, and "Reassurance," for young writers who itch, usually before they are ready, to say the words that will correct the world.*

BE NOBODY'S DARLING

Be nobody's darling;
Be an outcast.
Take the contradictions
Of your life
And wrap around
You like a shawl,
To parry stones
To keep you warm.

Watch the people succumb
To madness

*From *Revolutionary Petunias*.

With ample cheer;
Let them look askance at you
And you askance reply.

Be an outcast;
Be pleased to walk alone
(Uncool)
Or line the crowded
River beds
With other impetuous
Fools.

Make a merry gathering
On the bank
Where thousands perished
For brave hurt words
They said.

Be nobody's darling;
Be an outcast.
Qualified to live
Among your dead.

REASSURANCE

I must love the questions
themselves
as Rilke said
like locked rooms
full of treasure
to which my blind
and groping key
does not yet fit.

and await the answers
as unsealed
letters
mailed with dubious intent
and written in a very foreign
tongue.

and in the hourly making
of myself
no thought of Time
to force, to squeeze
the space
I grow into.

1972

. . . .

BEYOND THE PEACOCK:

THE RECONSTRUCTION OF

FLANNERY O'CONNOR

It was after a poetry reading I gave at a recently desegregated college in Georgia that someone mentioned that in 1952 Flannery O'Connor and I had lived within minutes of each other on the same Eatonton-to-Milledgeville road. I was eight years old in 1952 (she would have been 28) and we moved away from Milledgeville after less than a year. Still, since I have loved her work for many years, the coincidence of our having lived near each other intrigued me, and started me thinking of her again.

As a college student in the sixties I read her books endlessly, scarcely conscious of the difference between her racial and economic background and my own, but put them away in anger when I discovered that, while I was reading O'Connor—Southern, Catholic, and white—there were other women writers— some Southern, some religious, all black—I had not been allowed to know. For several years, while I searched for, found, and studied black women writers, I deliberately shut O'Connor out, feeling almost ashamed that she had reached me first. And yet, even when I no longer read her, I missed her, and realized that though the rest of America might not mind, having endured it so long, I would never be satisfied with a segregated literature. I would have to read Zora Hurston *and* Flannery O'Connor, Nella Larsen *and* Carson McCullers, Jean Toomer *and* William Faulkner, before I could begin to feel *well* read at all.

I thought it might be worthwhile, in 1974, to visit the two houses, Flannery O'Connor's and mine, to see what could be learned twenty-two years after we moved away and ten years after her death. It seemed right to go to my old house first—to set the priorities of vision, so to speak—and then to her house, to see, at the very least, whether her peacocks would still be around. To this bit of nostalgic exploration I invited my mother, who, curious about peacocks and abandoned houses, if not about literature and writers, accepted.

In her shiny new car, which at sixty-one she has learned to drive, we cruised down the wooded Georgia highway to revisit our past.

At the turnoff leading to our former house, we face a fence, a gate, a NO TRESPASSING sign. The car will not fit through the gate and beyond the gate is muddy pasture. It shocks me to remember that when we lived here we lived, literally, in a pasture. It is a memory I had repressed. Now, for a moment, it frightens me.

"Do you think we should enter?" I ask.

But my mother has already opened the gate. To her, life has no fences, except, perhaps, religious ones, and these we have decided not to discuss. We walk through pines rich with vines, fluttering birds, and an occasional wild azalea showing flashes of orange. The day is bright with spring, the sky cloudless, the road rough and clean.

"I would like to see old man Jenkins [who was our landlord]

come bothering me about some trespassing," she says, her head extremely up. "He never did pay us for the crop we made for him in fifty-two."

After five minutes of leisurely walking, we are again confronted with a fence, fastened gate, POSTED signs. Again my mother ignores all three, unfastens the gate, walks through.

"He never gave me my half of the calves I raised that year either," she says. And I chuckle at her memory and her style.

Now we are facing a large green rise. To our left calves are grazing; beyond them there are woods. To our right there is the barn we used, looking exactly as it did twenty-two years ago. It is high and weathered silver and from it comes the sweet scent of peanut hay. In front of it, a grove of pecans. Directly in front of us over the rise is what is left of the house.

"Well," says my mother, "it's still standing. And," she adds with wonder, "just look at my daffodils!"

In twenty-two years they have multiplied and are now blooming from one side of the yard to the other. It is a typical abandoned sharefarmer shack. Of the four-room house only two rooms are left; the others have rotted away. These two are filled with hay.

Considering the sad state of the house it is amazing how beautiful its setting is. There is not another house in sight. There are hills, green pastures, a ring of bright trees, and a family of rabbits hopping out of our way. My mother and I stand in the yard remembering. I remember only misery: going to a shabby segregated school that was once the state prison and that had, on the second floor, the large circular print of the electric chair that had stood there; almost stepping on a water moccasin on my way home from carrying water to my family in the fields; losing Phoebe, my cat, because we left this place hurriedly and she could not be found in time.

"Well, old house," my mother says, smiling in such a way

that I almost see her rising, physically, above it, "one good thing you gave us. It was right here that I got my first washing machine!"

In fact, the only pleasant thing I recall from that year was a field we used to pass on our way into the town of Milledgeville. It was like a painting by someone who loved tranquillity. In the foreground near the road the green field was used as pasture for black-and-white cows that never seemed to move. Then, farther away, there was a steep hill partly covered with kudzu—dark and lush and creeping up to cover and change fantastically the shapes of the trees. . . . When we drive past it now, it looks the same. Even the cows could be the same cows—though now I see that they *do* move, though not very fast and never very far.

What I liked about this field as a child was that in my life of nightmares about electrocutions, lost cats, and the surprise appearance of snakes, it represented beauty and unchanging peace.

"Of course," I say to myself, as we turn off the main road two miles from my old house, "that's Flannery's field." The instructions I've been given place her house on the hill just beyond it.

There is a garish new Holiday Inn directly across Highway 441 from Flannery O'Connor's house, and, before going up to the house, my mother and I decide to have something to eat there. Twelve years ago I could not have bought lunch for us at such a place in Georgia, and I feel a weary delight as I help my mother off with her sweater and hold out a chair by the window for her. The white people eating lunch all around us—staring though trying hard not to—form a blurred backdrop against which my mother's face is especially sharp. *This* is the proper perspective, I think, biting into a corn muffin; no doubt about it.

As we sip iced tea we discuss O'Connor, integration, the

inferiority of the corn muffins we are nibbling, and the care and raising of peacocks.

"Those things will sure eat up your flowers," my mother says, explaining why she never raised any.

"Yes," I say, "but they're a lot prettier than they'd be if somebody human had made them, which is why this lady liked them." This idea has only just occurred to me, but having said it, I believe it is true. I sit wondering why I called Flannery O'Connor a lady. It is a word I rarely use and usually by mistake, since the whole notion of ladyhood is repugnant to me. I can imagine O'Connor at a Southern social affair, looking very polite and being very bored, making mental notes of the absurdities of the evening. Being white she would automatically have been eligible for ladyhood, but I cannot believe she would ever really have joined.

"She must have been a Christian person then," says my mother. "She believed He made everything." She pauses, looks at me with tolerance but also as if daring me to object: "And she was *right*, too."

"She was a Catholic," I say, "which must not have been comfortable in the Primitive Baptist South, and more than any other writer she believed in everything, including things she couldn't see."

"Is that why you like her?" she asks.

"I like her because she could *write*," I say.

" 'Flannery' sounds like something to eat," someone said to me once. The word always reminds me of flannel, the material used to make nightgowns and winter shirts. It is very Irish, as were her ancestors. Her first name was Mary, but she seems never to have used it. Certainly "Mary O'Connor" is short on mystery. She was an Aries, born March 25, 1925. When she was sixteen, her father died of lupus, the disease that, years later, caused her own death. After her father died, O'Connor and her mother, Regina O'Connor, moved from Savannah, Georgia, to Milledgeville, where they lived in a townhouse built for Flannery O'Connor's grandfather, Peter Cline. This house, called "the Cline house," was built by slaves who made the bricks by hand. O'Connor's biographers are always impressed by this fact, as if it adds the blessed sign of aristocracy, but whenever I read it I think that those slaves were some of my own relatives, toiling in the stifling middle-Georgia heat, to erect her grandfather's house, sweating and suffering the swarming mosquitoes as the house rose slowly, brick by brick.

Whenever I visit antebellum homes in the South, with their spacious rooms, their grand staircases, their shaded back windows that, without the thickly planted trees, would look out onto the now vanished slave quarters in the back, this is invariably my thought. I stand in the backyard gazing up at the windows, then stand at the windows inside looking down into the backyard, and between the me that is on the ground and the me that is at the windows, History is caught.

O'Connor attended local Catholic schools and then Georgia Women's College. In 1945 she received a fellowship to the Writer's Workshop at the University of Iowa. She received her M.A. in 1947. While still a student she wrote stories that caused her to be recognized as a writer of formidable talent and integrity of craft. After a stay at Yaddo, the artists' colony in upstate New York, she moved to a furnished room in New York City. Later she lived and wrote over a garage at the Connecticut home of Sally and Robert Fitzgerald, who became, after her death, her literary executors.

Although, as Robert Fitzgerald states in the preface to O'Connor's *Everything That Rises Must Converge*, "Flannery was out to be a writer on her own and had no plans to go back to live in Georgia," staying out of Georgia for good was not possible. In December of 1950 she experienced a peculiar heaviness in her "typing arms." On the train home for the Christmas holidays she became so ill she was hospitalized immediately. It was disseminated lupus. In the fall of 1951, after nine wretched months in the hospital, she returned to Milledgeville. Because she could not climb the stairs at the Cline house her mother brought her to their country house, Andalusia, about five miles from town. Flannery O'Connor lived there with her mother for the next thirteen years. The rest of her life.

The word *lupus* is Latin for "wolf," and is described as "that which eats into the substance." It is a painful, wasting disease, and O'Connor suffered not only from the disease— which caused her muscles to weaken and her body to swell, among other things—but from the medicine she was given to fight the disease, which caused her hair to fall out and her hipbones to melt. Still, she managed—with the aid of crutches from 1955 on—to get about and to write, and left behind more than three dozen superb short stories, most of them prizewinners, two novels, and a dozen or so brilliant essays and speeches. Her book of essays, *Mystery and Manners*, which is primarily concerned with the moral imperatives of the serious writer of fiction, is the best of its kind I have ever read.

"When you make these trips back south," says my mother, as I give the smiling waitress my credit card, "just what is it exactly that you're looking for?"

"A wholeness," I reply.

"You look whole enough to me," she says.

"No," I answer, "because everything around me is split up, deliberately split up. History split up, literature split up, and people are split up too. It makes people do ignorant things. For example, one day I was invited to speak at a gathering of Mississippi librarians and before I could get started, one of the authorities on Mississippi history and literature got up and said she really *did* think Southerners wrote so well because 'we' lost the war. She was white, of course, but half the librarians in the room were black."

"I bet she was real old," says my mother. "They're the only ones still worrying over that war."

"So I got up and said no, 'we' didn't lose the war. '*You* all' lost the war. And you all's loss was our gain."

"Those old ones will just have to die out," says my mother.

"Well," I say, "I believe that the truth about any subject only comes when all the sides of the story are put together, and all their different meanings make one new one. Each writer writes the missing parts to the other writer's story. And the whole story is what I'm after."

"Well, I doubt if you can ever get the *true* missing parts of anything away from the white folks," my mother says softly, so as not to offend the waitress who is mopping up a nearby table; "they've sat on the truth so long by now they've mashed the life out of it."

"O'Connor wrote a story once called 'Everything That Rises Must Converge.' "

"What?"

"Everything that goes up comes together, meets, becomes one thing. Briefly, the story is this: an old white woman in her fifties—"

"That's not old! I'm older than that, and I'm not old!"

"Sorry. This middle-aged woman gets on a bus with her son, who likes to think he is a Southern liberal . . . he looks for a black person to sit next to. This horrifies his mother, who, though not old, has old ways. She is wearing a very hideous, very expensive hat, which is purple and green."

"Purple and *green?*"

"Very expensive. *Smart.* Bought at the best store in town. She says, 'With a hat like this, I won't meet myself coming and going.' But in fact, soon a large black woman, whom O'Connor describes as looking something like a gorilla, gets on the bus with a little boy, and she is wearing this same green-and-purple hat. Well, our not-so-young white lady is horrified, out*done.*"

"I *bet* she was. Black folks have money to buy foolish things with too, now."

"O'Connor's point exactly! Everything that rises, must converge."

"Well, the green-and-purple-hats people will have to converge without me."

"O'Connor thought that the South, as it became more 'progressive,' would become just like the North. Culturally bland, physically ravished, and, where the people are concerned, well, you wouldn't be able to tell one racial group from another. Everybody would want the same things, like the same things, and everybody would be reduced to wearing, symbolically, the same green-and-purple hats."

"And do you think this is happening?"

"I do. But that is not the whole point of the story. The white woman, in an attempt to save her pride, chooses to treat the incident of the identical hats as a case of monkey-see, monkey-do. She assumes she is not the monkey, of course. She ignores the idiotic-looking black woman and begins instead to flirt with the woman's son, who is small and black and *cute.* She fails to notice that the black woman is glowering at her. When they all get off the bus she offers the little boy a 'bright new penny.' And the child's mother knocks the hell out of her with her pocketbook."

"I bet she carried a large one."

"Large, and full of hard objects."

"Then what happened? Didn't you say the white woman's son was with her?"

"He had tried to warn his mother. 'These new Negroes are not like the old,' he told her. But she never listened. He thought he hated his mother until he saw her on the ground, then he felt sorry for her. But when he tried to help her, she didn't know him. She'd retreated in her mind to a historical time more congenial to her desires. 'Tell Grandpapa to come get me,' she says. Then she totters off, alone, into the night."

"Poor *thing*," my mother says sympathetically of this horrid woman, in a total identification that is *so* Southern and *so* black.

"That's what her son felt, too, and *that* is how you know it is a Flannery O'Connor story. The son has been changed by his mother's experience. He understands that, though she is a silly woman who has tried to live in the past, she is also a pathetic creature and so is he. But it is too late to tell her about this because she is stone crazy."

"What did the black woman do after she knocked the white woman down and walked away?"

"O'Connor chose not to say, and that is why, although this is a good story, it is, to me, only half a story. *You* might know the other half. . . ."

"Well, I'm not a writer, but there *was* an old white woman I once wanted to strike . . ." she begins.

"Exactly," I say.

I discovered O'Connor when I was in college in the North and took a course in Southern writers and the South. The perfection of her writing was so dazzling I never noticed that no black Southern writers were taught. The other writers we studied— Faulkner, McCullers, Welty—seemed obsessed with a racial past that would not let them go. They seemed to beg the question of their characters' humanity on every page. O'Connor's characters—whose humanity if not their sanity is taken for granted, and who are miserable, ugly, narrow-minded, atheistic, and of intense racial smugness and arrogance, with not a graceful, pretty one anywhere who is not, at the same time, a joke—shocked and delighted me.

It was for her description of Southern white women that I appreciated her work at first, because when she set her pen to them not a whiff of magnolia hovered in the air (and the tree itself might never have been planted), and yes, I could say, yes, these white folks without the magnolia (who are indifferent to the tree's existence), and these black folks without melons and superior racial patience, these are like Southerners that I know.

She was for me the first great modern writer from the South, and was, in any case, the only one I had read who wrote such sly, demythifying sentences about white women as: "The woman would be more or less pretty—yellow hair, fat ankles, muddy-colored eyes."

Her white male characters do not fare any better—all of them misfits, thieves, deformed madmen, idiot children, illiterates, and murderers, and her black characters, male and female, appear equally shallow, demented, and absurd. That she retained a certain distance (only, however, in her later, mature work) from the inner workings of her black characters seems to me all to her credit, since, by deliberately limiting her treatment of them to cover their observable demeanor and actions, she leaves them free, in the reader's imagination, to inhabit another landscape, another life, than the one she creates for them. This is a kind of grace many writers do not have when dealing with representatives of an oppressed people within a story, and their insistence on knowing everything, on being God, in fact, has burdened us with more stereotypes than we can ever hope to shed.

In her life, O'Connor was more casual. In a letter to her friend Robert Fitzgerald in the mid-fifties she wrote, "as the niggers say, I have the misery." He found nothing offensive, apparently, in including this unflattering (to O'Connor) statement in his Introduction to one of her books. O'Connor was then certain she was dying, and was in pain; one assumes she made this comment in an attempt at levity. Even so, I do not find it funny. In another letter she wrote shortly before she died she said: "Justice is justice and should not be appealed to along racial lines. The problem is not abstract for the Southerner, it's concrete: he sees it in terms of persons, not races—which way of seeing does away with easy answers." Of course this observation, though grand, does not apply to the racist treatment of blacks by whites in the South, and O'Connor should have added that she spoke only for herself.

But *essential* O'Connor is not about race at all, which is why it is so refreshing, coming, as it does, out of such a *racial* culture. If it can be said to be "about" anything, then it is "about" prophets and prophecy, "about" revelation, and "about" the impact of supernatural grace on human beings who don't have a chance of spiritual growth without it.

An indication that *she* believed in justice for the individual (if only in the corrected portrayal of a character she invented) is shown by her endless reworking of "The Geranium," the first story she published (in 1946), when she was twenty-one. She revised the story several times, renamed it at least twice, until, nearly twenty years after she'd originally published it (and significantly, I think, after the beginning of the Civil Rights Movement), it became a different tale. Her two main black characters, a man and a woman, underwent complete metamorphosis.

In the original story, Old Dudley, a senile racist from the South, lives with his daughter in a New York City building that has "niggers" living in it too. The black characters are described as being passive, self-effacing people. The black woman sits quietly, hands folded, in her apartment; the man, her husband, helps Old Dudley up the stairs when the old man is out of breath, and chats with him kindly, if condescendingly, about guns and hunting. But in the final version of the story, the woman walks around Old Dudley (now called Tanner) as if he's an open bag of garbage, scowls whenever she sees him, and "didn't look like any kind of woman, black or white, he had ever seen." Her husband, whom Old Dudley persists in calling "Preacher" (under the misguided assumption that to all black men it is a courtesy title), twice knocks the old man down. At the end of the story he stuffs Old Dudley's head, arms, and legs through the banisters of the stairway "as if in a stockade," and leaves him to die. The story's final title is "Judgment Day."

The quality added is rage, and, in this instance, O'Connor waited until she saw it *exhibited* by black people before she recorded it.

She was an artist who thought she might die young, and who then knew for certain she would. Her view of her characters pierces right through to the skull. Whatever her characters' color or social position she saw them as she saw herself, in the light of imminent mortality. Some of her stories, "The Enduring Chill" and "The Comforts of Home" especially, seem to be written out of the despair that must, on occasion, have come from this bleak vision, but it is for her humor that she is most enjoyed and remembered. My favorites are these:

> Everywhere I go I'm asked if I think the universities stifle writers. My opinion is that they don't stifle enough of them. There's many a best-seller that could have been prevented by a good teacher.
>
> —MYSTERY AND MANNERS

"She would of been a good woman, if it had been somebody there to shoot her every minute of her life."
—"The Misfit,"
<small>A GOOD MAN IS HARD TO FIND</small>

There are certain cases in which, if you can only learn to write poorly enough, you can make a great deal of money.
—MYSTERY AND MANNERS

It is the business of fiction to embody mystery through manners, and mystery is a great embarrassment to the modern mind.
—MYSTERY AND MANNERS

It mattered to her that she was a Catholic. This comes as a surprise to those who first read her work as that of an atheist. She believed in all the mysteries of her faith. And yet, she was incapable of writing dogmatic or formulaic stories. No religious tracts, nothing haloed softly in celestial light, not even any happy endings. It has puzzled some of her readers and annoyed the Catholic church that in her stories not only does good not triumph, it is not usually present. Seldom are there choices, and God never intervenes to help anyone win. To O'Connor, in fact, Jesus was God, and he won only by losing. She perceived that not much has been learned by his death by crucifixion, and that it is only by his continual, repeated dying—touching one's own life in a direct, searing way—that the meaning of that original loss is pressed into the heart of the individual.

In "The Displaced Person," a story published in 1954, a refugee from Poland is hired to work on a woman's dairy farm. Although he speaks in apparent gibberish, he is a perfect worker. He works so assiduously the woman begins to prosper beyond her greatest hopes. Still, because his ways are not her own (the

Displaced Person attempts to get one of the black dairy workers to marry his niece by "buying" her out of a Polish concentration camp), the woman allows a runaway tractor to roll over and kill him.

"As far as I'm concerned," she tells the priest, "Christ was just another D.P." He just didn't fit in. After the death of the Polish refugee, however, she understands her complicity in a modern crucifixion, and recognizes the enormity of her responsibility for other human beings. The impact of this new awareness debilitates her; she loses her health, her farm, even her ability to speak.

This moment of revelation, when the individual comes face to face with her own limitations and comprehends "the true frontiers of her own inner country," is classic O'Connor, and always arrives in times of extreme crisis and loss.

There is a resistance by some to read O'Connor because she is "too difficult," or because they do not share her religious "persuasion." A young man who studied O'Connor under the direction of Eudora Welty some years ago amused me with the following story, which may or may not be true:

"I don't think Welty and O'Connor understood each *other*," he said, when I asked if he thought O'Connor would have liked or understood Welty's more conventional art. "For Welty's part, wherever we reached a particularly dense and symbolic section of one of O'Connor's stories she would sigh and ask, 'Is there a Catholic in the class?' "

Whether one "understands" her stories or not, one knows her characters are new and wondrous creations in the world and that not one of her stories—not even the earliest ones in which her consciousness of racial matters had not evolved sufficiently to be interesting or to differ much from the insulting and ignorant racial stereotyping that preceded it—could have been written by anyone else. As one can tell a Bearden from a Keene or a Picasso from a Hallmark card, one can tell an O'Connor story from any story laid next to it. Her Catholicism did not in any way limit (by defining it) her art. After her great stories of sin, damnation, prophecy, and revelation, the stories one reads casually in the average magazine seem to be about love and roast beef.

Andalusia is a large white house at the top of a hill with a view of a lake from its screened-in front porch. It is neatly kept, and there are, indeed, peacocks strutting about in the sun. Behind it there is an unpainted house where black people must have lived. It was, then, the typical middle-to-upper-class arrangement: white folks up front, the "help," in a far shabbier house, within calling distance from the back door. Although an acquaintance of O'Connor's has told me no one lives there now —but that a caretaker looks after things—I go up to the porch and knock. It is not an entirely empty or symbolic gesture: I have come to this vacant house to learn something about myself in relation to Flannery O'Connor, and will learn it whether anyone is home or not.

What I feel at the moment of knocking is fury that someone is paid to take care of her house, though no one lives in it, and that her house still, in fact, stands, while mine—which of course we never owned anyway—is slowly rotting into dust. Her house becomes—in an instant—the symbol of my own disinheritance, and for that instant I hate her guts. All that she has meant to me is diminished, though her diminishment within me is against my will.

In Faulkner's backyard there is also an unpainted shack and a black caretaker still lives there, a quiet, somber man who, when asked about Faulkner's legendary "sense of humor" replied that, as far as he knew, "Mr. Bill never joked." For years, while reading Faulkner, this image of the quiet man in the backyard shack stretched itself across the page.

Standing there knocking on Flannery O'Connor's door, I do not think of her illness, her magnificent work in spite of it; I think: it all comes back to houses. To how people live. There are rich people who own houses to live in and poor people who do not. And this is wrong. Literary separatism, fashionable now among blacks as it has always been among whites, is easier to practice than to change a fact like this. I think: I would level this country with the sweep of my hand, if I could.

"Nobody can change the past," says my mother.

"Which is why revolutions exist," I reply.

My bitterness comes from a deeper source than my knowledge of the difference, historically, race has made in the lives of white and black artists. The fact that in Mississippi no one even remembers where Richard Wright lived, while Faulkner's house is maintained by a black caretaker is painful, but not unbearable. What comes close to being unbearable is that I know how damaging to my own psyche such injustice is. In an unjust society the soul of the sensitive person is in danger of deformity from just such weights as this. For a long time I will feel Faulkner's house, O'Connor's house, crushing me. To fight back will require a certain amount of energy, energy better used doing something else.

My mother has been busy reasoning that, since Flannery O'Connor died young of a lingering and painful illness, the hand of God has shown itself. Then she sighs. "Well, you know," she says, "it is true, as they say, that the grass is always greener on the other side. That is, until you find yourself over there."

In a just society, of course, clichés like this could not survive.

· "But grass *can* be greener on the other side and not be just an illusion," I say. "Grass on the other side of the fence might have good fertilizer, while grass on your side might have to grow, if it grows at all, in sand."

We walk about quietly, listening to the soft sweep of the peacocks' tails as they move across the yard. I notice how completely O'Connor, in her fiction, has described just this view of the rounded hills, the tree line, black against the sky, the dirt road that runs from the front yard down to the highway. I remind myself of her courage and of how much—in her art—she has helped me to see. She destroyed the last vestiges of sentimentality in white Southern writing; she caused white women to look ridiculous on pedestals, and she approached her black characters —as a mature artist—with unusual humility and restraint. She also cast spells and worked magic with the written word. The magic, the wit, and the mystery of Flannery O'Connor I know I will always love, I also know the meaning of the expression "Take what you can use and let the rest rot." If ever there was an expression designed to protect the health of the spirit, this is it.

As we leave O'Connor's yard the peacocks—who she said would have the last word—lift their splendid tails for our edification. One peacock is so involved in the presentation of his masterpiece he does not allow us to move the car until he finishes with his show.

"Peacocks are inspiring," I say to my mother, who does not seem at all in awe of them and actually frowns when she sees them strut, "but they sure don't stop to consider they might be standing in your way."

And she says, "Yes, and they'll eat up every bloom you have, if you don't watch out."

1975

. . . .

THE DIVIDED LIFE OF

JEAN TOOMER

In 1923, when he was twenty-nine years old, Jean Toomer published *Cane*, a book that sang naturally and effortlessly of the beauty, passion, and vulnerability of black, mostly Southern, life. In form it was unique: there were stories interspersed with poems, a novelette constructed like a play, and delicate line drawings that casually accented pages throughout. Some critics called the book a novel, some called it a prose poem, some did not know what to call it; but all agreed that *Cane* was original, and a welcome change from earlier fiction that took a didactic or hortatory position on black and interracial American life.

It was an immediate hit among those writers who would eventually make the Harlem Renaissance—including Langston Hughes and Zora Neale Hurston—who, apparently without knowing much about its author, accepted *Cane* as a work of genius and were influenced by it. Hughes was moved to explore the dramatic possibilities of interracial, intrafamilial relationships in the South in his plays and poems. Hurston was encouraged to portray the culture of rural black Southerners as generative, vibrant, and destined for a useful, if vastly changed, future in the modern world, though Toomer himself had considered *Cane* the "swan song" of that culture.

Not much was known about Toomer in black literary circles, because he never belonged to any; and shortly after *Cane* was published he no longer appeared even in white ones. By the time the Harlem Renaissance was in full swing, in the mid- and late 1920s, the book was out of print, largely forgotten, and its author an infrequently discussed mystery.

Toomer was still a mystery over forty years later, in 1969, when, at the height of the black studies movement, *Cane* was reissued and again captured the imagination of readers with its poetic complexity and sensitive treatment of black men and especially black women. By this time, the late Arna Bontemps, poet, novelist, and Curator of Special Collections at Fisk University, had access to Toomer's autobiographical writings: Toomer had died in 1967. Bontemps wrote sympathetically, albeit guardedly, of Toomer's long isolation in a Washington, D.C. brownstone, watching his grandparents decline, of the brief, three-month trip to Sparta, Georgia, that was the inspiration for *Cane*, and of the "crisis" about his racial identity. Some of the mystery surrounding Toomer's personality began to be dispelled.

This present collection of Toomer's writings, *The Wayward and the Seeking* (apparently there is much more), edited and shaped by Darwin T. Turner, also does much to clarify the Jean Toomer mystery. There is a large section of autobiographical fragments, three short stories, and many poems, including "The Blue Meridian," Toomer's definitive statement of his vision of America. Also included are two interesting and often provocative plays that illustrate both Toomer's sensitivity to women and his ultimate condescension toward them, as well as a selection of maxims and aphorisms commenting on nature and humanity from Toomer's previously published booklet *Essentials*.

Feminists will be intrigued by what Toomer writes about his mother and grandmother. His mother was an intelligent woman, utterly dominated by her father, whom she spent her whole, relatively short life trying to defy. She died when Toomer was fifteen, after the second of two mysterious at-home operations that, as described here, read like abortions. His grandmother was also dominated by her husband, until his health began to decline in old age. Then she, old and ill herself, blossomed magnificently from a sweet, silent shadow of her husband into a woman of high humor, memorable tales, satiric jibes at anything and everything. She is reported to have had "some dark blood."

It will no doubt be hard, if not impossible, for lovers of *Cane* to read *The Wayward and the Seeking* (the title is from one of Toomer's poems) without feelings of disappointment and loss. Disappointment because the man who wrote so piercingly of "Negro" life in *Cane* chose to live his own life as a white man, while Hughes, Hurston, Du Bois, and other black writers were celebrating the blackness in themselves as well as in their work. Loss because it appears this choice undermined Toomer's moral judgment: there were things in American life and in his own that he simply refused to see.

Toomer's refusal to acknowledge the racism around him is especially lamentable. He lived in Washington with his grandparents for nearly the first twenty years of his life, and when he left to attend the University of Wisconsin, he decided he would say nothing of his racial identity unless asked. If asked, he would say, basically, that he was an American. The subject "never came up," he writes, and within two weeks he was "taking this white world as a matter of course, forgetting that I had been in a colored group." He does not find it odd that when his schoolmates mistake him for an Indian they brutalize him so severely on the football field that he is forced to call time out for good. "If others had race prejudice that was their affair," he wrote, "as long as it did not manifest itself against me." Given this deliberate blindness, it is no wonder that the fiction he wrote after *Cane* depicts primarily white people and never documents their racism in any way; it is as if Toomer believed an absence of black people assured the absence of racism itself.

To many who read this collection Toomer will appear to be, as he saw himself, a visionary in his assumption that he was "naturally and inevitably" an American—a "prototype" of the new race now evolving on the American continent, "neither white nor black." They will note that it was not Toomer who ordained that a single drop of black blood makes one black. Toomer, looking more white than black, could as easily argue the opposite point: that several obvious drops of white blood make one white. They will think it heroic of Toomer to fling off racial labels and to insist on being simply "of the American race." They will not be bothered by the thought that, during Toomer's lifetime, only white people were treated simply as Americans.

Other readers will no doubt consider Toomer a racial opportunist, like his grandfather, P. B. S. Pinchback, Governor of Louisiana during Reconstruction, who, according to Toomer, settled in New Orleans before the Civil War and commanded a regiment of federal troops during the war. After "the war ended and the black man [was] freed and enfranchised," Pinchback saw his "opportunity in the political arena. He claimed he had Negro blood, linked himself with the Negro cause, and rose to power." Once having obtained power Pinchback did nothing of substance for the masses of black men who voted for him. He and his family lived richly among upper-class whites until his money began to dwindle from playing the horses too much. He then moved among "colored" people who were so nearly white that "they had never run up against the color line." It was among these white and near-white neighbors that Toomer grew up.

Like his grandfather, Toomer apparently used his "connection" to black people only once, when it was to his advantage to do so. When he was attempting to publish excerpts from *Cane,* he sent some stories to the *Liberator,* one of whose editors was black writer Claude McKay. He explained that though he was of French, Welsh, Negro, German, and Jewish and Indian ancestry, his "growing need for artistic expression" pulled him "deeper and deeper into the Negro group. And as my powers of receptivity increased, I found myself loving it in a way that I could never love the other. It has stimulated and fertilized whatever creative talent I may contain within me. A visit to Georgia last fall was the starting point of almost everything of worth that I have done. I heard folk-songs come from the lips of Negro peasants. I saw the rich dusk beauty that I had heard many false accents about, and of which till then, I was somewhat skeptical. And a deep part of my nature, a part that I had repressed, sprang suddenly to life and responded to them. Now I cannot conceive of myself as aloof and separated."

Once *Cane* was published, however, Toomer told a different story. When his publisher asked him to "feature" himself as a Negro for *Cane's* publicity, Toomer replied that as he was not a Negro, he could not feature himself as one. He dropped out of literary circles, joined a Gurdjieffian commune intent on self-realization, met the well-connected white novelist Margery Latimer and married her. She died a year later in childbirth. His second wife, the affluent Marjorie Content Toomer, also white, settled down with him on a farm among the "tolerant Quakers" of Bucks County, Pennsylvania, where, after seventy-three years of living as "an American," Toomer died in a nursing home.

A few of us will realize that *Cane* was not only his finest work but that it is also in part based on the essence of stories told to Toomer by his grandmother, she of the "dark blood" to whom the book is dedicated, and that many of the women in *Cane* are modeled on the tragic indecisiveness and weakness of his mother's life. *Cane* was for Toomer a double "swan song." He meant it to memorialize a culture he thought was dying, whose folk spirit he considered beautiful, but he was also saying good-bye to the "Negro" he felt dying in himself. *Cane* then is a parting gift, and no less precious because of that. I think Jean Toomer would want us to keep its beauty, but let him go.

1980

. . . .

A WRITER BECAUSE OF, NOT IN SPITE
OF, HER CHILDREN

Another writer and I were discussing the difficulty of working immediately after the birth of our children. "I wrote nothing for a year," I offered, "that didn't sound as though a baby were screaming right through the middle of it." "And I," she said, leaning forward, "was so stricken with melancholia whenever I tried to think of writing that I spent months in a stupor. Luckily," she added, still frowning at this dismal memory, "I always had full-time help." Having had a sitter only three afternoons a week, I thought she had a nerve comparing her hard time to mine.

What this woman and I needed to put our lives in perspective was a copy of Buchi Emecheta's book *Second Class Citizen.*

It was the dedication page of this novel that made me read it, because it is exactly the kind of dedication I could not imagine making myself.

To my dear children,
Florence, Sylvester, Jake, Christy and Alice,
without whose sweet background noises
this book would not have been written.

What kind of woman would think the "background noises" of *five* children "sweet"? I thought the dedication might camouflage the author's unadmitted maternal guilt, but Emecheta is a writer and a mother, and it is because she is both that she writes at all.

Adah, the central character of *Second Class Citizen*, has no memory of her existence before the age of eight. She is not positive she was eight, because, "you see, she was a girl. A girl who had arrived when everyone was expecting and predicting a boy. So, since she was such a disappointment to her parents, to her immediate family, to her tribe, nobody thought of recording her birth." Adah's "tribe" are the Ibos of Nigeria, and among the Ibos a woman's only function is to work hard around the house and have countless children, preferably boys.

It is her brother, Boy, who is routinely sent to school, while Adah is left home to learn the duties of a wife. Bright and intensely interested in learning to read, Adah sneaks off to school: because her desire to be educated is as pathetic as it is obvious, she is allowed to stay. Her parents are reminded by her teachers that, since Adah will be educated above the other girls in her age group, her bride price will be higher. In short, they will be able to make money off her.

The years pass in dreams of going to England (which Adah thinks is a kind of heaven), in hard work at home, and in study, which Adah loves. When it is time to apply to the university, however, Adah—who is now orphaned—discovers that because she has no home she will not be allowed to take the necessary exams. Because women who live alone in Ibo society are considered prostitutes, and because she needs a home to continue her education, Adah marries Francis, a lazy and spoiled perennial student who considers her his property. (And in Ibo society, she is.) Eager for elevation among her clan (a woman who has many sons eventually reaches the rank of man), Adah has two children in rapid succession, impressing everyone with her ability to reproduce as well as hold down a high-salaried civil-service job at the American consulate. When she follows Francis to London she discovers such speedy reproduction is not admired there. With children in tow and a husband who has accommodated himself to being a second-class citizen, resigned to living in a hovel (almost no one, English or otherwise, will rent to "Africans with children"), Adah must adapt to a country that is overwhelmingly racist, and to people who seem incapable of decent behavior toward their former subjects.

Ignoring her husband's advice that she too is now a second-class citizen and must accept work in a factory with the other African wives, Adah applies for a better job, in a library. To her husband's discomfiture, she gets it, but must soon give it up because she is pregnant again.

The horrors of Adah's life are many: Francis is physically abusive out of frustration at not passing the exams he came to England to study for; Adah's countrymen and -women are rude and unhelpful because they consider Adah, with her first-class job, a show-off; Adah's pregnancies are hard, and her children often sick. But through it all she manages to view her situation from a cultural perspective that precludes self-pity. Early on, she makes a distinction between her husband and her children: "But even if she had nothing to thank Francis for, she could still thank him for giving her her own children, because she had never really had anything before."

And it is here that Adah makes the decision that seems to me impressive and important for all artists with children. She reasons that since her children will someday be adults, she will fulfill the ambition of her life not only for herself, but also for them. The ambition of her life is to write a novel, and on the first day she has her oldest child in a nursery and her youngest two down for their naps, she begins writing it. Since this novel is written to the adults her children will become, it is okay with her if the distractions and joys they represent in her life, as children, become part of it. (I agree that it is healthier, in any case, to write for the adults one's children will become than for the children one's "mature" critics often are.)

In this way, she integrates the profession of writer into the cultural concept of mother/worker that she retains from Ibo society. Just as the African mother has traditionally planted crops, pounded maize, and done her washing with her baby strapped to her back, so Adah can write a novel with her children playing in the same room.

The first novel that Adah writes is destroyed by her husband. It would shame his parents, he claims, to have a daughter-in-law who writes. Adah leaves him and begins another book. To support herself she works in a local library, where she amuses herself listening to what are for her simplistic woes, which her British and American colleagues insist on revealing to her. She writes her novel in bits and pieces while her children are still asleep or not so quietly playing.

The book jacket makes clear the similarity between Adah's life and that of the author: "Buchi Emecheta was born in 1944 near Lagos, Nigeria, and she went to school and later married there. In 1962 she went to London, where, with her five children, she still lives, working among the black youth in Paddington. She finds time for writing by getting up at four every morning, before the demands of children and job take over."

The notion that this is remotely possible causes a rethinking of traditional Western ideas about how art is produced. Our culture separates the duties of raising children from those of creative work. I have, myself, always required an absolutely quiet and private place to work (preferably with a view of a garden). Others have required various versions of an ivory tower, a Yaddo, a MacDowell Colony.

Though *Second Class Citizen* is not stylistically exciting and is no doubt heavily autobiographical, it is no less valid as a novel. And a good one. It raises fundamental questions about how creative and prosaic life is to be lived and to what purpose, which is more than some books, written while one's children are banished from one's life, do. *Second Class Citizen* is one of the most informative books about contemporary African life that I have read.

1976

GIFTS OF POWER: THE WRITINGS OF

REBECCA JACKSON

In the summer of 1830, when Rebecca Cox Jackson was thirty-five years old, she awoke in panic to the loud thunder and flashing lightning of a severe storm. For five years thunderstorms had terrorized her, making her so sick she was forced to wait them out in bed. This time, even the sanctuary of her bed was not enough; she found herself cowering miserably at the top of the garret stairs of her house believing the next blast of thunder would knock her down them. In this condition she called earnestly to "the Lord" to forgive her all her sins, since she was about to die, and to have mercy in the next world on her poor sinner's soul. Instead of dying, however, with the utterance of this prayer her inner storm ceased, the clouded sky inside her cleared, and her heart became "light" with the forgiveness, mercy, and love of God. Her fear of storms left her permanently (she now believed the power of God's spirit would come to her in storms); and she ran from window to window throwing open the blinds to let the lightning stream in upon her. It was, she said, like "glory" to her soul.

This was Rebecca Jackson's first spiritual connection with the divine. She was to have many more.

Rebecca Cox was born in 1795 of free black parents in Philadelphia. Her mother died when she was thirteen, and she spent many years with a beloved grandmother, who also died while she was young. There is no record of her father. Her young adult life, indeed her life until she was nearly forty, was lived in the home of her older brother, Joseph Cox, an elder of the influential Bethel African Methodist Episcopal church, one of the first black churches in America, founded by Richard Allen. Her husband, Samuel Jackson, lived with her in her brother's house and was also deeply involved in the church. They had no children of their own.

After Jackson's spiritual conversion—as she acknowledged it in later years—she found she had been given spiritual "gifts." That she could tell the future through dreams, for example, and nothing was hidden from her "spirit eye." This meant that while speaking to other people or simply observing them (and frequently not even this) she was able to discern their innermost thoughts as well as ways to deal with them. "God" (manifested as an inner voice) spoke to her, she felt, directly, and as long as she did not hesitate to obey Him she could count on His help over any obstacle.

There were many obstacles.

For one thing, Jackson could neither read nor write, in a family and religious community that valued these skills perhaps above all others. As the eldest girl, responsible for the care of younger siblings after her mother died, as well as for her brother's several small children, there was no opportunity to attend school. How she was even to speak intelligently about God, hindered as she was by ignorance of His written word, she could not fathom. She was also a married woman.

It was her brother to whom she turned for help in learning to read, but, tired from his own work and often impatient with Jackson, he succeeded in making her feel even more backward and lost. He also attempted to censor or change what she dictated and wished him to write.

So I went to get my brother to write my letters and to read them. So he was awriting a letter in answer to one he had just read. I told him what to put in. Then I asked him to read. He did. I said, "Thee has put in more than I told thee. . . . I don't want thee to *word* my letter. I only want thee to *write* it." Then he said, "Sister, thee is the hardest one I ever wrote for!" These words, together with the manner that he wrote my letter, pierced my soul like a sword. . . . I could not keep from crying. And these words were spoken in my heart, "Be faithful, and the time shall come when you can write." These words were spoken in my heart as though a tender father spoke them. My tears were gone in a moment.

Incredibly, Jackson *was* taught to read and write by the spirit within her.

One day I was sitting finishing a dress in haste and in prayer. [Jackson earned her living as a dressmaker.] This word was spoken in my mind, "Who learned the first man on earth?" "Why, God." "He is unchangeable, and if He learned the first man to read, He can learn you." I laid down my dress, picked up my Bible, ran upstairs, opened it, and kneeled down with it pressed to my heart, prayed earnestly to Almighty God if it was consisting to His holy will, to learn me to read His holy word. And when I looked on the word, I began to read. And when I found I was reading, I was frightened—then I could not read another word. I closed my eyes again in prayer and then opened my eyes, began to read. So I done, until I read the whole chapter. I came down. "Samuel, I can read the Bible." "Woman, you are agoing crazy!" "Praise the God of heaven and earth, I can read His holy word!" Down I sat and read through. . . . When my brother came to dinner I told him, "I can read the Bible! I have read a whole chapter!" "One thee has heard the children read, till thee has got it by heart." What a wound that was to me, to think he would make so light of a gift of God!

From this time on, Rebecca Jackson found she could write her own letters and "read the Bible anywhere." Her scriptural interpretations, however, based solely on personal spiritual instruction, caused strife not only in her own family, but also in the entire religious community of which she was a part. She was a woman, after all, when the church did not permit women as preachers, who, as soon as she received the holy message, moved immediately to spread it. The pastors and elders of the established churches (all male) accused her of "chopping up the churches," since she declined to join any, and of being a heretic, "a woman aleading the men." There were many threats against her and attempts made on her life.

For the most part, Jackson's spiritual insights came from direct, frequently ecstatic, revelation in either a dreaming or a waking state. She was also literally instructed in matters both spiritual and temporal by a spirit who arrived almost daily to give her lessons. One of the most astonishing examples of this instruction (Jackson's "teacher" was a "fatherly" white man dressed in Quaker attire) is the following entry from her journal, "View of the Natural Atmosphere":

Monday evening, February 18, 1850, I was instructed concerning the atmosphere and its bounds. I saw its form—it is like the sea, which has her bounds. . . . It covered land and sea, so far above all moving things, and yet so far beneath the starry heavens. Its face is like the face of the sea, smooth and gentle when undisturbed by the wind. So is the atmosphere, when undisturbed by the power of the sun and moon. When agitated by these, it rages like the sea and sends forth its storms upon the earth. Nothing can live above it. A bird could no more live or fly above its face, than a fish can live or swim out of water. It is always calm and serene between its face and the starry heaven. The sight, to me, was beautiful.

Her dreams are filled with symbols and her own activity. She can fly through the air like a bird (though higher than birds, and, interestingly, white women), walk through walls, visit other realms, and converse with angels. She can touch a hot stove while awake and not be burned, or totter with eyes closed on the very lip of a steep cellar stair and not fall. She preaches the word of God as it is revealed to her and discovers she has the power to pray sick people well and sinful people holy. All glory for these wonders she gives to God alone and repeatedly describes herself as "a little child" or "a worm of the dust."

One of the biggest obstacles to Jackson's new life in Christ (Jesus, she is told, is the second Adam, and essentially a female spirit; the first Adam was essentially male and fell from grace because he permitted lust to replace spirit and therefore obedience to God) was the expectation of her husband that as his wife she must fulfill her sexual obligations toward him. But her inner voice insisted that though she might live with her husband and serve him in every other way, she could not indulge in what she termed "the sin of the fall." To do so would put her in the same category as Adam. Her husband was at first puzzled, then convinced of her holiness, then outraged anyhow. In his wilder moments, Jackson writes, he "sought my life, night and day." But, because her inner voice was always "leading" her, she was able to keep ahead of him, to know what he was "agoing to do" before he knew it himself.

A year after her conversion she left her husband and her brother's house. She became an itinerant minister who found "fellowship" (more accurately "sistership") among other black women who organized "praying bands" that met in small groups in each other's houses to pray, discuss the scripture and sing, and sustain each other in the arduous task of following the "true" voice within them. (Spiritual consciousness-raising groups, one might say.) It was at this time that Jackson formed a relationship with a younger woman, Rebecca Perot. These two women lived together, ate together, traveled together, prayed together, and slept together until the end of Jackson's life, some thirty-odd years after they met.

It was with Rebecca Perot that Jackson became a resident member of the community of Shakers at Watervliet, New York. The Shakers, a religious group that believed in nothing secular —least of all government and man-made laws (they would not fight in America's wars; indeed, they did not recognize the country of America)—were ecstatics who shared the same spiritual views as Rebecca Jackson: they believed God was spirit ("As well ask how Jesus could be a man as how can Jesus be a woman. God is spirit") and should be worshiped as one, preferably in silence unless the spirit itself directs otherwise. They believed in confession and repentance of sin as a prerequisite of inner peace. They believed in physical and moral cleanliness, in plain dress, in meditation and silence, and in living separate from the world. But more important than any of these, from Rebecca Jackson's point of view, they believed in celibacy; the only religious group she ever heard of that did.

During her time with the Shakers, Jackson knew much spiritual richness and love. For the first time in her life she felt understood and warmly treasured as one who revealed obvious gifts from God. As much as she had been despised in the A.M.E. churches for her stand on celibacy (in her view, an absolute necessity if one wanted to lead a spiritual life), she was embraced by the Shakers, who agreed with her that inasmuch as Jesus Christ was unmarried and celibate, this was the example he wished his people to follow.

With the passing of time, however, disagreements surfaced, primarily because Jackson felt compelled *always* to follow her own inner voice or "invisible lead" and could not follow the Shaker leaders unless instructed by her inner lead to do so. Shortly before the Civil War she was commanded by her inner voice to minister to her own people—ravaged by slavery and persecution—whose destitution she felt the Shakers did not adequately address. But when she requested leave to follow the commandment, the Shaker leadership would not give her its blessing to do so. She and Perot left Watervliet anyway, though Jackson was accused of apostasy, of attempting to lead others "in her own gift."

With time, the rift was healed. Rebecca Jackson received instruction from her inner lead that she might accept orders and instruction from the Shaker elders and eldresses. After this submission she was given a Shaker blessing to minister to black people in a black Shaker settlement, which she established in Philadelphia in the 1870s. With this blessing came the authority of being a recognized religious group, as well as a Shaker promise to render aid to the new settlement in time of trouble. There is no record that Jackson either requested or received such aid.

·   ·   ·

A core group of sisters lived together in a single large house, supporting themselves by daywork, as seamstresses or laundresses in the city . . . [Shaker records tell us]. White Shakers, visiting from Watervliet and New Lebanon in 1872, described the residence of the family in slightly awestruck terms, as "almost palatial" with its modern plumbing, central heating, "a large drawing room, sufficient for twenty souls to sit down," a carpeted meeting room with "marble" mantels . . . "very nice, almost extravagantly so." Their description of the services that took place that evening . . . is also thoroughly admiring.

In 1878 eight black women, three black children, and three white women (one of them Jewish) lived in the Shaker commune, members of Rebecca Jackson and Rebecca Perot's spiritual family.

The little band of Shaker sisters survived after Rebecca Jackson's death, in 1871, at least until 1908, when the last reports of the group were recorded.

Gifts of Power is an extraordinary document. It tells us much about the spirituality of human beings, especially of the interior spiritual resources of our mothers, and, because of this, makes an invaluable contribution to what we know of ourselves. A simple review could not begin to do it justice, for it is a contribution of many facets, some readily comprehended, some not. What, for instance, are we to make of Rebecca Jackson's obviously gnostic beliefs (that the "resurrection" occurs in life, not after death; that the spirit of "Christ" is manifested through the "mind" in visions and dreams and not through the bureaucracy of the church) a hundred years before the Nag Hammadi "Gnostic Gospels, the Secret Teachings of Christ" was found? What are we to make of her discovery that she had not only a divine Father but also a divine Mother—which is consistent with pre-Western Indian and African religious belief? What are we to make of the reasons that suggest why so many black women (Rebecca Jackson only one of them*) abandoned the early black churches to find religious au.iences of their own? (The established churches insisted on "civilized" worship, everyone singing at the same time out of the same book; whereas the women wanted the passion and glory of spontaneous *inspired* worship and song, behavior the male leaders of the churches called "heathenish." What the male leaders termed "progress" in the black church, i.e., subdued, calm, rather Presbyterian behavior, the women called "letting the devil into the church.") What are we to make of Jackson's ability to "manufacture" spiritually a "father" she had never had? And what are we to make of the remarkable general power of Rebecca Jackson herself—a woman whose inner spirit directed her to live her own life, creating it from scratch, leaving husband, home, family, and friends, to do so?

Jean McMahon Humez has done a magnificent job in editing *Gifts of Power.* There is only one point at which I stopped, while reading her splendid and thorough introduction, to question her obviously deep knowledge of her material. It is when she discusses the relationship between Rebecca Jackson and Rebecca Perot (known among the Shakers as "the two Rebeccas"). Unlike other black women who were spiritual leaders and were single and traveled alone, Rebecca, Humez writes, "after breaking with her husband and brother . . . lived and traveled throughout the rest of her life in close relationship with a single cherished, intimate woman friend who shared her religious ideas. *Perhaps, had she been born in the modern age, she would have been an open lesbian"* (my italics).

*Others included Sojourner Truth, Amanda Berry Smith, and Jerena Lee.

79

Though women ministers who worshiped and lived with other women were perceived by the male leaders of the early churches as "closeted lesbians," because they followed their own inner voices rather than the "fathers" of the church, there is nothing in these writings that seems to make Jackson one. It would be wonderful if she were, of course. But it would be just as wonderful if she were not. One wonders why, since Jackson mentions more than once her "deadness" to sexuality or "lust," Humez implies she was a lesbian? The example she gives of "erotic" activity on Jackson's part is a dream Jackson relates which involves Rebecca Perot's long hair. In the dream another woman combs all her hair out, and Rebecca Jackson is upset because she had worked so hard on Perot's hair and "had got it so long."

Considering that our culture has always treasured long hair nearly as much as reading, and frequently *as* much, I submit that this does not qualify as an erotic dream. A more telling dream, in my opinion, is one related by Rebecca *Perot,* in which she saw herself as queen and Rebecca Jackson as king of Africa.

What I am questioning is a nonblack scholar's attempt to label something lesbian that the black woman in question has not. Even if Rebecca Jackson and Rebecca Perot *were* erotically bound, what was their own word for it? (What would be the name that must have been as black and positive as "bull-dagger" —in more modern times—is black and negative?) Did they see it as a rejection of men? Did it (whatever they did alone together) infringe on their notion of celibacy? Was the "lesbianism" the simple fact that Jackson and Perot lived together? And would this mean that any two women who lived together are lesbians? Is the "lesbianism" the fact that Jackson and Perot lived with other women and founded a religious settlement comprised entirely of women (and their children)? If the "lesbianism" is any of these things, then the charge that the women were "closeted lesbians" was well founded. But the women did not accept this label when it was made, and I think we should at least wonder whether they would accept it now, particularly since the name they *did* accept, *and embrace,* which caused them so much suffering and abuse, was *celibate.* Of course celibates, like lesbians, have a hard time proving they exist. My own guess is that, like Virginia Woolf, whom many claim as a lesbian but who described herself as a "eunuch," the two Rebeccas became spiritual sisters partly *because* they cared little for sex, which Jackson repeatedly states.

The word "lesbian" may not, in any case, be suitable (or comfortable) for black women, who surely would have begun their woman-bonding earlier than Sappho's residency on the Isle of Lesbos. Indeed, I can imagine black women who love women (sexually or not) hardly thinking of what Greeks were doing; but, instead, referring to themselves as "whole" women, from "wholly" or "holy." Or as "round" women—women who love other women, yes, but women who also have concern, in a culture that oppresses all black people (and this would go back very far), for their fathers, brothers, and sons, no matter how they feel about them as males. My own term for such women would be "womanist." At any rate, the word they chose would have to be both spiritual and concrete and it would have to be organic, characteristic, not simply applied. A word that said more than that they choose women over men. More than that they choose to live separate from men. In fact, to be consistent with black cultural values (which, whatever their shortcomings, still have considerable worth) it would have to be a word that affirmed connectedness to the entire community and the world, rather than separation, *regardless* of who worked and slept with whom. All things considered, the main problem with Lesbos as a point of common reference for women who love women is not, as I had once thought, that it was inhabited by Greek women whose servants, like their culture, were probably stolen from Egypt, but that it is an island. The symbolism of this, for a black person, is far from positive.

But this is a small complaint and perhaps an esoteric one. I simply feel that naming our own experience after our own fashion (as well as rejecting whatever does not seem to suit) is the least we can do—and in this society may well be our only tangible sign of personal freedom. It was her grasp of the importance of this that caused Rebecca Jackson to write down her spiritual "travels" that all might witness her individual path. This, that makes her an original. This, that makes us thankful to receive her as a gift of power in herself.

1981

. . . .

ZORA NEALE HURSTON:

A CAUTIONARY TALE AND

A PARTISAN VIEW

I became aware of my need of Zora Neale Hurston's work some
time before I knew her work existed. In late 1970 I was writing
a story that required accurate material on voodoo practices
among rural Southern blacks of the thirties; there seemed none
available I could trust. A number of white, racist anthropologists
and folklorists of the period had, not surprisingly, disappointed
and insulted me. They thought blacks inferior, peculiar, and
comic, and for me this undermined, no, *destroyed,* the relevance
of their books. Fortunately, it was then that I discovered *Mules
and Men,* Zora's book on folklore, collecting, herself, and her
small, all-black community of Eatonville, Florida. Because she
immersed herself in her own culture even as she recorded its
"big old lies," i.e., folk tales, it was possible to see how she and
it (even after she had attended Barnard College and become a
respected writer and apprentice anthropologist) fit together.
The authenticity of her material was verified by her familiarity

with its context, and I was soothed by her assurance that she was exposing not simply an adequate culture but a superior one. That black people can be on occasion peculiar and comic was knowledge she enjoyed. That they could be racially or culturally inferior to whites never seems to have crossed her mind.

The first time I heard Zora's *name*, I was auditing a black-literature class taught by the great poet Margaret Walker, at Jackson State College in Jackson, Mississippi. The reason this fact later slipped my mind was that Zora's name and accomplishments came and went so fast. The class was studying the usual "giants" of black literature: Chesnutt, Toomer, Hughes, Wright, Ellison, and Baldwin, with the hope of reaching LeRoi Jones very soon. Jessie Fauset, Nella Larsen, Ann Petry, Paule Marshall (unequaled in intelligence, vision, craft by anyone of her generation, to put her contributions to our literature modestly), and Zora Neale Hurston were names appended, like verbal footnotes, to the illustrious all-male list that paralleled them. As far as I recall, none of their work was studied in the course. Much of it was out of print, in any case, and remains so. (Perhaps Gwendolyn Brooks and Margaret Walker herself were exceptions to this list; both poets of such obvious necessity it would be impossible to overlook them. And their work—owing to the political and cultural nationalism of the sixties—was everywhere available.)

When I read *Mules and Men* I was delighted. Here was this perfect book! The "perfection" of which I immediately tested on my relatives, who are such typical black Americans they are useful for every sort of political, cultural, or economic survey. Very regular people from the South, rapidly forgetting their Southern cultural inheritance in the suburbs and ghettos of Boston and New York, they sat around reading the book themselves, listening to me read the book, listening to each other read the book, and a kind of paradise was regained. For what Zora's book did was this: it gave them back all the stories they had forgotten or of which they had grown ashamed (told to us years ago by our parents and grandparents—not one of whom could *not* tell a story to make you weep, or laugh) and showed how marvelous, and, indeed, priceless, they are. This is not exaggerated. No matter how they read the stories Zora had collected, no matter how much distance they tried to maintain between themselves, as new sophisticates, and the lives their parents and grandparents lived, no matter how they tried to remain cool toward all Zora revealed, in the end they could not hold back the smiles, the laughter, the joy over who she was showing them to be: descendants of an inventive, joyous, courageous, and outrageous people; loving drama, appreciating wit, and, most of all, relishing the pleasure of each other's loquacious and *bodacious* company.

This was my first indication of the quality I feel is most characteristic of Zora's work: racial health; a sense of black people as complete, complex, *undiminished* human beings, a sense that is lacking in so much black writing and literature. (In my opinion, only Du Bois showed an equally consistent delight in the beauty and spirit of black people, which is interesting when one considers that the angle of his vision was completely the opposite of Zora's.) Zora's pride in black people was so pronounced in the ersatz black twenties that it made other blacks suspicious and perhaps uncomfortable (after all, *they* were still infatuated with things European). Zora was interested in Africa, Haiti, Jamaica, and—for a little racial diversity (Indians) —Honduras. She also had a confidence in herself as an individual that few people (anyone?), black or white, understood. This was because Zora grew up in a community of black people who had enormous respect for themselves and for their ability to govern themselves. Her own father had written the Eatonville town laws. This community affirmed her right to exist, and loved her as an extension of its self. For how many other black Americans is this true? It certainly isn't true for any that I know. In her easy self-acceptance, Zora was more like an uncolonized African than she was like her contemporary American blacks, most of whom believed, at least during their formative years, that their blackness was something wrong with them.

On the contrary, Zora's early work shows she grew up pitying whites because the ones she saw lacked "light" and soul. It is impossible to imagine Zora envying anyone (except tongue in cheek), and least of all a white person for being white. Which is, after all, if one is black, a clear and present calamity of the mind.

Condemned to a desert island for life, with an allotment of ten books to see me through, I would choose, unhesitatingly, two of Zora's: *Mules and Men,* because I would need to be able to pass on to younger generations the life of American blacks as legend and myth; and *Their Eyes Were Watching God,* because I would want to enjoy myself while identifying with the black heroine, Janie Crawford, as she acted out many roles in a variety of settings, and functioned (with spectacular results!) in romantic and sensual love. *There is no book more important to me than this one* (including Toomer's *Cane,* which comes close, but from what I recognize is a more perilous direction).

Having committed myself to Zora's work, loving it, in fact, I became curious to see what others had written about her. This was, for the young, impressionable, barely begun writer I was, a mistake. After reading the misleading, deliberately belittling, inaccurate, and generally irresponsible attacks on her work and her life by almost everyone, I became for a time paralyzed with confusion and fear. For if a woman who had given so much of obvious value to all of us (and at such risks: to health, reputation, sanity) could be so casually pilloried and consigned to a sneering oblivion, what chance would someone else—for example, myself—have? I was aware that I had much less gumption than Zora.

For a long time I sat looking at this fear, and at what caused it. Zora was a woman who wrote and spoke her mind—as far as one could tell, practically always. People who knew her and were unaccustomed to this characteristic in a woman, who was, moreover, a. sometimes in error, and b. successful, for the most part, in her work, attacked her as meanly as they could. Would I also be attacked if I wrote and spoke my mind? And if I dared open my mouth to speak, must I always be "correct"? And by whose standards? Only those who have read the critics' opinions of Zora and her work will comprehend the power of these questions to riddle a young writer with self-doubt.

Eventually, however, I discovered that I repudiate and despise the kind of criticism that intimidates rather than instructs the young; and I dislike fear, especially in myself. I did then what fear rarely fails to force me to do: I fought back. I began to fight for Zora and her work; for what I knew was good and must not be lost to us.

Robert Hemenway was the first critic I read who seemed indignant that Zora's life ended in poverty and obscurity; that her last days were spent in a welfare home and her burial paid for by "subscription." Though Zora herself, as he is careful to point out in his book *Zora Neale Hurston: A Literary Biography*, remained gallant and unbowed until the end. It was Hemenway's efforts to define Zora's legacy and his exploration of her life that led me, in 1973, to an overgrown Fort Pierce, Florida graveyard in an attempt to locate and mark Zora's grave. Although by that time I considered her a native American genius, there was nothing grand or historic in my mind. It was, rather, a duty I accepted as naturally mine—as a black person, a woman, and a writer—because Zora was dead and I, for the time being, was alive.

. . .

Zora was funny, irreverent (she was the first to call the Harlem Renaissance literati the "niggerati"), good-looking, sexy, and once sold hot dogs in a Washington park just to record accurately how the black people who bought the hot dogs talked. (A letter I received a month ago from one of her old friends in D.C. brought this news.) She would go anywhere she had to go: Harlem, Jamaica, Haiti, Bermuda, to find out anything she simply had to know. She loved to give parties. Loved to dance. Would wrap her head in scarves as black women in Africa, Haiti, and everywhere else have done for centuries. On the other hand, she loved to wear hats, tilted over one eye, and pants and boots. (I have a photograph of her in pants, boots, and broadbrim that was given to me by her brother, Everette. She has her foot up on the running board of a car—presumably hers, and bright red —and looks racy.) She would light up a fag—which wasn't done by ladies then (and, thank our saints, as a young woman she was never a lady) on the street.

Her critics disliked even the "rags" on her head. (They seemed curiously incapable of telling the difference between an African-American queen and Aunt Jemima.) They disliked her apparent sensuality: the way she tended to marry or not marry men, but enjoyed them anyway—while never missing a beat in her work. They hinted slyly that Zora was gay, or at least bisexual —how else could they account for her drive? Though there is not, perhaps unfortunately, a shred of evidence that this was true. The accusation becomes humorous—and of course at all times irrelevant—when one considers that what she *did* write was one of the sexiest, most "healthily" rendered heterosexual love stories in our literature. In addition, she talked too much, got things from white folks (Guggenheims, Rosenwalds, and footstools) much too easily, was slovenly in her dress, and appeared maddeningly indifferent to other people's opinions of her. With her easy laughter and her Southern drawl, her belief in doing "cullud" dancing authentically, Zora seemed—among these genteel "New Negroes" of the Harlem Renaissance—*black.* No wonder her presence was always a shock. Though almost everyone agreed she was a delight, not everyone agreed such audacious black delight was permissible, or, indeed, quite the proper image for the race.

Zora was before her time, in intellectual circles, in the life style she chose. By the sixties everyone understood that black women could wear beautiful cloths on their beautiful heads and care about the authenticity of things "cullud" *and* African. By the sixties it was no longer a crime to receive financial assistance —in the form of grants and fellowships—for one's work. (Interestingly, those writers who complained that Zora "got money from white folks" were often themselves totally supported, down to the food they ate—or, in Langston Hughes's case, *tried* to eat, after his white "Godmother" discarded him—by white patrons.) By the sixties, nobody cared that marriage didn't last forever. No one expected it to. And I do believe that now, in the seventies, we do not expect (though we may wish and pray) every black person who speaks *always* to speak *correctly* (since this is impossible): and if we *do* expect it, we deserve all the silent leadership we are likely to get.

During the early and middle years of her career Zora was a cultural revolutionary simply because she was always herself. Her work, so vigorous among the rather pallid productions of many of her contemporaries, comes from the essence of black folk life. During her later life she became frightened of the life she had always dared bravely before. Her work too became reactionary, static, shockingly misguided and timid. (This is especially true of her last novel, *Seraphs on the Sewannee*, which is not even about black people, which is no crime, but *is* about white people for whom it is impossible to care, which is.)

A series of misfortunes battered Zora's spirit and her health. And she was broke.

Being broke made all the difference.

Without money of one's own in a capitalist society, there is no such thing as independence. This is one of the clearest lessons of Zora's life, and why I consider the telling of her life "a cautionary tale." We must learn from it what we can.

Without money, an illness, even a simple one, can undermine the will. Without money, getting into a hospital is problematic and getting out without money to pay for the treatment is nearly impossible. Without money, one becomes dependent on other people, who are likely to be—even in their kindness—erratic in their support and despotic in their expectations of return. Zora was forced to rely, like Tennessee Williams's Blanche, "on the kindness of strangers." Can anything be more dangerous, if the strangers are forever in control? Zora, who worked so hard, was never able to make a living from her work.

She did not complain about not having money. She was not the type. (Several months ago I received a long letter from one of Zora's nieces, a bright ten-year-old, who explained to me that her aunt was so proud that the only way the family could guess she was ill or without funds was by realizing they had no idea where she was. Therefore, none of the family attended either Zora's sickbed or her funeral.) Those of us who have had "grants and fellowships from 'white folks' " know this aid is extended in precisely the way welfare is extended in Mississippi. One is asked, *curtly*, more often than not: How much do you need *just to survive?* Then one is—if fortunate—given a third of that. What is amazing is that Zora, who became an orphan at nine, a runaway at fourteen, a maid and manicurist (because of necessity and not from love of the work) before she was twenty—with one dress—managed to become Zora Neale Hurston, author and anthropologist, at all.

For me, the most unfortunate thing Zora ever wrote is her autobiography. After the first several chapters, it rings false. One begins to hear the voice of someone whose life required the assistance of too many transitory "friends." A Taoist proverb states that *to act sincerely with the insincere is dangerous.* (A mistake blacks as a group have tended to make in America.) And so we have Zora sincerely offering gratitude and kind words to people one knows she could not have respected. But this unctuousness, so out of character for Zora, is also a result of dependency, a sign of her powerlessness, her inability to pay back her debts with anything but words. They must have been bitter ones for her. In her dependency, it should be remembered, Zora was not alone—because it is quite true that America does not support or honor us as human beings, let alone as blacks, women, and artists. We have taken help where it was offered because we are committed to what we do and to the survival of our work. Zora was committed to the survival of her people's cultural heritage as well.

In my mind, Zora Neale Hurston, Billie Holiday, and Bessie Smith form a sort of unholy trinity. Zora *belongs* in the tradition of black women singers, rather than among "the literati," at least to me. There were the extreme highs and lows of her life, her undaunted pursuit of adventure, passionate emotional and sexual experience, and her love of freedom. Like Billie and Bessie she followed her own road, believed in her own gods, pursued her own dreams, and refused to separate herself from "common" people. It would have been nice if the three of them had had one another to turn to, in times of need. I close my eyes and imagine them: Bessie would be in charge of all the money; Zora would keep Billie's masochistic tendencies in check and prevent her from singing embarrassing anything-for-a-man songs, thereby preventing Billie's heroin addiction. In return, Billie could be, along with Bessie, the family that Zora felt she never had.

We are a people. A people do not throw their geniuses away. And if they are thrown away, it is our duty *as artists and as witnesses for the future* to collect them again for the sake of our children, and, if necessary, bone by bone.

1979

. . . .

LOOKING FOR ZORA

On January 16, 1959, Zora Neale Hurston, suffering from the effects of a stroke and writing painfully in longhand, composed a letter to the "editorial department" of Harper & Brothers inquiring if they would be interested in seeing "the book I am laboring upon at present—a life of Herod the Great." One year and twelve days later, Zora Neale Hurston died without funds to provide for her burial, a resident of the St. Lucie County, Florida, Welfare Home. She lies today in an unmarked grave in a segregated cemetery in Fort Pierce, Florida, a resting place generally symbolic of the black writer's fate in America.

Zora Neale Hurston is one of the most significant unread authors in America, the author of two minor classics and four other major books.
—*Robert Hemenway,*
"Zora Hurston and the Eatonville Anthropology,"
in THE HARLEM RENAISSANCE REMEMBERED

．　　　．　　　．

On August 15, 1973, I wake up just as the plane is lowering over Sanford, Florida, which means I am also looking down on Eatonville, Zora Neale Hurston's birthplace. I recognize it from Zora's description in *Mules and Men:* "the city of five lakes, three croquet courts, three hundred brown skins, three hundred good swimmers, plenty guavas, two schools, and no jailhouse." Of course I cannot see the guavas, but the five lakes are still there, and it is the lakes I count as the plane prepares to land in Orlando.

From the air, Florida looks completely flat, and as we near the ground this impression does not change. This is the first time I have seen the interior of the state, which Zora wrote about so well, but there are the acres of orange groves, the sand, mangrove trees, and scrub pine that I know from her books. Getting off the plane I walk through the humid air of midday into the tacky but air-conditioned airport. I search for Charlotte Hunt, my companion on the Zora Hurston expedition. She lives in Winter Park, Florida, very near Eatonville, and is writing her graduate dissertation on Zora. I see her waving—a large, pleasant-faced white woman in dark glasses. We have written to each other for several weeks, swapping our latest finds (mostly hers) on Zora, and trying to make sense out of the mass of information obtained (often erroneous or simply confusing) from Zora herself—through her stories and autobiography—and from people who wrote about her.

Eatonville has lived for such a long time in my imagination that I can hardly believe it will be found existing in its own right. But after twenty minutes on the expressway, Charlotte turns off and I see a small settlement of houses and stores set with no particular pattern in the sandy soil off the road. We stop in front of a neat gray building that has two fascinating signs: EATON-VILLE POST OFFICE and EATONVILLE CITY HALL.

Inside the Eatonville City Hall half of the building, a slender, dark-brown-skin woman sits looking through letters on a desk. When she hears we are searching for anyone who might have known Zora Neale Hurston, she leans back in thought. Because I don't wish to inspire foot-dragging in people who might know something about Zora they're not sure they should tell, I have decided on a simple, but I feel profoundly *useful,* lie.

"I am Miss Hurston's niece," I prompt the young woman, who brings her head down with a smile.

"I think Mrs. Moseley is about the only one still living who might remember her," she says.

"Do you mean *Mathilda* Moseley, the woman who tells those 'woman-is-smarter-than-man' lies in Zora's book?"

"Yes," says the young woman. "Mrs. Moseley is real old now, of course. But this time of day, she should be at home."

I stand at the counter looking down on her, the first Eatonville resident I have spoken to. Because of Zora's books, I feel I know something about her; at least I know what the town she grew up in was like years before she was born.

"Tell me something," I say. "Do the schools teach Zora's books here?"

"No," she says, "they don't. I don't think most people know anything about Zora Neale Hurston, or know about any of the great things she did. She was a fine lady. I've read all of her books myself, but I don't think many other folks in Eatonville have."

"Many of the church people around here, as I understand it," says Charlotte in a murmured aside, "thought Zora was pretty loose. I don't think they appreciated her writing about them."

"Well," I say to the young woman, "thank you for your help." She clarifies her directions to Mrs. Moseley's house and smiles as Charlotte and I turn to go.

The letter to Harper's does not expose a publisher's rejection of an unknown masterpiece, but it does reveal how the bright promise of the Harlem Renaissance deteriorated for many of the writers who shared in its exuberance. It also indicates the personal tragedy of Zora Neale Hurston: Barnard graduate, author of four novels, two books of folklore, one volume of autobiography, the most important collector of Afro-American folklore in America, reduced by poverty and circumstance to seek a publisher by unsolicited mail.
—*Robert Hemenway*

Zora Hurston was born in 1901, 1902, or 1903—depending on how old she felt herself to be at the time someone asked.
—*Librarian, Beinecke Library,*
   Yale University

The Moseley house is small and white and snug, its tiny yard nearly swallowed up by oleanders and hibiscus bushes. Charlotte and I knock on the door. I call out. But there is no answer. This strikes us as peculiar. We have had time to figure out an age for Mrs. Moseley—not dates or a number, just old. I am thinking of a quivery, bedridden invalid when we hear the car. We look behind us to see an old black-and-white Buick— paint peeling and grillwork rusty—pulling into the drive. A neat old lady in a purple dress and with white hair is straining at the wheel. She is frowning because Charlotte's car is in the way.

Mrs. Moseley looks at us suspiciously. "Yes, I knew Zora Neale," she says, unsmilingly and with a rather cold stare at Charlotte (who, I imagine, feels very *white* at that moment), "but that was a long time ago, and I don't want to talk about it."

"Yes, ma'am," I murmur, bringing all my sympathy to bear on the situation.

"Not only that," Mrs. Moseley continues, "I've been sick. Been in the hospital for an operation. Ruptured artery. The doctors didn't believe I was going to live, but you see me alive, don't you?"

"Looking well, too," I comment.

Mrs. Moseley is out of her car. A thin, sprightly woman with nice gold-studded false teeth, uppers and lowers. I like her because she stands there *straight* beside her car, with a hand on her hip and her straw pocketbook on her arm. She wears white T-strap shoes with heels that show off her well-shaped legs.

"I'm eighty-two years old, you know," she says. "And I just can't remember things the way I used to. Anyhow, Zora Neale left here to go to school and she never really came back to live. She'd come here for material for her books, but that was all. She spent most of her time down in South Florida."

"You know, Mrs. Moseley, I saw your name in one of Zora's books."

"You did?" She looks at me with only slightly more interest. "I read some of her books a long time ago, but then people got to borrowing and borrowing and they borrowed them all away."

"I could send you a copy of everything that's been reprinted," I offer. "Would you like me to do that?"

"No," says Mrs. Moseley promptly. "I don't read much any more. Besides, all of that was so long ago. . . ."

Charlotte and I settle back against the car in the sun. Mrs. Moseley tells us at length and with exact recall every step in her recent operation, ending with: "What those doctors didn't know—when they were expecting me to die (and they didn't even think I'd live long enough for them to have to take out my stitches!)—is that Jesus is the best doctor, and if *He* says for you to get well, that's all that counts."

With this philosophy, Charlotte and I murmur quick assent: being Southerners and church bred, we have heard that belief before. But what we learn from Mrs. Moseley is that she does not remember much beyond the year 1938. She shows us a picture of her father and mother and says that her father was Joe Clarke's brother. Joe Clarke, as every Zora Hurston reader knows, was the first mayor of Eatonville; his fictional counterpart is Jody Starks of *Their Eyes Were Watching God*. We also get directions to where Joe Clarke's store *was*—where Club Eaton is now. Club Eaton, a long orange-beige nightspot we had seen on the main road, is apparently famous for the good times in it regularly had by all. It is, perhaps, the modern equivalent of the store porch, where all the men of Zora's childhood came to tell "lies," that is, black folk tales, that were "made and used on the spot," to take a line from Zora. As for Zora's exact birthplace, Mrs. Moseley has no idea.

After I have commented on the healthy growth of her hibiscus bushes, she becomes more talkative. She mentions how much she *loved* to dance, when she was a young woman, and talks about how good her husband was. When he was alive, she says, she was completely happy because he allowed her to be completely free. "I was so free I had to pinch myself sometimes to tell if I was a married woman."

Relaxed now, she tells us about going to school with Zora. "Zora and I went to the same school. It's called Hungerford High now. It *was* only to the eighth grade. But our teachers were so good that by the time you left you knew college subjects. When I went to Morris Brown in Atlanta, the teachers there were just teaching me the same things I had already learned right in Eatonville. I wrote Mama and told her I was going to come home and help her with her babies. I wasn't learning anything new."

"Tell me something, Mrs. Moseley," I ask. "Why do you suppose Zora was against integration? I read somewhere that she was against school desegregation because she felt it was an insult to black teachers."

"Oh, one of them [white people] came around asking me about integration. One day I was doing my shopping. I heard 'em over there talking about it in the store, about the schools. And I got on out of the way because I knew if they asked me, they wouldn't like what I was going to tell 'em. But they came up and asked me anyhow. 'What do you think about this integration?' one of them said. I acted like I thought I had heard wrong. 'You're asking *me* what *I* think about integration?' I said. 'Well, as you can see, I'm just an old colored woman'—I was seventy-five or seventy-six then—'and this is the first time anybody ever asked me about integration. And nobody asked my grandmother what she thought, either, but her daddy was one of you all.' " Mrs. Moseley seems satisfied with this memory of her rejoinder. She looks at Charlotte. "I have the blood of three races in my veins," she says belligerently, "white, black, and Indian, and nobody asked me *anything* before."

"Do you think living in Eatonville made integration less appealing to you?"

"Well, I can tell you this: I have lived in Eatonville all my life, and I've been in the governing of this town. I've been everything but mayor and I've been *assistant* mayor. Eatonville was and is an all-black town. We have our own police department, post office, and town hall. Our own school and good teachers. Do I need integration?

"They took over Goldsboro, because the black people who lived there never incorporated, like we did. And now I don't even know if any black folks live there. They built big houses up there around the lakes. But we didn't let that happen in Eaton-ville, and we don't sell land to just anybody. And you see, we're still here."

When we leave, Mrs. Moseley is standing by her car, wav-ing. I think of the letter Roy Wilkins wrote to a black newspaper blasting Zora Neale for her lack of enthusiasm about the integra-tion of schools. I wonder if he knew the experience of Eatonville she was coming from. Not many black people in America have come from a self-contained, all-black community where loyalty and unity are taken for granted. A place where black pride is nothing new.

There is, however, one thing Mrs. Moseley said that both-ered me.

"Tell me, Mrs. Moseley," I had asked, "why is it that thirteen years after Zora's death, no marker has been put on her grave?"

And Mrs. Moseley answered: "The reason she doesn't have a stone is because she wasn't buried here. She was buried down in South Florida somewhere. I don't think anybody really knew where she was."

Only to reach a wider audience, need she ever write books —because she is a perfect book of entertainment in herself. In her youth she was always getting scholarships and things from wealthy white people, some of whom simply paid her just to sit around and represent the Negro race for them, she did it in such a racy fashion. She was full of sidesplitting anecdotes, humorous tales, and tragicomic stories, remem-bered out of her life in the South as a daughter of a travel-ing minister of God. She could make you laugh one minute and cry the next. To many of her white friends, no doubt, she was a perfect "darkie," in the nice meaning they give the term—that is, a naïve, childlike, sweet, humorous, and highly colored Negro.

But Miss Hurston was clever, too—a student who didn't let college give her a broad "a" and who had great scorn for all pretensions, academic or otherwise. That is why she was such a fine folklore collector, able to go among the people and never act as if she had been to school at all. Almost nobody else could stop the average Harlemite on Lenox Avenue and measure his head with a strange-looking, anthropological device and not get bawled out for the attempt, except Zora, who used to stop anyone whose head looked interesting, and measure it.
—*Langston Hughes,*
THE BIG SEA

What does it matter what white folks must have thought about her?
—*Student, black women writers class*
Wellesley College

Mrs. Sarah Peek Patterson is a handsome, red-haired woman in her late forties, wearing orange slacks and gold earrings. She is the director of Lee-Peek Mortuary in Fort Pierce, the establishment that handled Zora's burial. Unlike most black funeral homes in Southern towns that sit like palaces among the general poverty, Lee-Peek has a run-down, *small* look. Perhaps this is because it is painted purple and white, as are its Cadillac chariots. These colors do not age well. The rooms are cluttered and grimy, and the bathroom is a tiny, stale-smelling prison, with a bottle of black hair dye (apparently used to touch up the hair of the corpses) dripping into the face bowl. Two pine burial boxes are resting in the bathtub.

Mrs. Patterson herself is pleasant and helpful.

"As I told you over the phone, Mrs. Patterson," I begin, shaking her hand and looking into her penny-brown eyes, "I am Zora Neale Hurston's niece, and I would like to have a marker put on her grave. You said, when I called you last week, that you could tell me where the grave is."

By this time I am, of course, completely into being Zora's niece, and the lie comes with perfect naturalness to my lips. Besides, as far as I'm concerned, she *is* my aunt—and that of all black people as well.

"She was buried in 1960," exclaims Mrs. Patterson. "That was when my father was running this funeral home. He's sick now or I'd let you talk to him. But I know where she's buried. She's in the old cemetery, the Garden of the Heavenly Rest, on Seventeenth Street. Just when you go in the gate there's a circle, and she's buried right in the middle of it. Hers is the only grave in that circle—because people don't bury in that cemetery any more."

She turns to a stocky, black-skinned woman in her thirties, wearing a green polo shirt and white jeans cut off at the knee. "This lady will show you where it is," she says.

"I can't tell you how much I appreciate this," I say to Mrs. Patterson, as I rise to go. "And could you tell me something else? You see, I never met my aunt. When she died, I was still a junior in high school. But could you tell me what she died of, and what kind of funeral she had?"

"I don't know exactly what she died of," Mrs. Patterson says. "I know she didn't have any money. Folks took up a collection to bury her. . . . I believe she died of malnutrition."

"Malnutrition?"

Outside, in the blistering sun, I lean my head against Charlotte's even more blistering car top. The sting of the hot metal only intensifies my anger. *"Malnutrition,"* I manage to mutter.

"Hell, our condition hasn't changed *any* since Phillis Wheatley's time. *She* died of malnutrition!"

"Really?" says Charlotte. "I didn't know that."

One cannot overemphasize the extent of her commitment. It was so great that her marriage in the spring of 1927 to Herbert Sheen was short-lived. Although divorce did not come officially until 1931, the two separated amicably after only a few months, Hurston to continue her collecting, Sheen to attend Medical School. Hurston never married again.
—*Robert Hemenway*

"What is your name?" I ask the woman who has climbed into the back seat.

"Rosalee," she says. She has a rough, pleasant voice, as if she is a singer who also smokes a lot. She is homely, and has an air of ready indifference.

"Another woman came by here wanting to see the grave," she says, lighting up a cigarette. "She was a little short, dumpty white lady from one of these Florida schools. Orlando or Daytona. But let me tell you something before we gets started. All I know is where the cemetery is. I don't know one thing about that grave. You better go back in and ask her to draw you a map."

A few moments later, with Mrs. Patterson's diagram of where the grave is, we head for the cemetery.

We drive past blocks of small, pastel-colored houses and turn right onto Seventeenth Street. At the very end, we reach a tall curving gate, with the words "Garden of the Heavenly Rest" fading into the stone. I expected, from Mrs. Patterson's small drawing, to find a small circle—which would have placed Zora's grave five or ten paces from the road. But the "circle" is over an acre large and looks more like an abandoned field. Tall weeds choke the dirt road and scrape against the sides of the car. It doesn't help either that I step out into an active ant hill.

"I don't know about y'all," I say, "but I don't even believe this." I am used to the haphazard cemetery-keeping that is traditional in most Southern black communities, but this neglect is staggering. As far as I can see there is nothing but bushes and weeds, some as tall as my waist. One grave is near the road, and Charlotte elects to investigate it. It is fairly clean, and belongs to someone who died in 1963.

Rosalee and I plunge into the weeds; I pull my long dress up to my hips. The weeds scratch my knees, and the insects have a feast. Looking back, I see Charlotte standing resolutely near the road.

"Aren't you coming?" I call.

"No," she calls back. "I'm from these parts and I know what's out there." She means snakes.

"Shit," I say, my whole life and the people I love flashing melodramatically before my eyes. Rosalee is a few yards to my right.

"How're you going to find anything out here?" she asks. And I stand still a few seconds, looking at the weeds. Some of them are quite pretty, with tiny yellow flowers. They are thick and healthy, but dead weeds under them have formed a thick gray carpet on the ground. A snake could be lying six inches from my big toe and I wouldn't see it. We move slowly, very slowly, our eyes alert, our legs trembly. It is hard to tell where the center of the circle is since the circle is not really round, but more like half of something round. There are things crackling and hissing in the grass. Sandspurs are sticking to the inside of my skirt. Sand and ants cover my feet. I look toward the road and notice that there are, indeed, *two* large curving stones, making an entrance and exit to the cemetery. I take my bearings from them and try to navigate to exact center. But the center of anything can be very large, and a grave is not a pinpoint. Finding the grave seems positively hopeless. There is only one thing to do:

"Zora!" I yell, as loud as I can (causing Rosalee to jump). "Are you out here?"

"If she is, I sho hope she don't answer you. If she do, I'm gone."

"Zora!" I call again. "I'm here. Are you?"

"If she is," grumbles Rosalee, "I hope she'll keep it to herself."

"Zora!" Then I start fussing with her. "I hope you don't think I'm going to stand out here all day, with these snakes watching me and these ants having a field day. In fact, I'm going to call you just one or two more times." On a clump of dried grass, near a small bushy tree, my eye falls on one of the largest bugs I have ever seen. It is on its back, and is as large as three of my fingers. I walk toward it, and yell "Zo-ra!" and my foot sinks into a hole. I look down. I am standing in a sunken rectangle that is about six feet long and about three or four feet wide. I look up to see where the two gates are.

"Well," I say, "this is the center, or approximately anyhow. It's also the only sunken spot we've found. Doesn't this look like a grave to you?"

"For the sake of not going no farther through these bushes," Rosalee growls, "yes, it do."

"Wait a minute," I say, "I have to look around some more to be sure this is the only spot that resembles a grave. But you don't have to come."

Rosalee smiles—a grin, really—beautiful and tough.

"Naw," she says, "I feels sorry for you. If one of these snakes got ahold of you out here by yourself I'd feel *real* bad." She laughs. "I done come this far, I'll go on with you."

"Thank you, Rosalee," I say. "Zora thanks you too."

"Just as long as she don't try to tell me in person," she says, and together we walk down the field.

The gusto and flavor of Zora Neal[e] Hurston's storytelling, for example, long before the yarns were published in "Mules and Men" and other books, became a local legend which might . . . have spread further under different conditions. A tiny shift in the center of gravity could have made them best-sellers.
—*Arna Bontemps,*
PERSONALS

Bitter over the rejection of her folklore's value, especially in the black community, frustrated by what she felt was her failure to convert the Afro-American world view into the forms of prose fiction, Hurston finally gave up.
—*Robert Hemenway*

When Charlotte and I drive up to the Merritt Monument Company, I immediately see the headstone I want.

"How much is this one?" I ask the young woman in charge, pointing to a tall black stone. It looks as majestic as Zora herself must have been when she was learning voodoo from those root doctors down in New Orleans.

"Oh, *that* one," she says, "that's our finest. That's Ebony Mist."

"Well, how much is it?"

"I don't know. But wait," she says, looking around in relief, "here comes somebody who'll know."

A small, sunburned man with squinty green eyes comes up. He must be the engraver, I think, because his eyes are contracted into slits, as if he has been keeping stone dust out of them for years.

"That's Ebony Mist," he says. "That's our best."

"How much is it?" I ask, beginning to realize I probably *can't* afford it.

He gives me a price that would feed a dozen Sahelian drought victims for three years. I realize I must honor the dead, but between the dead great and the living starving, there is no choice.

"I have a lot of letters to be engraved," I say, standing by the plain gray marker I have chosen. It is pale and ordinary, not at all like Zora, and makes me momentarily angry that I am not rich.

We go into his office and I hand him a sheet of paper that has:

ZORA NEALE HURSTON

"A GENIUS OF THE SOUTH"

NOVELIST   FOLKLORIST

ANTHROPOLOGIST

1901   1960

"A genius of the South" is from one of Jean Toomer's poems.

"Where is this grave?" the monument man asks. "If it's in a new cemetery, the stone has to be flat."

"Well, it's not a new cemetery and Zora—my aunt—doesn't need anything flat, because with the weeds out there, you'd never be able to see it. You'll have to go out there with me."

He grunts.

"And take a long pole and 'sound' the spot," I add. "Because there's no way of telling it's a grave, except that it's sunken."

"Well," he says, after taking my money and writing up a

receipt, in the full awareness that he's the only monument dealer for miles, "you take this flag" (he hands me a four-foot-long pole with a red-metal marker on top) "and take it out to the cemetery and put it where you think the grave is. It'll take us about three weeks to get the stone out there."

I wonder if he knows he is sending me to another confrontation with the snakes. He probably does. Charlotte has told me she will cut my leg and suck out the blood if I am bit.

"At least send me a photograph when it's done, won't you?"

He says he will.

Hurston's return to her folklore-collecting in December of 1927 was made possible by Mrs. R. Osgood Mason, an elderly white patron of the arts, who at various times also helped Langston Hughes, Alain Locke, Richmond Barthe, and Miguel Covarrubias. Hurston apparently came to her attention through the intercession of Locke, who frequently served as a kind of liaison between the young black talent and Mrs. Mason. The entire relationship between this woman and the Harlem Renaissance deserves extended study, for it represents much of the ambiguity involved in white patronage of black artists. All her artists were instructed to call her "Godmother"; there was a decided emphasis on the "primitive" aspects of black culture, apparently a holdover from Mrs. Mason's interest in the Plains Indians. In Hurston's case there were special restrictions imposed by her patron: although she was to be paid a handsome salary for her folklore collecting, she was to limit her correspondence and publish nothing of her research without prior approval.
—Robert Hemenway

> You have to read the chapters Zora *left out* of her autobio-
> graphy.
> —*Student, Special Collections Room*
>   *Beinecke Library, Yale University*

Dr. Benton, a friend of Zora's and a practicing M.D. in
Fort Pierce, is one of those old, good-looking men whom I
always have trouble not liking. (It no longer bothers me that
I may be constantly searching for father figures; by this time, I
have found several and dearly enjoyed knowing them all.) He is
shrewd, with steady brown eyes under hair that is almost white.
He is probably in his seventies, but doesn't look it. He carries
himself with dignity, and has cause to be proud of the new clinic
where he now practices medicine. His nurse looks at us with
suspicion, but Dr. Benton's eyes have the penetration of a scal-
pel cutting through skin. I guess right away that if he knows
anything at all about Zora Hurston, he will not believe I am her
niece. "Eatonville?" Dr. Benton says, leaning forward in his
chair, looking first at me, then at Charlotte. "Yes, I know Eatonville; I grew up not far from there. I knew the whole bunch of
Zora's family." (He looks at the shape of my cheekbones, the
size of my eyes, and the nappiness of my hair.) "I knew her
daddy. The old man. He was a hard-working, Christian man.
Did the best he could for his family. He was the mayor of
Eatonville for a while, you know.

"My father was the mayor of Goldsboro. You probably
never heard of it. It never incorporated like Eatonville did, and
has just about disappeared. But Eatonville is still all black."

He pauses and looks at me. "And you're Zora's niece," he
says wonderingly.

"Well," I say with shy dignity, yet with some tinge, I hope,
of a nineteenth-century blush, "I'm illegitimate. That's why I
never knew Aunt Zora."

I love him for the way he comes to my rescue. "You're *not* illegitimate!" he cries, his eyes resting on me fondly. "All of us are God's children! Don't you even *think* such a thing!"

And I hate myself for lying to him. Still, I ask myself, would I have gotten this far toward getting the headstone and finding out about Zora Hurston's last days without telling my lie? Actually, I probably would have. But I don't like taking chances that could get me stranded in central Florida.

"Zora didn't get along with her family. I don't know why. Did you read her autobiography, *Dust Tracks on a Road*?"

"Yes, I did," I say. "It pained me to see Zora pretending to be naïve and grateful about the old white 'Godmother' who helped finance her research, but I loved the part where she ran off from home after falling out with her brother's wife."

Dr. Benton nods. "When she got sick, I tried to get her to go back to her family, but she refused. There wasn't any real hatred; they just never had gotten along and Zora wouldn't go to them. She didn't want to go to the county home, either, but she had to, because she couldn't do a thing for herself."

"I was surprised to learn she died of malnutrition."

Dr. Benton seems startled. "Zora *didn't* die of malnutrition," he says indignantly. "Where did you get that story from? She had a stroke and she died in the welfare home." He seems peculiarly upset, distressed, but sits back reflectively in his chair. "She was an incredible woman," he muses. "Sometimes when I closed my office, I'd go by her house and just talk to her for an hour or two. She was a well-read, well-traveled woman and always had her own ideas about what was going on. . . ."

"I never knew her, you know. Only some of Carl Van Vechten's photographs and some newspaper photographs . . . What did she look like?"

"When I knew her, in the fifties, she was a big woman, *erect*. Not quite as light as I am [Dr. Benton is dark beige], and about five foot, seven inches, and she weighed about two hundred pounds. Probably more. She . . ."

"What! Zora was *fat!* She wasn't, in Van Vechten's pictures!"

"Zora loved to eat," Dr. Benton says complacently. "She could sit down with a mound of ice cream and just eat and talk till it was all gone."

While Dr. Benton is talking, I recall that the Van Vechten pictures were taken when Zora was still a young woman. In them she appears tall, tan, and healthy. In later newspaper photographs—when she was in her forties—I remembered that she seemed heavier and several shades lighter. I reasoned that the earlier photographs were taken while she was busy collecting folklore materials in the hot Florida sun.

"She had high blood pressure. Her health wasn't good. . . . She used to live in one of my houses—on School Court Street. It's a block house. . . . I don't recall the number. But my wife and I used to invite her over to the house for dinner. *She always ate well,*" he says emphatically.

"That's comforting to know," I say, wondering where Zora ate when she wasn't with the Bentons.

"Sometimes she would run out of groceries—after she got sick—and she'd call me. 'Come over here and see 'bout me,' she'd say. And I'd take her shopping and buy her groceries.

"She was always studying. Her mind—before the stroke—just worked all the time. She was always going somewhere, too. She once went to Honduras to study something. And when she died, she was working on that book about Herod the Great. She was so intelligent! And really had perfect expressions. Her English was beautiful." (I suspect this is a clever way to let me know Zora herself didn't speak in the "black English" her characters used.)

"I used to read all of her books," Dr. Benton continues,

"but it was a long time ago. I remember one about . . . it was called, I think, 'The Children of God' [*Their Eyes Were Watching God*], and I remember Janie and Teapot [Teacake] and the mad dog riding on the cow in that hurricane and bit old Teapot on the cheek. . . ."

I am delighted that he remembers even this much of the story, even if the names are wrong, but seeing his affection for Zora I feel I must ask him about her burial. "Did she *really* have a pauper's funeral?"

"She *didn't* have a pauper's funeral!" he says with great heat. "Everybody around here *loved* Zora."

"We just came back from ordering a headstone," I say quietly, because he *is* an old man and the color is coming and going on his face, "but to tell the truth, I can't be positive what I found is the grave. All I know is the spot I found was the only grave-size hole in the area."

"I remember it wasn't near the road," says Dr. Benton, more calmly. "Some other lady came by here and we went out looking for the grave and I took a long iron stick and poked all over that part of the cemetery but we didn't find anything. She took some pictures of the general area. Do the weeds still come up to your knees?"

"And beyond," I murmur. This time there isn't any doubt. Dr. Benton feels ashamed.

As he walks us to our car, he continues to talk about Zora. "She couldn't really write much near the end. She had the stroke and it left her weak; her mind was affected. She couldn't think about anything for long.

"She came here from Daytona, I think. She owned a houseboat over there. When she came here, she sold it. She lived on that money, then she worked as a maid—for an article on maids she was writing—and she worked for the *Chronicle* writing the horoscope column.

"I think black people here in Florida got mad at her because she was for some politician they were against. She said this politician *built* schools for blacks while the one they wanted just talked about it. And although Zora wasn't egotistical, what she thought, she thought; and generally what she thought, she said."

When we leave Dr. Benton's office, I realize I have missed my plane back home to Jackson, Mississippi. That being so, Charlotte and I decide to find the house Zora lived in before she was taken to the county welfare home to die. From among her many notes, Charlotte locates a letter of Zora's she has copied that carries the address: 1734 School Court Street. We ask several people for directions. Finally, two old gentlemen in a dusty gray Plymouth offer to lead us there. School Court Street is not paved, and the road is full of mud puddles. It is dismal and squalid, redeemed only by the brightness of the late afternoon sun. Now I can understand what a "block" house is. It is a house shaped like a block, for one thing, surrounded by others just like it. Some houses are blue and some are green or yellow. Zora's is light green. They are tiny—about fifty by fifty feet, squatty with flat roofs. The house Zora lived in looks worse than the others, but that is its only distinction. It also has three ragged and dirty children sitting on the steps.

"Is this where y'all live?" I ask, aiming my camera.

"No, ma'am" they say in unison, looking at me earnestly. "We live over yonder. This Miss So-and-So's house; but she in the horspital."

We chatter inconsequentially while I take more pictures. A car drives up with a young black couple in it. They scowl fiercely at Charlotte and don't look at me with friendliness, either. They get out and stand in their doorway across the street. I go up to them to explain. "Did you know Zora Hurston used to live right across from you?" I ask.

"Who?" They stare at me blankly, then become curiously attentive, as if they think I made the name up. They are both Afroed and he is somberly dashikied.

I suddenly feel frail and exhausted. "It's too long a story," I say, "but tell me something: is there anybody on this street who's lived here for more than thirteen years?"

"That old man down there," the young man says, pointing. Sure enough, there is a man sitting on his steps three houses down. He has graying hair and is very neat, but there is a weakness about him. He reminds me of Mrs. Turner's husband in *Their Eyes Were Watching God*. He's rather "vanishing"-looking, as if his features have been sanded down. In the old days, before black was beautiful, he was probably considered attractive, because he has wavy hair and light-brown skin; but now, well, light skin has ceased to be its own reward.

After the preliminaries, there is only one thing I want to know: "Tell me something," I begin, looking down at Zora's house. "Did Zora like flowers?"

He looks at me queerly. "As a matter of fact," he says, looking regretfully at the bare, rough yard that surrounds her former house, "she was crazy about them. And she was a great gardener. She loved azaleas, and that running and blooming vine [morning-glories], and she really loved that night-smelling flower [gardenia]. She kept a vegetable garden year-round, too. She raised collards and tomatoes and things like that.

"Everyone in this community thought well of Miss Hurston. When she died, people all up and down this street took up a collection for her burial. We put her away nice."

"Why didn't somebody put up a headstone?"

"Well, you know, one was never requested. Her and her family didn't get along. They didn't even come to the funeral."

"And did she live down there by herself?"

"Yes, until they took her away. She lived with—just her and her companion, Sport."

My ears perk up. "Who?"

"Sport, you know, her dog. He was her only companion. He was a big brown-and-white dog."

When I walk back to the car, Charlotte is talking to the young couple on their porch. They are relaxed and smiling.

"I told them about the famous lady who used to live across the street from them," says Charlotte as we drive off. "Of course they had no idea Zora ever lived, let alone that she lived across the street. I think I'll send some of her books to them."

"That's real kind of you," I say.

I am not tragically colored. There is no great sorrow dammed up in my soul, nor lurking behind my eyes. I do not mind at all. I do not belong to the sobbing school of Negrohood who hold that nature somehow has given them a lowdown dirty deal and whose feelings are all hurt about it. . . . No, I do not weep at the world—I am too busy sharpening my oyster knife.
—*Zora Neale Hurston,*
  "How It Feels To Be Colored Me,"
  WORLD TOMORROW, *1928*

There are times—and finding Zora Hurston's grave was one of them—when normal responses of grief, horror, and so on do not make sense because they bear no real relation to the depth of the emotion one feels. It was impossible for me to cry when I saw the field full of weeds where Zora is. Partly this is because I have come to know Zora through her books and she was not a teary sort of person herself; but partly, too, it is because there is a point at which even grief feels absurd. And at this point, laughter gushes up to retrieve sanity.

It is only later, when the pain is not so direct a threat to one's own existence, that what was learned in that moment of comical lunacy is understood. Such moments rob us of both youth and vanity. But perhaps they are also times when greater disciplines are born.

1975

PART
TWO

If you bring forth what is within you, what is within you will save you. If you do not bring forth what is within you, what is within you will destroy you.

—*Jesus,*
THE GNOSTIC GOSPELS,
Elaine Pagels, ed.

. . . .

THE CIVIL RIGHTS MOVEMENT:

WHAT GOOD WAS IT?

[I wrote the following essay in the winter of 1966–67 while sharing one room above Washington Square Park in New York with a struggling young Jewish law student who became my husband. It was my first published essay and won the three-hundred-dollar first prize in the annual *American Scholar* essay contest. The money was almost magically reassuring to us in those days of disaffected parents, outraged friends, and one-item meals, and kept us in tulips, peonies, daisies, and lamb chops for several months.]

. . .

Someone said recently to an old black lady from Mississippi, whose legs had been badly mangled by local police who arrested her for "disturbing the peace," that the Civil Rights Movement was dead, and asked, since it was dead, what she thought about it. The old lady replied, hobbling out of his presence on her cane, that the Civil Rights Movement was like herself, "if it's dead, it shore ain't ready to lay down!"

This old lady is a legendary freedom fighter in her small town in the Delta. She has been severely mistreated for insisting on her rights as an American citizen. She has been beaten for singing Movement songs, placed in solitary confinement in prisons for talking about freedom, and placed on bread and water for praying aloud to God for her jailers' deliverance. For such a woman the Civil Rights Movement will never be over as long as her skin is black. It also will never be over for twenty million others with the same "affliction," for whom the Movement can never "lay down," no matter how it is killed by the press and made dead and buried by the white American public. As long as one black American survives, the struggle for equality with other Americans must also survive. This is a debt we owe to those blameless hostages we leave to the future, our children.

Still, white liberals and deserting Civil Rights sponsors are quick to justify their disaffection from the Movement by claiming that it is all over. "And since it is over," they will ask, "would someone kindly tell me what has been gained by it?" They then list statistics supposedly showing how much more advanced segregation is now than ten years ago—in schools, housing, jobs. They point to a gain in conservative politicians during the last few years. They speak of ghetto riots and of the survey that shows that most policemen are admittedly too anti-Negro to do their jobs in ghetto areas fairly and effectively. They speak of every area that has been touched by the Civil Rights Movement as somehow or other going to pieces.

They rarely talk, however, about human attitudes among Negroes that have undergone terrific changes just during the past seven to ten years (not to mention all those years when there was a Movement and only the Negroes knew about it). They seldom speak of changes in personal lives because of the influence of people in the Movement. They see general failure and few, if any, individual gains.

They do not understand what it is that keeps the Movement from "laying down" and Negroes from reverting to their former *silent* second-class status. They have apparently never stopped to wonder why it is always the white man—on his radio and in his newspaper and on his television—who says that the Movement is dead. If a Negro were audacious enough to make such a claim, his fellows might hanker to see him shot. The Movement is dead to the white man because it no longer interests him. And it no longer interests him because he can afford to be uninterested: he does not have to live by it, with it, or for it, as Negroes must. He can take a rest from the news of beatings, killings, and arrests that reach him from North and South —if his skin is white. Negroes cannot now and will never be able to take a rest from the injustices that plague them, for they— not the white man—are the target.

Perhaps it is naïve to be thankful that the Movement "saved" a large number of individuals and gave them something to live for, even if it did not provide them with everything they wanted. (Materially, it provided them with precious little that they wanted.) When a movement awakens people to the possibilities of life, it seems unfair to frustrate them by then denying what they had thought was offered. But what was offered? What was promised? What was it all about? What good did it do? Would it have been better, as some have suggested, to leave the Negro people as they were, unawakened, unallied with one another, unhopeful about what to expect for their children in some future world?

I do not think so. If knowledge of my condition is all the freedom I get from a "freedom movement," it is better than unawareness, forgottenness, and hopelessness, the existence that is like the existence of a beast. Man only truly lives by knowing;

otherwise he simply performs, copying the daily habits of others, but conceiving nothing of his creative possibilities as a man, and accepting someone else's superiority and his own misery.

When we are children, growing up in our parents' care, we await the spark from the outside world. Sometimes our parents provide it—if we are lucky—sometimes it comes from another source far from home. We sit, paralyzed, surrounded by our anxiety and dread, hoping we will not have to grow up into the narrow world and ways we see about us. We are hungry for a life that turns us on; we yearn for a knowledge of living that will save us from our innocuous lives that resemble death. We look for signs in every strange event; we search for heroes in every unknown face.

It was just six years ago that I began to be alive. I had, of course, been living before—for I am now twenty-three—but I did not really know it. And I did not know it because nobody told me that I—a pensive, yearning, typical high-school senior, but Negro—existed in the minds of others as I existed in my own. Until that time my mind was locked apart from the outer contours and complexion of my body as if it and the body were strangers. The mind possessed both thought and spirit—I wanted to be an author or a scientist—which the color of the body denied. I had never seen myself and existed as a statistic exists, or as a phantom. In the white world I walked, less real to them than a shadow; and being young and well hidden among the slums, among people who also did not exist—either in books or in films or in the government of their own lives—I waited to be called to life. And, by a miracle, I was called.

There was a commotion in our house that night in 1960. We had managed to buy our first television set. It was battered and overpriced, but my mother had gotten used to watching the afternoon soap operas at the house where she worked as maid, and nothing could satisfy her on days when she did not work but a continuation of her "stories." So she pinched pennies and bought a set.

I remained listless throughout her "stories," tales of pregnancy, abortion, hypocrisy, infidelity, and alcoholism. All these men and women were white and lived in houses with servants, long staircases that they floated down, patios where liquor was served four times a day to "relax" them. But my mother, with her swollen feet eased out of her shoes, her heavy body relaxed in our only comfortable chair, watched each movement of the smartly coiffed women, heard each word, pounced upon each innuendo and inflection, and for the duration of these "stories" she saw herself as one of them. She placed herself in every scene she saw, with her braided hair turned blond, her two hundred pounds compressed into a sleek size-seven dress, her rough dark skin smooth and *white*. Her husband became "dark and handsome," talented, witty, urbane, charming. And when she turned to look at my father sitting near her in his sweat shirt with his smelly feet raised on the bed to "air," there was always a tragic look of surprise on her face. Then she would sigh and go out to the kitchen looking lost and unsure of herself. My mother, a truly great woman who raised eight children of her own and half a dozen of the neighbors' without a single complaint, was convinced that she did not exist compared to "them." She subordinated her soul to theirs and became a faithful and timid supporter of the "Beautiful White People." Once she asked me, in a moment of vicarious pride and despair, if I didn't think that "they" were "jest naturally smarter, prettier, better." My mother asked this: a woman who never got rid of any of her children, never cheated on my father, was never a hypocrite if she could help it, and never even tasted liquor. She could not even bring herself to blame "them" for making her believe what they wanted her to believe: that if she did not look like them, think like them, be sophisticated and corrupt-for-comfort's-sake like them, she was a nobody. Black was not a color on my mother; it was a shield that made her invisible.

Of course, the people who wrote the soap-opera scripts always made the Negro maids in them steadfast, trusty, and wise in a home-remedial sort of way; but my mother, a maid for nearly forty years, never once identified herself with the scarcely glimpsed black servant's face beneath the ruffled cap. Like everyone else, in her daydreams at least, she thought she was free.

Six years ago, after half-heartedly watching my mother's soap operas and wondering whether there wasn't something more to be asked of life, the Civil Rights Movement came into my life. Like a good omen for the future, the face of Dr. Martin Luther King, Jr., was the first black face I saw on our new television screen. And, as in a fairy tale, my soul was stirred by the meaning for me of his mission—at the time he was being rather ignominiously dumped into a police van for having led a protest march in Alabama—and I fell in love with the sober and determined face of the Movement. The singing of "We Shall Overcome"—that song betrayed by nonbelievers in it—rang for the first time in my ears. The influence that my mother's soap operas might have had on me became impossible. The life of Dr. King, seeming bigger and more miraculous than the man himself, because of all he had done and suffered, offered a pattern of strength and sincerity I felt I could trust. He had suffered much because of his simple belief in nonviolence, love, and brotherhood. Perhaps the majority of men could not be reached through these beliefs, but because Dr. King kept trying to reach them in spite of danger to himself and his family, I saw in him the hero for whom I had waited so long.

What Dr. King promised was not a ranch-style house and an acre of manicured lawn for every black man, but jail and finally freedom. He did not promise two cars for every family, but the courage one day for all families everywhere to walk without shame and unafraid on their own feet. He did not say that one day it will be us chasing prospective buyers out of our prosperous well-kept neighborhoods, or in other ways exhibiting our snobbery and ignorance as all other ethnic groups before us have done; what he said was that we had a right to live anywhere in this country we chose, and a right to a meaningful well-paying job to provide us with the upkeep of our homes. He did not say we had to become carbon copies of the white American middle class; but he did say we had the right to become whatever we wanted to become.

Because of the Movement, because of an awakened faith in the newness and imagination of the human spirit, because of "black and white together"—for the first time in our history in some human relationship on and off TV—because of the beatings, the arrests, the hell of battle during the past years, I have fought harder for my life and for a chance to be myself, to be something more than a shadow or a number, than I had ever done before in my life. Before, there had seemed to be no real reason for struggling beyond the effort for daily bread. Now there was a chance at that other that Jesus meant when He said we could not live by bread alone.

I have fought and kicked and fasted and prayed and cursed and cried myself to the point of existing. It has been like being born again, literally. Just "knowing" has meant everything to me. Knowing has pushed me out into the world, into college, into places, into people.

Part of what existence means to me is knowing the difference between what I am now and what I was then. It is being capable of looking after myself intellectually as well as financially. It is being able to tell when I am being wronged and by whom. It means being awake to protect myself and the ones I love. It means being a part of the world community, and being *alert* to which part it is that I have joined, and knowing how to change to another part if that part does not suit me. To know is to exist; to exist is to be involved, to move about, to see the world with my own eyes. This, at least, the Movement has given me.

The hippies and other nihilists would have me believe that it is all the same whether the people in Mississippi have a movement behind them or not. Once they have their rights, they say, they will run all over themselves trying to be just like everybody else. They will be well fed, complacent about things of the spirit, emotionless, and without that marvelous humanity and "soul" that the Movement has seen them practice time and time again. "What has the Movement done," they ask, "with the few people it has supposedly helped?" "Got them white-collar jobs, moved them into standardized ranch houses in white neighborhoods, given them nondescript gray flannel suits?" "What are these people now?" they ask. And then they answer themselves, "Nothings!"

I would find this reasoning—which I have heard many, many times from hippies and nonhippies alike—amusing if I did not also consider it serious. For I think it is a delusion, a cop-out, an excuse to disassociate themselves from a world in which they feel too little has been changed or gained. The real question, however, it appears to me, is not whether poor people will adopt the middle-class mentality once they are well fed; rather, it is whether they will ever be well fed enough to be able to choose whatever mentality they think will suit them. The lack of a movement did not keep my mother from *wishing* herself bourgeois in her daydreams.

There is widespread starvation in Mississippi. In my own state of Georgia there are more hungry families than Lester Maddox would like to admit—or even see fed. I went to school with children who ate red dirt. The Movement has prodded and pushed some liberal senators into pressuring the government for food so that the hungry may eat. Food stamps that were two dollars and out of the reach of many families not long ago have been reduced to fifty cents. The price is still out of the reach of some families, and the government, it seems to a lot of people, could spare enough free food to feed its own people. It angers people in the Movement that it does not; they point to the billions in wheat we send free each year to countries abroad. Their government's slowness while people are hungry, its unwillingness to believe that there are Americans starving, its stingy cutting of the price of food stamps, make many Civil Rights workers throw up their hands in disgust. But they do not give up. They do not withdraw into the world of psychedelia. They apply what pressure they can to make the government give away food to hungry people. They do not plan so far ahead in their disillusionment with society that they can see these starving families buying identical ranch-style houses and sending their snobbish children to Bryn Mawr and Yale. They take first things first and try to get them fed.

They do not consider it their business, in any case, to say what kind of life the people they help must lead. How one lives is, after all, one of the rights left to the individual—when and if he has opportunity to choose. It is not the prerogative of the middle class to determine what is worthy of aspiration. There is also every possibility that the middle-class people of tomorrow will turn out ever so much better than those of today. I even know some middle-class people of today who are not *all* bad.

I think there are so few Negro hippies because middle-class Negroes, although well fed, are not careless. They are required by the treacherous world they live in to be clearly aware of whoever or whatever might be trying to do them in. They are middle class in money and position, but they cannot afford to be middle class in complacency. They distrust the hippie movement because they know that it can do nothing for Negroes as a group but "love" them, which is what all paternalists claim to do. And since the only way Negroes can survive (which they cannot do, unfortunately, on love alone) is with the support of the group, they are wisely wary and stay away.

A white writer tried recently to explain that the reason for the relatively few Negro hippies is that Negroes have built up a "super-cool" that cracks under LSD and makes them have a "bad trip." What this writer doesn't guess at is that Negroes are needing drugs less than ever these days for any kind of trip. While the hippies are "tripping," Negroes are going after power, which is so much more important to their survival and their children's survival than LSD and pot.

Everyone would be surprised if the Israelis ignored the Arabs and took up "tripping" and pot smoking. In this country we are the Israelis. Everybody who can do so would like to forget this, of course. But for us to forget it for a minute would be fatal. "We Shall Overcome" is just a song to most Americans, *but we must do it.* Or die.

What good was the Civil Rights Movement? If it had just given this country Dr. King, a leader of conscience, for once in our lifetime, it would have been enough. If it had just taken black eyes off white television stories, it would have been enough. If it had fed one starving child, it would have been enough.

If the Civil Rights Movement is "dead," and if it gave us nothing else, it gave us each other forever. It gave some of us bread, some of us shelter, some of us knowledge and pride, all of us comfort. It gave us our children, our husbands, our brothers, our fathers, as men reborn and with a purpose for living. It broke the pattern of black servitude in this country. It shattered the phony "promise" of white soap operas that sucked away so many pitiful lives. It gave us history and men far greater than Presidents. It gave us heroes, selfless men of courage and strength, for our little boys and girls to follow. It gave us hope for tomorrow. It called us to life.

Because we live, it can never die.

1967

THE UNGLAMOROUS BUT WORTHWHILE
DUTIES OF THE BLACK REVOLUTIONARY
ARTIST, OR OF THE BLACK WRITER
WHO SIMPLY WORKS AND WRITES

[This is a paper I presented to the Black Students' Association of Sarah Lawrence College on February 12, 1970. I began with "Greetings from the great sovereign state of Mississippi," which brought laughter.]

When I came to Sarah Lawrence in 1964, I was fleeing from Spelman College in Atlanta, a school that I considered opposed to change, to freedom, and to understanding that by the time most girls enter college they are already women and should be treated as women. At Sarah Lawrence I found all that I was looking for at the time—freedom to come and go, to read leisurely, to go my own way, dress my own way, and conduct my personal life as I saw fit. It was here that I wrote my first published short story and my first book, here that I learned to feel what I thought had some meaning, here that I felt no teacher or administrator breathing down my neck.

I thought I had found happiness and peace in my own time.

And for that time, perhaps, I had. It was not until after I had graduated and gone south to Mississippi that I began to realize that my lessons at Sarah Lawrence had left crucial areas empty, and had, in fact, contributed to a blind spot in my education that needed desperately to be cleared if I expected to be a whole woman, a full human being, a black woman full of self-awareness and pride. I realized, sometime after graduation, that when I had studied contemporary writers and the South at this college—taught by a warm, wonderful woman whom I much admired—the writings of Richard Wright had not been studied and that instead I had studied the South from Faulkner's point of view, from Feibleman's, from Flannery O'Connor's. It was only after trying to conduct the same kind of course myself —with black students—that I realized that such a course simply cannot *be* taught if *Black Boy* is not assigned and read, or if "The Ethics of Living Jim Crow" is absent from the reading list.

I realized further that when I had been yearning, while here, to do a paper on pan-Africanism in my modern world history class, my Harvard-trained teacher had made no mention of W. E. B. Du Bois (who attended Harvard too, in the nineteenth century, no doubt because he had never heard of him).

I also realized that I had wasted five of my hard-to-come-by dollars one semester when I bought a supposedly "comprehensive" anthology of English and American verse which had been edited by a Sarah Lawrence faculty member. A nice man, a handsome one even, who had not thought to include a single poem by a black poet. I believe this man, who *was* really very nice, did not know there *were* black poets, or, if he did, believed like Louis Simpson that "poetry that is identifiably Negro is not important." I've yet to figure out *exactly* what that means, but it sounds ugly and has effectively kept black poets out of "comprehensive" anthologies, where the reader would have the opportunity to decide whether their poems are "important" or not.

I began to feel that subtly and without intent or malice, I had been miseducated. For where my duty as a black poet, writer, and teacher would take me, people would have little need of Keats and Byron or even Robert Frost, but much need of Hughes, Bontemps, Gwendolyn Brooks, and Margaret Walker.

So for the past four years I've been in still another college. This time simply a college of books—musty old books that went out of print years ago—and of old people, the oldest old black men and women I could find, and a college of the young; students and dropouts who articulate in various bold and shy ways that they believe themselves to be without a valuable history, without a respectable music, without writing or poetry that speaks to them.

My enrollment in this newest college will never end, and for that I am glad. And each day I look about to see what can and should be done to make it a bigger college, a more inclusive one, one more vital and long living. There are things our people should know, books they should read, poems they should know by heart. I think now of *Black Reconstruction* by Du Bois, of *Cane* by Jean Toomer, of *Mules and Men* by Zora Neale Hurston. Ten years ago, the one copy of *Black Reconstruction* that could be found in Atlanta was so badly battered and had been pasted back together so many times that a student could check it out of the library for only thirty minutes, and was then not allowed to take it outside the reading room. *Cane* by Jean Toomer and *Mules and Men* by Zora Neale Hurston I found tucked away behind locked doors in the library of Lincoln University. Knowing both books were out of print at the time, I Xeroxed them and stole somebody's rights, but it was the least

I could do if I wanted to read them over and over again, which I did.

Today it gives me pleasure to see a Black Students' Association at Sarah Lawrence. That must mean there are many black students to pay dues. When I was here there were six of us and none of us was entirely black. Much has clearly changed, here as in the rest of the country. But when I look about and see what work still remains I can only be mildly, though sincerely, impressed.

Much lip service has been given the role of the revolutionary black writer but now the words must be turned into work. For, as someone has said, "Work is love made visible." There are the old people, Toms, Janes, or just simply old people, who need us to put into words for them the courage and dignity of their lives. There are the students who need guidance and direction. Real guidance and real direction, and support that doesn't get out of town when the sun goes down.

I have not labeled myself yet. I would like to call myself revolutionary, for I am always changing, and growing, it is hoped for the good of more black people. I do call myself black when it seems necessary to call myself anything, especially since I believe one's work rather than one's appearance adequately labels one. I used to call myself a poet, but I've come to have doubts about that. The truest and most enduring impulse I have is simply to write. It seems necessary for me to forget all the titles, all the labels, and all the hours of talk and to concentrate on the mountain of work I find before me. My major advice to young black artists would be that they shut themselves up somewhere away from all debates about who they are and what color they are and just turn out paintings and poems and stories and novels. Of course the kind of artist we are required to be cannot do this. Our people are waiting. *But there must be an awareness of what is Bull and what is Truth*, what is practical and what is designed ultimately to paralyze our talents. For example, it is unfair to the people we expect to reach to give them a beautiful poem if they are unable to read it.

And so, what is the role of the black revolutionary artist? Sometimes it is the role of remedial reading teacher. I will never forget one of the girls in my black studies course last year at Jackson State. All year long she had been taught by one of the greatest black poets still living: Margaret Walker. I took over the class when Miss Walker was away for the quarter. We were reading "For My People" and this girl came to the section that reads:

> Let a new earth rise. Let another world be born. Let a bloody peace be written in the sky. Let a second generation full of courage issue forth, let a people loving freedom come to growth, let a beauty full of healing and a strength of final clenching be the pulsing in our spirits and our blood. Let the martial songs be written, let the dirges disappear. Let a race of men now rise and take control!

"What do you think?" I asked the girl. (She had read the poem very well.) She shook her head. "What is the matter?" I asked. She said, "Oh, these older poets! They never write poems that tell us to fight!" Then I realized that she had read the poem, even read it passionately, and had not understood a word of what it was about. "What is a 'martial song' "? I asked. "What is a disappearing dirge?" The girl was completely thrown by the words.

I recall a young man (bearded, good-looking), a Muslim, he said, who absolutely refused to read Faulkner. "We in the revolution now," he said, "We don't have to read no more white folks." "Read thine enemy," I prodded, to no avail. And this same young man made no effort, either, to read Hughes or

Ellison or McKay or Ernest Gaines, who is perhaps the most gifted young black writer working today. His problem was that the revolutionary rhetoric so popular today had convinced him of his own black perfection and of the imperfection of everybody and everything white, but it had not taught him how to read. The belief that he was already the complete man had stunted this young man's growth. And when he graduates from college, as he will, he will teach your children and mine, and still not know how to read, nor will he be inclined to learn.

The real revolution is always concerned with the least glamorous stuff. With raising a reading level from second grade to third. With simplifying history and writing it down (or reciting it) for the old folks. With helping illiterates fill out food-stamp forms—for they must eat, revolution or not. The dull, frustrating work with our people is the work of the black revolutionary artist. It means, most of all, staying close enough to them to be there whenever they need you.

But the work of the black artist is also to create and to preserve what was created before him. It is knowing the words of James Weldon Johnson's "Negro National Anthem" and even remembering the tune. It is being able to read "For My People" with tears in the eyes, comprehension in the soul. It is sending small tokens of affection to our old and ancient poets whom renown has ignored. One of the best acts of my entire life was to take a sack of oranges to Langston Hughes when he had the flu, about two weeks before he died.

We must cherish our old men. We must revere their wisdom, appreciate their insight, love the humanity of their words. They may not all have been heroes of the kind we think of today, but generally it takes but a single reading of their work to know that they were all men of sensitivity and soul.

Only a year or so ago did I read this poem, by Arna Bontemps, "The Black Man Talks of Reaping":

I have sown beside all waters in my day.
I planted deep within my heart the fear
That wind or fowl would take the grain away.
I planted safe against this stark, lean year.

I scattered seed enough to plant the land
In rows from Canada to Mexico.
But for my reaping only what the hand
Can hold at once is all that I can show.

Yet what I sowed and what the orchard yields
My brother's sons are gathering stalk and root,
Small wonder then my children glean in fields
They have not sown, and feed on bitter fruit.

It requires little imagination to see the author as a spiritual colossus, arms flung wide, as in a drawing by Charles White, to encompass all the "Adams and the Eves and their countless generations," bearing the pain of the reaping but brooding on the reapers with great love.

Where *was* this poem in all those poetry anthologies I read with eager heart and hushed breath? It was not there, along with all the others that were not there. But it must, and will, be always in my heart. And if, in some gray rushing day, all our black books are burned, it must be in my head and I must be able to drag it out and recite it, though it be bitter to the tongue and painful to the ears. For that is also the role of the black revolutionary artist. He must be a walking filing cabinet of poems and songs and stories, of people, of places, of deeds and misdeeds.

In my new college of the young I am often asked, "What is the place of hate in writing?" After all we have been through in this country it is foolish and in any case useless to say hate has no place. Obviously, it has. But we must exercise our noblest impulses with our hate, not to let it destroy us or destroy our *truly precious heritage,* which is not, by the way, a heritage of bigotry or intolerance. I've found, in my own writing, that a little hatred, keenly directed, is a useful thing. Once spread about, however, it becomes a web in which I would sit caught and paralyzed like the fly who stepped into the parlor. The artist must remember that some individual men, like Byron de la Beckwith or Sheriff Jim Clark, should be hated, and that some corporations like Dow and General Motors should be hated too. Also the Chase Manhattan Bank and the Governor of Mississippi. However, there are men who should be loved, or at least respected on their merits, and groups of men, like the American Friends, who should not be hated. The strength of the artist is his courage to look at every old thing with fresh eyes and his ability to re-create, as true to life as possible, that great middle ground of people between Medgar Evers's murderer, Byron de la Beckwith, and the fine old gentleman John Brown.

I am impressed by people who claim they can see every person and event in strict terms of black and white, but generally their work is not, in my long-contemplated and earnestly considered opinion, either black or white, but a dull, uniform gray. It is boring because it is easy and requires only that the reader be a lazy reader and a prejudiced one. Each story or poem has a formula, usually two-thirds "hate whitey's guts" and one-third "I am black, beautiful, strong, and almost always right." Art is not flattery, necessarily, and the work of any artist must be more difficult than that. A man's life can rarely be summed up in one word; even if that word is black or white. And it is the duty of the artist to present the man *as he is.* One should recall that Bigger Thomas was many great and curious things, but he was neither good nor beautiful. He was real, and that is sufficient.

Sometimes, in my anger and frustration at the world we live in, I ask myself, What is real and what is not? And now it seems to me that what is real is what is happening. What is real is what did happen. What happened to me and happens to me is most real of all. I write then, out of that. I write about the old men that I knew (I love old men), and the great big beautiful women with arms like cushions (who would really rather look like Pat Nixon), and of the harried fathers and mothers and the timid, hopeful children. And today, in Mississippi, it seems I sometimes relive my Georgia childhood. I see the same faces, hear the same soft voices, take a nip, once in a while, of the same rich mellow corn, or wine. And when I write about the people there, in the strangest way it is as if I am not writing about them at all, but about myself. The artist then is the voice of the people, but she is also The People.

1971

. . . .

THE ALMOST YEAR

What *can* a well-intentioned upper-middle-class white family do to calm the frustrations, cool the anger, assuage the rage of a black ghetto child who comes to live with them? "Commit suicide," late-sixties militants might suggest. From a black point of view there are indeed few options. The author of *The Almost Year*, Florence Engel Randall, in a book that is remarkably free of cant, stereotypes, déjà vu, and white liberal guilt-ridden sermonizing, seeks to find a way in which black abused and poor and white privileged and rich can meet and exchange some warmth of themselves. For warmth, perhaps, is all that either side has to give.

A black girl from the ghetto spends "an almost year," from September to June, with the Mallorys, a wealthy white suburban family. She hates the idea—and them. However, her aunt and only means of support leaves her with them while she goes looking for a better job. The Mallorys find the girl hostile to preferential treatment, or any other kind. Whatever advances they make toward her are quickly checked.

Yet the Mallorys are, for God's sake, sincere. They try every way they know to make the poor child feel at home. They feed her well, they offer her clothes the Mallory teen-ager has out-grown. But to the black girl there is too much food, too many clothes. The Mallorys seem to be drowning in an abundance of essentials. And though she can recognize their sincerity, she cannot respond to it; the house, the cars, the beautiful lake, the ducks, the oceans of fallen leaves (where the black girl lives there are no trees) get in her way. Unable to approach the Mallorys as anything other than a pariah the black girl recoils from them, meeting their every expression of concern with disdain.

In her rage the girl conjures up a poltergeist, who takes possession of the Mallory house. Unfortunately, one cannot believe in this ghost who champions (seemingly) the black girl's cause. And it is just as well, because black misery and rage are not yet the stuff of fairy-tale conclusions. Indeed, one wonders if the author intended to create a believable poltergeist; for near the end of the book, after much house shaking and dish rattling, the black girl opens the dreaded attic door and confronts "a small dark wraith." Herself. And in this fearful journey it is Mrs. Mallory who walks beside her, the girl at last *allowing* this white woman to touch her, and, more important, to share and face down the fear that had stalked the Mallory household. The warmth generated between them lays the poltergeist to rest, banishes fear.

This warmth, this touching to banish fear of each other, is what the black girl will carry back to the ghetto with her— certainly not the lovely suburban estate of the Mallorys. Nor are the Mallorys going to share their monetary wealth with her. Nor are they going to kill themselves. Nor are they going to lead a revolution that will free the black girl from her street without trees.

What is the value of one hour's warmth in nine months of coldness? Of nine months in a beautiful house but a lifetime in a slum? What value has friendship that is content to see one comfortable *part of the time?* Indeed, is it friendship?

What one yearns for (and must have if we are to share this earth as unashamed friends) is a Mallory family that is radically involved in changing society, not merely giving succor to its oppressed. This book, marvelous as it is, accepts shared warmth as enough. One could share warmth with the Mallorys but one really could not depend on them in any radically meaningful way. The girl knows this, as she moves back into the slums with her aunt. And the Mallorys, for all their understanding and good intentions, would hardly notice if a black girl called to them from a Harlem tenement window as they rode the train downtown to catch a show.

1971

CHOICE: A TRIBUTE TO
DR. MARTIN LUTHER KING, JR.

[This address was made in 1972 at a Jackson, Mississippi restaurant that refused to serve people of color until forced to do so by the Civil Rights Movement a few years before.]

My great-great-great-grandmother walked as a slave from Virginia to Eatonton, Georgia—which passes for the Walker ancestral home—with two babies on her hips. She lived to be a hundred and twenty-five years old and my own father knew her as a boy. (It is in memory of this walk that I choose to keep and to embrace my "maiden" name, Walker.)

There is a cemetery near our family church where she is buried; but because her marker was made of wood and rotted years ago, it is impossible to tell exactly where her body lies. In the same cemetery are most of my mother's people, who have lived in Georgia for so long nobody even remembers when they came. And all of my great-aunts and -uncles are there, and my grandfather and grandmother, and, very recently, my own father.

If it is true that land does not belong to anyone until they have buried a body in it, then the land of my birthplace belongs to me, dozens of times over. Yet the history of my family, like that of all black Southerners, is a history of dispossession. We loved the land and worked the land, but we never owned it; and even if we bought land, as my great-grandfather did after the Civil War, it was always in danger of being taken away, as his was, during the period following Reconstruction.

My father inherited nothing of material value from his father, and when I came of age in the early sixties I awoke to the bitter knowledge that in order just to continue to love the land of my birth, I was expected to leave it. For black people —including my parents—had learned a long time ago that to stay willingly in a beloved but brutal place is to risk losing the love and being forced to acknowledge only the brutality.

It is a part of the black Southern sensibility that we treasure memories; for such a long time, that is all of our homeland those of us who at one time or another were forced away from it have been allowed to have.

I watched my brothers, one by one, leave our home and leave the South. I watched my sisters do the same. This was not unusual; abandonment, except for memories, was the common thing, except for those who "could not do any better," or those whose strength or stubbornness was so colossal they took the risk that others could not bear.

In 1960, my mother bought a television set, and each day after school I watched Hamilton Holmes and Charlayne Hunter as they struggled to integrate—fair-skinned as they were—the University of Georgia. And then, one day, there appeared the face of Dr. Martin Luther King, Jr. What a funny name, I thought. At the moment I first saw him, he was being hand-cuffed and shoved into a police truck. He had dared to claim his rights as a native son, and had been arrested. He displayed no fear, but seemed calm and serene, unaware of his own extraordinary courage. His whole body, like his conscience, was at peace.

At the moment I saw his resistance I knew I would never be able to live in this country without resisting everything that sought to disinherit me, and I would never be forced away from the land of my birth without a fight.

He was The One, The Hero, The One Fearless Person for whom we had waited. I hadn't even realized before that we *had* been waiting for Martin Luther King, Jr., but we had. And I knew it for sure when my mother added his name to the list of people she prayed for every night.

I sometimes think that it was literally the prayers of people like my mother and father, who had bowed down in the struggle for such a long time, that kept Dr. King alive until five years ago. For years we went to bed praying for his life, and awoke with the question "Is the 'Lord' still here?"

The public acts of Dr. King you know. They are visible all around you. His voice you would recognize sooner than any other voice you have heard in this century—this in spite of the fact that certain municipal libraries, like the one in downtown Jackson, do not carry recordings of his speeches, and the librarians chuckle cruelly when asked why they do not.

You know, if you have read his books, that his is a complex and revolutionary philosophy that few people are capable of understanding fully or have the patience to embody in themselves. Which is our weakness, which is our loss.

And if you know anything about good Baptist preaching, you can imagine what you missed if you never had a chance to hear Martin Luther King, Jr., preach at Ebeneezer Baptist Church.

You know of the prizes and awards that he tended to think very little of. And you know of his concern for the disinherited: the American Indian, the Mexican-American, and the poor American white—for whom he cared much.

You know that this very room, in this very restaurant, was closed to people of color not more than five years ago. And that we eat here together tonight largely through his efforts and his blood. We accept the common pleasures of life, assuredly, in his name.

But add to all of these things the one thing that seems to me second to none in importance: He gave us back our heritage. He gave us back our homeland; the bones and dust of our ancestors, who may now sleep within our caring *and* our hearing. He gave us the blueness of the Georgia sky in autumn as in summer; the colors of the Southern winter as well as glimpses of the green of vacation-time spring. Those of our relatives we used to invite for a visit we now can ask to stay. . . . He gave us full-time use of our own woods, and restored our memories to those of us who were forced to run away, as realities we might each day enjoy and leave for our children.

He gave us continuity of place, without which community is ephemeral. He gave us home.

1973

CORETTA KING: REVISITED

I met Coretta Scott King for the first time in 1962 when I was a freshman at Spelman College in Atlanta and lived a few blocks from the neat but rather worn neighborhood where Coretta and Martin Luther King, Jr., lived. A group of us from Spelman were going to the World Youth Peace Festival in Helsinki that summer, and our adviser, a white peace activist from California, thought we should meet Mrs. King, who seemed, at that time, the only black woman in Atlanta actively and publicly engaged in the pursuit of peace.

I recall vividly our few minutes in the King home, a modest, almost bare-looking house with exceedingly nondescript furniture. I was delighted that the furniture was so plain, because it was the same kind of stuff most black people had and not the stylish plastic-covered French provincial that sat unused in many black middle-class homes. I felt quite comfortable on the sofa. Coretta that day was quick, bright-eyed, slim, and actually bubbly; and very girlish-looking with her face free of make-up, shining a little, and her long hair tied back in a simple, slightly curly, ponytail. She herself was on her way to a peace conference in Geneva. And, in addition, she was aglow with thoughts of an upcoming musical recital.

As she talked briefly to us, I sat on the sofa and stared at her, much too shy myself to speak. I was satisfied just to witness her exuberance, her brightness, her sparkle and smiles, as she talked about the peace movement, her music, and all her plans. She gave us several words of encouragement about our journey, the first trip abroad for all of us, but I don't recall what they were. She did not, and we did not, mention her husband. But she was so clearly a happy woman I couldn't help wishing I could sneak out of the living room and through the rest of the house, because I was positive he was there.

I have often thought that if it had not been for her husband, Dr. King, I would have come of age believing in nothing and no one. As it was, my life, like that of millions of black young Southerners, seemed to find its beginning and its purpose at the precise moment I first heard him speak. Through the years, like thousands of others, I followed him, unquestioningly, for my belief in him overcame even my disbelief in America. When he was assassinated in 1968 it was as if the last light in my world had gone out. But in 1962 people of eighteen, as I was then, felt at the beginning of things. The future looked difficult, but bright. We had a tough, young, fearless friend and brother who stood with us and for us. We hoped bluntly, as eighteen-year-olds will, that his wife was good enough for him. How lucky you are that he belongs to you! I had thought, looking at Coretta then, beginning to admit grudgingly that my hero had married a person, and not just a wife.

When I saw Coretta again it was at Dr. King's funeral, when my husband and I marched behind her husband's body in anger and despair. We could only see her from a distance, as she sat on a platform on the Morehouse campus. In my heart I said good-bye to the nonviolence she still professed. I was far less calm than she appeared to be. The week after that long, four-mile walk across Atlanta, and after the tears and anger and the feeling of turning gradually to stone, I lost the child I had been carrying. I did not even care. It seemed to me, at the time, that if "he" (it was weeks before my tongue could form his name) must die no one deserved to live, not even my own child. I thought, as I lay on my bed listening to the rude Mississippi accents around me, that with any luck I could lose myself. I do not recall wanting very much to live. A week later, however, I saw Coretta's face again, on television, and perhaps it was my imagination, but she sounded so much like her husband that for a minute I thought I was hearing his voice. . . . "I come to New York today with a strong feeling that my dearly beloved husband, who was snatched suddenly from our midst slightly more than three weeks ago now, would have wanted me to be present today. Though my heart is heavy with grief from having suffered an irreparable loss, my faith in the redemptive will of God is stronger today than ever before."

I knew then that my grief was really self-pity; something I don't believe either Martin or Coretta had time to feel. I was still angry, confused, and, unlike Coretta, I have wandered very far, I think, from my belief in God if not from my faith in humanity, but she pulled me to my feet, as her husband had done in a different way, and forced me to acknowledge the debt I owed, not only to her husband's memory but also to the living continuation of his work.

Coretta was surprised, when I arrived to interview her for this article, that I remembered so well our first meeting in her home, for she had long since forgotten it. The first thing I noticed was that her eyes have changed. They are reserved, almost cool, and she is tense; perhaps because she has been written about so often and because she is bored with it. She is not as slim as she was in 1962, but then, neither am I. Her hair this time falls down against her cheeks and is held back by a magenta-colored headband. Her dress is colorfully striped and her lipstick is very red.

I am embarrassed because I have dared to list among my interview questions things like "Do you enjoy dancing?" "Can you bougaloo?" "Do you save trading stamps?" I also want to know her favorite color and her horoscope sign. She rightly comments that even though people who are curious about her might like to know these things the questions themselves are "not important." I feel rather foolish when she says this, and hasten to explain that what I am most concerned about is what direction her music career—Mrs. King studied at the New England Conservatory of Music and often sings in concert—is taking. After that, I add, beginning to brighten a bit, for her look now is much less severe, I would like to know whether she thinks a woman can maintain her art—in her case, her singing—without having to sacrifice it to her husband's ambitions, her children's needs, or society's expectations. I want to know her opinion of why black women have been antagonistic toward women's liberation. As a black woman myself, I say, I do not understand this because black women among all women have been oppressed almost beyond recognition—oppressed by *everyone*. Until recently, I comment, black women didn't even know what a real black woman looked like, because most black women were lightening their skin and straightening their hair. Ticking off another item on my shamefully long list—her assistant, Mrs. Bennett, had made it quite clear to me when I arrived that an hour of interviewing was the limit—I ask about the role she feels she has in the world, in this country, in her family, and in her immediate community.

Coretta's voice in conversation is quite different from the way it sounds when she gives speeches. It is softer and not as flatly Southern. When she talks she seems very calm and sure, though not relaxed, and she is cautious and careful that her precise meaning is expressed and understood. I have the feeling that she is far more fragile than she seems and the oddly eerie suggestion enters my head that the Coretta I am speaking with is not at all the one her children and family know. It strikes me that perhaps the reaction to overwhelming publicity must be a vigilant guarding of the private person. I try hard not to stare while Coretta talks, but I find I can't help it. I would have stared at Mary McLeod Bethune the same way. Coretta has changed a lot since 1962 but she continues to believe in and carry on her husband's work along with her own. I am trying to see where so much strength is coming from.

She leans back in her camel-colored swivel chair under-neath the large oil portrait of her husband and pauses briefly to touch one of the many piles of correspondence on her desk. She begins at a mutual point of reference: the day we first met, nearly ten years ago. "I was on my way then," she recalls, "to the Seventeen-Nation Disarmament Conference in Geneva. Fifty American women had been invited and I was going as a delegate. I was also scheduled, the following Sunday, to give a recital in Cincinnati. Of course this presented something of a problem, because I would be away from the children for a week, but I thought it was important that I go. However, I wouldn't have gone had my husband not encouraged me to go." She smiles, slightly, and explains. "Periodically Martin and I would have these discussions about my being so involved in my singing and speaking and being away from home so much. We always agreed that when both of us were under a lot of pressure to be away from home I would be the one to curtail my activities. I wasn't too unhappy about this. It was really a question of knowing what our priorities were. And since my top priority has always been my family there was never any conflict.

"Of course Martin had a problem throughout his career because he couldn't be with his family more. He never felt comfortable about being away so much. I don't think anybody who must be away from home a lot can really resolve this. But what you have to do is spend as much time with your family as you can and make the time that you spend meaningful. When Martin spent time with the children he gave himself so completely that they had a great feeling of love and security. I think this can best be done by individuals who feel secure within themselves and who are committed to what they are doing. People who have a sense of direction and who feel that what they're doing is the most important thing they *can* be doing. There was never a question in our minds that we were not doing the most important thing we could be doing for ourselves and for a better society for our children, all children, to grow up in."

At this point something goes wrong with my tape recorder and I lean forward to fix it, explaining with some vexation that I am the world's worst manipulator of simple gadgetry. Coretta charitably admits she's no genius with mechanical things either.

While waiting for the tape to rewind I tell her that her husband often crops up in my work and is very often in my thoughts. I tell her that in my novel, a copy of which I just gave her, one of the characters mentions that although Dr. King was constantly harassed and oppressed by the white world he was always gentle with his wife and children. I tell her how important I feel this is: that black men not take out their anger and frustration on their wives and children. A temptation that is all too obvious.

Coretta's face is thoughtful as she says, "Maybe I shouldn't say this, because I don't *know* it, it's just a feeling I have . . . but few black men seem to feel secure enough as men that they can make women feel like women. It was such a good feeling that Martin gave me, since the first time I met him. He was such a strong man that I felt like a woman, I could *be* a woman, and let him be a man. Yet he too was affected by the system, as a black man; but in spite of everything he always came through as a man, a person of dignity. . . . I miss this now, very much. Since my husband's death I've had to struggle on alone, and I can appreciate now, more than ever, how important it is to have somebody to share things with, to have someone who cares, someone who is concerned."

A rather ardent feminist myself I would like to spend a lot of time on the subjects of black woman and women's liberation. But Coretta only states that she understands the black woman's reluctance to be involved in liberating herself when all black people are still not free. Of course, she says, and laughs with humor and exasperation, "it *is* annoying to have men constantly saying things like 'I know that must be a woman driver!' " She also believes that if women become irrevocably involved in social issues they will find themselves powerful as activists *and* as women. She thinks that women will liberate themselves to the extent of their involvement in the struggle for change and social justice. To me this sounds very logical, but I am stuck with the suspicion that, as with black people, there must be for women a new and self-given definition. I fear that many people, including many women, do not know, in fact, what Woman is.

We do, however, share a vast appreciation for the black woman, liberated or not. I think we both realize that in the majority of black women in the South we have been seeing women whose souls have been liberated for generations. In fact, it is when Coretta mentions some words of gentle courage from some old woman she has met somewhere that her eyes fill with tears. "The black woman," she says, "has a special role to play. Our heritage of suffering and our experience in having to struggle against all odds to raise our children gives us a greater capacity for understanding both suffering and the need and meaning of compassion. We have, I think, a kind of stamina, a determination, which makes us strong." Then she says something that I feel is particularly true: "Women, in general, are not a part of the corruption of the past, so they can give a new kind of leadership, a new image for mankind. But if they are going to be bitter or vindictive they are not going to be able to do this. But they're capable of tremendous compassion, love, and forgiveness, which, if they use it, can make this a better world. When you think of what some black women have gone through, and then look at how beautiful they still are! It is incredible that they still believe in the values of the race, that they have retained a love of justice, that they can still feel the deepest compassion, not only for themselves but for anybody who is oppressed; this is a kind of miracle, something we have that we must preserve and must pass on."

Coretta was born and raised in Marion, Alabama, a small town not far from the larger one of Selma, which her husband was later to make infamous. When she speaks of her upbringing in the "heart of Dixie" there is no bitterness in her voice. Like many blacks from the South she is able to dismiss or feel pity for white racists because she realizes they are sick. Instead, her voice warms with pride and respect for her father, who survived against fantastic odds. Not only did Obidiah Scott survive; he prevailed.

The Scotts owned a farm in Marion, and Coretta's father raised thousands of chickens. When his sawmill was mysteriously burned out only days after he purchased it he bought himself a truck and began a small pulpwood business. Recently, at seventy-one, Obie Scott ran for highway commissioner in his home town, something he wouldn't have dreamed of doing as short a time as six or seven years ago. He lost in the election, and Coretta thinks losing "got to him," but the important thing, she says, is that he still has the courage to try to change things in the South so that all people can live there in harmony and peace.

"My father is a *most* industrious man," says Coretta. "If he'd been white he'd be the mayor of Marion, Alabama." From what she has told me about him I think she underestimates Obidiah Scott: if he had been white I doubt if he'd have stopped with the Alabama governorship.

Although active in several political campaigns, Coretta appears to have enjoyed her swing through her home state, in support of local black candidates, including her father, most. She explains that she gave a number of "Freedom Concerts" which her children helped her sing, and that they enjoyed campaigning as much as she. What emerges about Coretta is that the fabric of her life is finely knit. Each part is woven firmly into another part. Her office, which is in the basement of her house, is where she directs the business of the Martin Luther King, Jr. Memorial Center. When her children come home from school they troop downstairs to see her. She will usually stop whatever she is doing to talk to them. Her music is a skill that she uses for a variety of good causes: her Freedom Concerts bring out the crowds at local elections for black candidates; her other concerts are given to raise money for the memorial to her husband that she insists he must have. Her singing is also her means of reaching other peoples who can understand the beauty of her voice if not the words she sings.

The hour I was allotted for the interview has long since ended. But Coretta, much more relaxed now, is willing to discuss a few other topics that seemed to grow, organically, from answers she has given to my questions. About black people in power and the whites who work with them she says: "I don't believe that black people are going to misuse power in the way it has been misused. I think they've learned from their experiences. And we've seen instances where black and white work together very effectively. This is true even in places where you have a black majority, in Hancock County, Georgia, for example, or Fayette, Mississippi, where Charles Evers is mayor." About nonviolence she says, "It is very difficult to get people beyond the point of seeing nonviolence as something you do on marches and in demonstrations. It is harder to get people to the point of organizing to bring pressure to bear on changing society. People who think nonviolence is easy don't realize that it's a spiritual discipline that requires a great deal of strength, growth, and purging of the self so that one can overcome almost any obstacle for the good of all without being concerned about one's own welfare."

I am glad, while we're talking, to hear Coretta, the mother, talking to her oldest son, Marty, fourteen, who calls her on the phone. It seems he has been left at his school several miles away, it is pouring rain, and he wants somebody to come immediately to pick him up. Coretta is concerned but firm. She tells him that since he has missed the ride home that was arranged for him he will just have to wait until she can send someone for him. He protests. She restates her solution; he will have to wait. Period.

We spend a few minutes discussing her role in life as she sees it. I am not surprised that what she would like to do is inspire other women to take a more active role in the peace movement, in the election of acceptable candidates, and in being involved in making the decisions that will affect their lives and the lives of their children. She says that she and Martin used to talk a lot about trying to organize women and she regrets that he never had time to get around to addressing women as women. "We have never used," she says, "the womanpower that we had."

While I am gathering up my paraphernalia to leave,

Coretta comes from behind her desk and we chat a few moments about the pictures of her family that line the walls of her office. There is one that is especially charming, of her and her husband and the children on an outing in the park. Coretta's face in the photograph is radiant, although she ruefully comments that it was a hassle that day getting everybody dressed up so they could have the picture made. Outside her office she introduces me to Dr. King's sister, Mrs. Farris, whom I had known slightly at Spelman. Mrs. Farris brings the presence of her brother strongly to mind; she has both his dignity and his calm. She is a woman of few words but they are pertinent ones. She assists Mrs. King with the bookkeeping.

When I leave the red-brick house on Sunset Avenue, the rain that had been beating down heavily all day has let up. And, though there is no promise of sun, there is a feeling that spring has already come to the winter-colored slopes of Atlanta. "You *Southern* black people," someone had said to me several weeks before, "are very protective of Martin King and Coretta." I think about this as I leave the place where Martin King no longer lives except in the hearts of all the people who work there in his name.

As my plane takes off, I think of all the ways Martin and Coretta King's lives have touched mine. I think of that spring day so few, so many, years ago, and of Coretta's willingness to encourage a group of young women who were about to become involved in an exciting but somewhat frightening experience. I think of the years when I and most black Georgians, including atheists and agnostics, went to bed praying for Martin King's safety, and how we awoke each morning stronger because he was still with us. It was Martin, more than anyone, who exposed the hidden beauty of black people in the South, and caused us to look again at the land our fathers and mothers knew. The North is not for us. We will not be forced away from what is ours.

Martin King, with Coretta at his side, gave the South to black people, and reduced the North to an option. And, though I realize the South belonged to me all the time, it has a newness in my eyes. I gaze down from the plane on the blood-red hills of Georgia and Alabama and finally, home, Mississippi, knowing that when I arrive the very ground may tremble and convulse but I will walk upright, forever.

1971

. . . .

CHOOSING TO STAY AT HOME:
TEN YEARS AFTER THE MARCH
ON WASHINGTON

Our bus left Boston before dawn on the day of the March. We were a jolly, boisterous crowd who managed to shout the words to "We Shall Overcome" without a trace of sadness or doubt. At least on the surface. Underneath our bravado there was anxiety: Would Washington be ready for us? Would there be violence? Would we *be* Overcome? Could *we* Overcome? At any rate, we felt confident enough to try.

It was the summer of my sophomore year in college in Atlanta and I had come to Boston as I usually did to find a job that would allow me to support myself through another year of school. No one else among my Boston relatives went to the March, but all of them watched it eagerly on TV. When I returned that night they claimed to have seen someone exactly like me among those milling about just to the left of Martin Luther King, Jr. But of course I was not anywhere near him. The crowds would not allow it. I was, instead, perched on the limb of a tree far from the Lincoln Memorial, and although I managed to see very little of the speakers, I could hear everything.

For a speech and drama term paper the previous year my teacher had sent his class to Atlanta University to hear Martin Luther King lecture. "I am not interested in his politics," he warned, "only in his speech." And so I had written a paper that contained these lines: "Martin Luther King, Jr. is a surprisingly effective orator, although *terribly* under the influence of the Baptist church so that his utterances sound overdramatic and too weighty to be taken seriously." I also commented on his lack of humor, his expressionless "oriental" eyes, and the fascinating fact that his gray sharkskin suit was completely without wrinkles —causing me to wonder how he had gotten into it. It was a surprise, therefore, to find at the March on Washington that the same voice that had seemed ponderous and uninspired in a small lecture hall was now as electrifying in its tone as it was in its message.

Martin King was a man who truly had his tongue wrapped around the roots of Southern black religious consciousness, and when his resounding voice swelled and broke over the heads of the thousands of people assembled at the Lincoln Memorial I felt what a Southern person brought up in the church *always* feels when those cadences—not the words themselves, necessarily, but the rhythmic spirals of passionate emotion, followed by even more passionate pauses—roll off the tongue of a really first-rate preacher. I felt my soul rising from the sheer force of Martin King's eloquent goodness.

There are those who are asking the devotees of civil rights, "When will you be satisfied?" We can never be satisfied as long as the Negro is the victim of the unspeakable horrors of police brutality. We can never be satisfied as long as our bodies, heavy with the fatigue of travel, cannot gain lodging in the motels of the highways and the hotels of the cities. We cannot be satisfied as long as the Negro's basic mobility is from a smaller ghetto to a larger one. We can never be satisfied as long as our children are stripped of their selfhood and robbed of their dignity by signs stating "For white only." We cannot be satisfied as long as a Negro in Mississippi cannot vote and a Negro in New York believes he has nothing for which to vote. No, we are not satisfied and we will not be satisfied until justice rolls down like waters and righteousness like a mighty stream.

And when he spoke of "letting freedom ring" across "the green hills of Alabama and the red hills of Georgia" I saw again what he was always uniquely able to make me see: that I, in fact, had claim to the land of my birth. Those red hills of Georgia were mine, and nobody was going to force me away from them until I myself was good and ready to go.

. . . Some of you have come here out of great trials and tribulations. Some of you have come fresh from narrow jail cells. Some of you have come from areas where your quest for freedom left you battered by storms of persecution and staggered by the winds of police brutality. . . . Go back to Mississippi, go back to Alabama, go back . . . to Georgia . . . knowing that somehow this situation can and will be changed. . . . This is our hope. This is the faith that I go back to the South with. With this faith we will be able to hew out of the mountain of despair a stone of hope.

Later I was to read that the March on Washington was a dupe of black people, that the leaders had sold out to the

Kennedy administration, and that all of us should have felt silly for having participated. But whatever the Kennedy administration may have done had nothing to do with the closeness I felt that day to my own people, to King and John Lewis and thousands of others. And it is impossible to regret hearing that speech, because no black person I knew had ever encouraged anybody to "Go back to Mississippi . . . ," and I knew if this challenge were taken up by the millions of blacks who normally left the South for better fortunes in the North, a change couldn't help but come.

This may not seem like much to other Americans, who constantly move about the country with nothing but restlessness and greed to prod them, but to the Southern black person brought up expecting to be run away from home—because of lack of jobs, money, power, and respect—it was a notion that took root in willing soil. We would fight to stay where we were born and raised and destroy the forces that sought to disinherit us. We would proceed with the revolution from our own homes.

I thought of my seven brothers and sisters who had already left the South and I wanted to know: Why did they have to leave home to find a better life?

I was born and raised in Eatonton, Georgia, which is in the center of the state. It is also the birthplace of Joel Chandler Harris, and visitors are sometimes astonished to see a large iron rabbit on the courthouse lawn. It is a town of two streets, and according to my parents its social climate had changed hardly at all since they were children. That being so, on hot Saturday afternoons of my childhood I gazed longingly through the window of the corner drugstore where white youngsters sat on stools in air-conditioned comfort and drank Cokes and nibbled ice-cream cones. Black people could come in and buy, but what they bought they couldn't eat inside. When the first motel was built in Eatonton in the late fifties the general understanding of *place* was so clear the owners didn't even bother to put up a "Whites Only" sign.

I was an exile in my own town, and grew to despise its white citizens almost as much as I loved the Georgia countryside where I fished and swam and walked through fields of black-eyed Susans, or sat in contemplation beside the giant pine tree my father "owned," because when he was a boy and walking five miles to school during the winter he and his schoolmates had built a fire each morning in the base of the tree, and the tree still lived—although there was a blackened triangular hole in it large enough for me to fit inside. This was my father's tree, and from it I had a view of fields his people had worked (and briefly owned) for generations, and could walk—in an afternoon—to the house where my mother was born; a leaning, weather-beaten ruin, it was true, but as essential to her sense of existence as one assumes Nixon's birthplace in California is to him. Probably more so, since my mother has always been careful to stay on good terms with the earth she occupies. But I would have to leave all this. Take my memories and run north. For I would not be a maid, and could not be a "girl," or a frightened half-citizen, or any of the things my brothers and sisters had already refused to be.

In those days few blacks spent much time discussing hatred of white people. It was understood that they were—generally—vicious and unfair, like floods, earthquakes, or other natural catastrophes. Your job, if you were black, was to live with that knowledge like people in San Francisco live with the San Andreas Fault. You had as good a time (and life) as you could, under the circumstances.

Not having been taught black history—except for the once-a-year hanging up of the pictures of Booker Washington, George Washington Carver, and Mary McLeod Bethune that

marked Negro History Week—we did not know how much of
the riches of America we had missed. Somehow it was hard to
comprehend just how white folks—lazy as all agreed they were
—always managed to get ahead. When Hamilton Holmes and
Charlayne Hunter were first seen trying to enter the University
of Georgia, people were stunned: Why did they want to go to
that whitefolks' school? If they wanted to go somewhere let 'em
go to a school black money had built! It was a while before they
could connect their centuries of unpaid labor with white "progress," but as soon as they did they saw Hamp and Charlayne as
the heroes they were.

I had watched Charlayne and Hamp every afternoon on
the news when I came home from school. Their daring was
infectious. When I left home for college in Atlanta in 1961 I
ventured to sit near the front of the bus. A white woman (may
her fingernails now be dust!) complained to the driver and he
ordered me to move. But even as I moved, in confusion and
anger and tears, I knew he had not seen the last of me.

My only regret when I left Atlanta for New York two and
a half years later was that I would miss the Saturday-morning
demonstrations downtown that had become indispensable to
education in the Atlanta University Center. But in 1965 I went
back to Georgia to work part of the summer in Liberty County,
helping to canvass voters and in general looking at the South to
see if it was worth claiming. I suppose I decided it *was* worth
something, because later, in 1966, I received my first writing
fellowship and made eager plans to leave the country for Sene-
gal, West Africa—but I never went. Instead I caught a plane to
Mississippi, where I knew no one personally and only one
woman by reputation. That summer marked the beginning of
a realization that I could never live happily in Africa—or anywhere else—until I could live freely in Mississippi.

I was also intrigued by the thought of what continuity of

place could mean to the consciousness of the emerging writer. The Russian writers I admired had one thing in common: a sense of the Russian soul that was directly rooted in the soil that nourished it. In the Russian novel, land itself is a personality. In the South, Faulkner, Welty, and O'Connor could stay in their paternal homes and write because although their neighbors might think them weird—and in Faulkner's case, trashy—they were spared the added burden of not being able to use a public toilet and did not have to go through intense emotional struggle over where to purchase a hamburger. What if Wright had been able to stay in Mississippi? I asked this not because I assumed an alternative direction to his life (since I readily admit that Jackson, Mississippi, with the stilling of gunfire, bombings, and the surge and pound of black street resistance, is about the most boring spot on earth), but because it indicates Wright's lack of choice. And that a man of his talent should lack a choice is offensive. Horribly so.

Black writers had generally left the South as soon as possible. The strain of creation and constant exposure to petty insults and legally encouraged humiliations proved too great. But their departure impoverished those they left behind. I realized this more fully when I arrived in Jackson to live and discovered Margaret Walker, the author of *For My People,* already there, a natural force, creating work under unimaginable pressures and by doing so keeping alive, in the thousands of students who studied under her, not only a sense of art but also the necessity of claiming one's birthright at the very source. I do not know if, in her case, settling in the South was purely a matter of choice or preference, but in the future—for other black artists—it might and *must* be.

And so, ten years after the March on Washington, the question is: How much has the mountain of despair dwindled? What shape and size is the stone of hope?

I know it is annoying this late in the day to hear of more "symbols" of change, but since it is never as late in the day in Mississippi as it is in the rest of the country I will indulge in a few:

One afternoon each week I drive to downtown Jackson to have lunch with my husband at one of Jackson's finest motels. It has a large cool restaurant that overlooks a balalaika-shaped swimming pool, and very good food. My husband, Mel Leventhal, a human-rights lawyer who sues a large number of racist institutions a year (and wins) (and who is now thinking of suing the Jackson Public Library, because a. they refused to issue me a library card in my own name, and b. the librarian snorted like a mule when I asked for a recording of Dr. King's speeches—which the library didn't have), has his own reasons for coming here, and the least of them is that the cooks provide excellent charbroiled cheeseburgers. He remembers "testing" the motel's swimming pool in 1965 (before I knew him)—the angry insults of the whites as blacks waded in, and the tension that hung over everyone as the whites vacated the pool and stood about menacingly. I remember the cold rudeness of the waitresses in the restaurant a year later and recall wondering if "testing" would ever end. (We were by no means alone in this: one of the new black school-board members still lunches at a different downtown restaurant each day—because she has been thrown out of all of them.) It is sometimes hard to eat here because of those memories, but in Mississippi (as in the rest of America) racism is like that local creeping kudzu vine that swallows whole forests and abandoned houses; if you don't keep pulling up the roots it will grow back faster than you can destroy it.

One day we sat relaxing in the restaurant and as we ate watched a young black boy of about fifteen swimming in the pool. Unlike the whites of the past, the ones in the pool did not get out. And the boy, when he was good and tired, crawled up alongside the pool, turned on his back, drew up his knees—in his tight trunks—and just lay there, oblivious to the white faces staring down at him from the restaurant windows above.

"I could *swear* that boy doesn't know what a castration complex is," I said, thinking how the bravest black "testers" in the past had seemed to crouch over themselves when they came out of the water.

We started to laugh, thinking of what a small, insignificant thing this sight should have been. It reminded us of the day we saw a young black man casually strolling down a street near the center of town arm in arm with his high-school sweetheart, a tiny brunette. We had been with a friend of ours who was in no mood to witness such "incorrect" behavior, and who moaned, without a trace of humor: "Oh, why is it that as soon as you do start seeing signs of freedom they're the wrong ones!"

But would one really prefer to turn back the clock? I thought of the time, when I was a child, when black people were not allowed to use the town pool, and the town leaders were too evil to permit the principal of my school to build a pool for blacks *on his own property.* And when my good friend a teen-ager from the North (visiting his grandmother, naturally) was beaten and thrown into prison because he stooped down on Main Street in broad daylight to fix a white girl's bicycle chain. And now, thinking about these two different boys, I was simply glad that they are still alive, just as I am glad we no longer have to "test" public places to eat, or worry that a hostile waitress will spit in our soup. They will inherit Emmett Till soon enough. For the moment, at least, their childhood is not being destroyed, nor do they feel hemmed in by the memories that plague us.

It is memory, more than anything else, that sours the sweetness of what has been accomplished in the South. What we cannot forget and will never forgive. My husband has said that for her sixth birthday he intends to give our daughter a completely *safe* (racially) Mississippi, and perhaps that is possible. For her. For us, safety is not enough any more.

I thought of this one day when we were debating whether to go for a swim and boat ride in the Ross Barnett Reservoir, this area's largest recreational body of water. But I remembered state troopers descending on us the first time we went swimming there, in 1966 (at night), and the horror they inspired in me; and I also recall too well the man whose name the reservoir bears. Not present fear but memory makes our visits there infrequent. For us, every day of our lives here has been a "test." Only for coming generations will enjoyment of life in Mississippi seem a natural right. But for just this possibility people have given their lives, freely. And continue to give them in the day-by-day, year-by-year hard work that is the expression of their will and of their love.

Blacks are coming home from the North. My brothers and sisters have bought the acres of pines that surround my mother's birthplace. Blacks who thought automatically of leaving the South ten years ago are now staying. There are more and better jobs, caused by more, and more persistent, lawsuits: we have learned for all time that nothing of value is ever given up voluntarily. The racial climate is as good as it is in most areas of the North (one would certainly hesitate before migrating to parts of Michigan or Illinois), and there is still an abundance of fresh air and open spaces—although the frenetic rate of economic growth is likely to ugly up the landscape here as elsewhere. It is no longer a harrowing adventure to drive from Atlanta to Texas; as long as one has money one is not likely to be refused service in "the motels of the highways and the hotels of the cities." The last holdouts are the truck stops, whose owners are being dragged into court at a regular rate. Police brutality—the newest form of lynching—is no longer accepted as a matter of course; black people react violently against it and the city administrations worry about attracting business and their cities' "progressive" image. Black people can and do vote (poll watchers still occasionally being needed), and each election year brings its small harvest of black elected officials. The public schools are among the most integrated in the nation, and of course those signs "White Only" and "Colored" will not hurt my daughter's heart as they bruised mine—because they are gone.

Charles Evers, the famous mayor of Fayette, is thinking—again—of running for the Mississippi governorship. James Meredith is—again—thinking of running for the same position. They make their intentions known widely on local TV. Charles Evers said in June, at the tenth commemoration of his brother Medgar's assassination, "I don't think any more that I will be shot." Considering the baldness of his political aspirations and his tenacity in achieving his goals, this is a telling statement. The fear that shrouded Mississippi in the sixties is largely gone. "If Medgar could see what has happened in Mississippi in the last few years," said his widow, Myrlie Evers, "I think he'd be surprised and pleased."

The mountain of despair *has* dwindled, and the stone of hope has size and shape, and can be fondled by the eyes and by the hand. But freedom has always been an elusive tease, and in the very act of grabbing for it one can become shackled. I think Medgar Evers and Martin Luther King, Jr., would be dismayed by the lack of radicalism in the new black middle class, and discouraged to know that a majority of the black people helped most by the Movement of the sixties has abandoned itself to the pursuit of cars, expensive furniture, large houses, and the finest Scotch. That in fact the very class that owes its new affluence to the Movement now refuses to support the organizations that made its success possible, and has retreated from its concern for black people who are poor. Ralph Abernathy recently resigned as head of the Southern Christian Leadership Conference because of lack of funds and an $80,000.00 debt. This is more than a shame; it is a crime.

A friend of mine from New York who was in SNCC in the sixties came to Mississippi last week to find "spiritual nourishment." "But I found no nourishment," he later wrote, "because Mississippi has changed. It is becoming truly American. What is worse, it is becoming the North."

Unfortunately, this is entirely possible, and causes one to search frantically for an alternative direction. One senses instinctively that the beauty of the Southern landscape will not be saved from the scars of greed, because Southerners are as greedy as anyone else. And news from black movements in the North is far from encouraging. In fact, a movement *backward* from the equalitarian goals of the sixties seems a facet of nationalist groups. In a recent article in *The Black Scholar*, Barbara Sizemore writes:

> The nationalist woman cannot create or initiate. Her main life's goal is to inspire and encourage man and his children. Sisters in this movement must beg for permission to speak and function as servants to men, their masters and leaders, as teachers and nurses. Their position is similar to that of the sisters in the Nation of Islam. When Baraka is the guiding spirit at national conferences only widows and wives of black martyrs such as Malcolm X and Martin Luther King, Jr. and Queen Mother Moore can participate. Other women are excluded.

This is heartbreaking. Not just for black women who have struggled so *equally* against the forces of oppression, but for all those who believe subservience of any kind is death to the spirit. But we are lucky in our precedents; for I know that Sojourner Truth, Harriet Tubman—or Fannie Lou Hamer or Mrs. Winson Hudson—would simply ignore the assumption that "permission to speak" *could be given them,* and would fight on for freedom of all people, tossing "white only" signs and "men only" signs on the same trash heap. For in the end, freedom is a personal and lonely battle, and one faces down fears of today so that those of tomorrow might be engaged. And that is also my experience with the South.

And if I leave Mississippi—as I will one of these days—it will not be for the reasons of the other sons and daughters of my parents. Fear will have no part in my decision, nor will lack of freedom to express my womanly thoughts. It will be because the pervasive football culture bores me, and the proliferating Kentucky Fried Chicken stands appall me, and neon lights have begun to replace the trees. It will be because the sea is too far away and there is not a single mountain here. But most of all, it will be because I have freed myself to go; and it will be My Choice.

1973

. . . .

GOOD MORNING, REVOLUTION:

UNCOLLECTED WRITINGS

OF SOCIAL PROTEST

In her introduction to this extremely important collection of Langston Hughes's previously uncollected revolutionary work, Faith Berry, its editor, makes the following observation: "Langston Hughes was best known as a folk poet, pursuing the theme 'I, too, sing America.' But that image, which he accepted though did not choose, is only part of his legacy.

"During a career which covered four decades, in which he tried every literary genre, he wrote some of the most revolutionary works by any American writer of his generation. He was called the 'poet laureate of the Negro race,' but never for reasons which included his most radical verse. Editors, publishers and critics who hailed him as 'poet laureate' ignored that part of his canon which did not fit his popular image. Seen from their perspective, his revolutionary prose and poetry represented an aberration, an isolated phase of his career." However, as Berry demonstrates, Langston Hughes's revolutionary "phase" spanned forty years, and lasted as long as he lived.

For those who have misjudged the nature of Langston Hughes's political commitment, and they are many, this comment by Saunders Redding in the foreword of this book will relieve some of the guilt: "Hughes was a revolutionary writer and poet. If, heretofore, the fact has not been operative in the making of his reputation, it is in part Hughes' own fault. *That was the way he wanted it*" (my italics). The plot, as they say, thickens. What does Redding mean?

It appears that Langston, with his characteristic warmth toward any idea he felt beneficial to poor and colored peoples, liked very much the revolutionary social and political changes he witnessed in Russia in the early thirties. What is more, he fell in love with the idea of Revolution itself; and with the firm touch of a true believer, he personalized it:

> Good morning, Revolution:
> You're the very best friend
> I ever had.
> We gonna pal around together from now on.

The long poem "Good Morning, Revolution," from which this verse is taken, was published in *New Masses* in 1932. Two years later, in the same publication, Hughes wrote:

REVOLUTION

> Great mob that knows no fear—
> Come here!
> And raise your hand
> Against this man
> Of iron and steel and gold

Who's bought and sold
You—
Each one—
For the last thousand years.
Come here.
Great mob that knows no fear.
And tear him limb from limb.
Split his golden throat from
Ear to ear,
And end his time forever,
Now—
This year—
Great mob that knows no fear.

But it was his outright admiration of the Soviet Union that caused him trouble, as was true of many writers who found themselves, in the fifties, hounded by McCarthyism. Although Langston was never a member of the Communist Party, Berry writes, he fell victim "to that era of unparalleled paranoia, when anyone who ever had expressed praise of Russia was branded a public enemy and treated as such. In March 1953, summoned to testify before Joseph McCarthy's Senate Committee on Government Operations, he was pressed to answer such questions as 'Would you tell this committee frankly as to whether or not there was ever a period of time in your life when you believed in the Soviet form of government?' "

Being black and with perfectly good sense, good eyesight, and a highly educated sensibility about racial and economic matters, Langston had found "the Soviet form of government" quite appealing, having as it did clear advantages over the Jim Crow system of democracy he was used to in America. In an essay called "The Soviet Union and Color" Langston wrote: "In a museum in Ashkabad, capitol of Turkmenia, I saw signs on the wall as curiosities for the school kids to look at: SARTS KEEP OUT, in both the Turkomen and Russian language. I was told that in the old days these signs were at the entrances of the big beautiful public park in the heart of Ashkabad. In Tzarist times that park was only for Europeans—white people, not for the native peoples whom whites contemptuously named "sarts," a word equivalent to our worst anti-Negro terms.

"As I stood looking at these signs in a museum now, but once very real barriers to the colored peoples of Turkmenia, I remembered parks I had seen in my own America where I could not enter—public parks in cities like Charleston and Memphis and Dallas. Even today after a great world war for democracy such parks still exist in our United States. They are gone in the Soviet Union."

It was not only the liberation from racism that delighted him. Langston found that the Soviet Union was the only country in the world where he could have his teeth filled without charge (and he was constantly plagued with tooth troubles and had toothache all over the world); and it pleased him that women, who in Asiatic Russia had been used for their husbands' pleasure in harems, had thrown off their veils and were going to school, and could not be bought and sold as they had been before the Revolution.

From his writings it was obvious that he preferred the free medicine, free parks, and free women in the Soviet Union to people calling him "boy" at home. So, Berry writes: "As a result of the McCarthy hearings, for several years, Hughes' name was on a list of 'un-American' authors whose books were banned from U.S.I.A. libraries throughout the world. His books were also banned from the schools and libraries of certain states that passed anti-Communist laws. An influential lecture bureau, which long had scheduled his speaking engagements, canceled his contract. His public appearances often were met with pickets carrying signs with the words 'traitor,' 'red,' and 'Communist sympathizer.' "

And so, this sensitive man, who made his living from writing, surprised Saunders Redding at the All-African Writers Conference in Africa in 1962, because, although hundreds of representatives from African countries were eager to hear his revolutionary poems against colonialism and imperialism, Langston would not read them. He "stuck instead to his conventional verses on conventional themes."

Some of Langston's best poems are in this collection, and they point to his basic impatience for Revolution, an impatience that was only partly racial.

GOD TO HUNGRY CHILD

Hungry child,
I didn't make this world for you.
You didn't buy any stock in my railroad.
You didn't invest in my corporation.
Where are your shares in standard oil?
I made the world for the rich
And the will-be-rich
And the have-always-been-rich,
Not for you,
Hungry child.

TIRED

I am so tired of waiting,
Aren't you,
For the world to become good
And beautiful and kind?
Let us take a knife

And cut the world in two—
And see what worms are eating
At the rind.

Berry's finely edited book restores Langston's political thought to its proper context, which is to say to his autobiography, *The Big Sea* and *I Wonder as I Wander,* and should be read along with these volumes as a part Langston left out. However, I am left wondering if Langston's silence on his revolutionary writing was attributable *solely* to the reluctance of his publishers to publish it or to the attacks he endured during the McCarthy era. The behavior of a man as complex as Langston Hughes is never easily understood. I think it is possible that while his enthusiasm for revolution did not change, his enthusiasm for the Soviet Union did. Several people he knew in Russia were purged or imprisoned or killed. This experience was bound to have an impact on a man who, since childhood, was incapable of violence: it made him physically sick.

Langston Hughes was also a man with an exquisite sense of justice and an extraordinary degree of tolerance toward *individuals,* qualities more hardened revolutionaries—those who understand they must shoot people and so go right ahead—scarcely have time to cultivate. He was also committed to his own personal and artistic freedom. Or perhaps he reached that point all serious revolutionary writers reach, where the knowledge that children starve to death in a world of plenty seems to demand a gun across the barricades, not a speech across the podium, not a pen across a page. Writing or speaking about actions that he was not prepared, himself, to take may have seemed to make a mockery of his integrity. But even if these things are true—and I offer them merely as considerations a great artist may have had—they do not negate the fact that Langston saw the coming of revolution in America as a good, long-overdue event and was generally impressed with what he saw of revolutions in other countries.

When he was in China in 1949 Langston saw small children sold on the streets for sex and sold to factories for labor, their parents too poor to feed them. They say this is no longer true, in China. Good Morning, Revolution.

1976

. . . .

MAKING THE MOVES AND
THE MOVIES WE WANT

The scene is a fictional West African village. Women are being dragged from their homes and shoved to the ground by African soldiers pointing rifles. Their homes are torched and blaze against the sky. The women huddle together as the soldiers shoot over their heads, mocking their helplessness and fear. Eventually, after the village has been destroyed, the soldiers are signaled back to their Jeep by their commander, a European mercenary.

Then one of the women rises, places her basket of plantains on her head, hoists her baby more firmly against her back, and walks off quietly through the woods. Her shortcut takes her to the side of the main road just as the soldiers come roaring by. They shout jauntily at her. She waves at them. But as they pass in a cloud of dust, she raises a submachine gun she had kept hidden in the brush, and kills them all. Then she picks up her basket, puts it back on her head (her baby still resting comfortably against her back), and walks away.

Though the remainder of *Countdown at Kusini* is not as strong as this serious, unequivocal opening, it is a production to be happy about, to learn from, and—with its irrepressible music and nonstop action—to enjoy.

It is the first major motion picture ever produced by an organization of black women, Delta Sigma Theta. With a history of political activism that includes participation in the feminist and suffragist demonstrations of 1913, the eighty-five thousand members of American-based Delta Sigma Theta, the largest black sorority in the world, decided they would no longer accept the degraded images of black people—and especially black women—being foisted on them from the movie screen. Instead they would raise the money themselves, *from among themselves,* to make the kind of movie they wanted: one that reflected contemporary values and concerns of black people, and the ungilded magnificence and political activism of black women. *Countdown at Kusini,* from a script by Ossie Davis (who also directed), Ladi Ladebo, and Al Freeman, Jr., and based on a story by John Storm Roberts, is the result.

Kusini explores the themes of revolution, guerrilla warfare, and the relation of Afro-Americans to the African struggle against foreign domination. Afro-American musician Red Salter (Greg Morris) is touring in Africa when he gets involved in revolution. Foreign corporations are attempting to destroy the local anticolonialist struggle by assassinating Motapo (Ossie Davis), a revered guerrilla freedom fighter. Salter is enticed by revolutionary Leah Matazima (Ruby Dee) into running guns and transporting Motapo between hiding places.

The movie is often painful: ideals are betrayed, friends of the revolution are murdered. But it is basically an upbeat, joyous film, with incredible vistas of Africa (filming was done entirely in Nigeria; many of the actors are African), and African ceremonies, music, and customs. One leaves the theater ready to join the next revolutionary battle, not in dejection over how much there is to be done, but in awe of the possibilities for change once an oppressed people decides to rise.

Nearly all the flaws in *Kusini* are both obvious and instructive: Ossie Davis, as Motapo (a composite of Patrice Lamumba, Amilcar Cabral, and Martin Luther King), is essentially detached from the character. He plays Motapo as patronizing, too aware of his role as "liberator" of his people. He does not project a depth of feeling, and certainly not enough of it to get through a revolution. Ruby Dee's Leah, Motapo's tough, beautiful corevolutionist, is often distractingly overdressed for her role in a poor, embattled country. Otherwise she is superb, so real as a woman determined to get oppressors off her back that one is moved to reach out and take her hand.

The film's major flaw is the casting of Greg Morris (who in his plasticity is reminiscent of Richard Nixon) as the Afro-American musician turned gunrunner for the cause. Morris— Barney Collier in the TV series "Mission: Impossible!"—is so awkward and jerky as the *macho* lover of Leah (who is obviously more woman that he will ever be able to understand, much less dominate) that the audience, both times I saw the film, chuckled at his efforts.

Another flaw is the obligatory put-down of "the ugly honky woman" (mindlessly pursuing the plastic black hero) in favor of the black woman, Leah, who does not need this sort of cheap build-up.

Countdown at Kusini is an impressive beginning in moviemaking by the black women of Delta Sigma Theta. I hope they will give us, from now on, at least one such meaningful movie a year.

1976

. . . .

LULLS

Atlanta, Georgia, January 15, 1976

My cousin is driving me through the city. She is slender and brown, an aggressive, vocal driver, at ease with the idiosyncrasies of other drivers, calm at high speed. After a snowy morning in New York, the sunny weather in Atlanta is like spring. "What brings you to Atlanta?" she asks, driving down a hill that affords a sweeping view of the "New Atlanta," from "the world's tallest hotel" (recently completed) to bright murals that cover the walls of several of the city's lower buildings. It is the murals I like; the hotel building—as straight and round as a black finger pointed at the sky—seems imitative in its height, and redundant.

My cousin's name is Faye.* I have not seen her in ten years. Standing on an Atlanta street corner, resting after a mile-long

---

*Many names and identifying characteristics have been changed to protect the privacy of my friends and relatives.

march from Ebeneezer Baptist Church in support of the right of every American to have a job and also in commemoration of Martin Luther King, Jr.'s forty-seventh birthday, I had, while listening to the mellow voice of Atlanta's black mayor, Maynard Jackson, felt a gentle tug on my arm. "Are you my cousin Alice Walker?" she had asked. For an answer I gave her a hug. We stood smiling at each other for the duration of the rally. Then she whisked me away in her car.

"I had been thinking about how unemployment is killing what remains of the quality of black and/or poor life," I said. "Then I heard about the March for Jobs in Atlanta. I couldn't resist. I also wanted to visit places like Atlanta, Mississippi, and Boston to see what black people are thinking and doing in what appears to be a lull in political protest."

"I almost didn't come today," she said. "Marching is such a drag once you realize that every time you're out here ruining your feet, your President and congressmen are off skiing somewhere. The last thing they're thinking about is poor folks pounding the street *begging*—not for food, not for a handout—but for work. Still, it's a good occasion to bump into relatives and friends, and better than doing nothing. What did you think of it?"

Through much of the march I had thought of the FBI and the CIA. I had focused on J. Edgar Hoover and imagined him —an evil geni spread fumelike over the sky—grinning down on all our former marches, planning ways to make even the greatest of them come to nothing. I had thought of Martin Luther King, Jr., so maligned by so many, fearing—during his last "Mountain Top" days—that he could not remain with us through our final marches, through our arrival (wherever we might arrive), because once black people heard the tapes the FBI threatened to play for us about his sexual "escapades" we would no longer want or believe in him. I had thought how wrong such a fear would have been. Black people had heard rumors about King's sexual "appetite" for years, had read stories that had him making love to strange women "Super-fly" style in bathtubs, yet the majority of us had understood perfectly the character assassination being attempted, and had wished him only joy in whatever part of his life he had left to himself, any modicum of pleasure. At least I had felt that way.

"I felt silly, marching," I said. "The songs stuck in my throat. When someone started singing 'We Shall Overcome' I actually choked. But then I found myself singing anyway, because if black people still want to sing, if they can still dig up the heart, who am I not to sing with them?"

The only stanza of the former black movement anthem nobody could get past their lips was the "black and white together" one. It was quickly replaced by "Full Employment Now." I was struck by that. That, and the fact that the person singing near our group who had the purest voice, the sweetest voice, was a young man, barely in his twenties, who was obviously a junkie. At the sudden high force of this young man's voice people in my line of marchers halted, as if an angel from the Movement's past had come to join them. As one person we turned to welcome him, the only singer, it seemed, still capable of infusing the old, righteous energy into our songs. He had reeled under the euphoria of his drug, even as he marched.

What does this *mean*, I'd wondered, clutching my hand-bag tightly, annoyed at this reflex action even as I gazed with sorrow at his sensitive, though lost, dark face; aware it might not be long before I *knew*.

Faye has been a student of French literature at Brown University since we last saw each other. "It was a disaster," she says. "I thought I'd go crazy. I wanted to study French-speaking Haitian poets, and of course all I ever got was Proust."

After Brown there was a year in Lyon "studying and

loafing." She has been married—briefly and badly—divorced, and is now studying in an Atlanta seminary to become a minister. She already has a church in her hometown, and this coming Sunday she will preach. "God and I are on excellent terms," she says cheerfully, as if it explains the way she drives. She also runs a day-care center, and as she speeds past the brightly decorated buildings she points out the kind of art, the lively colors, she wants for her children's walls.

I am amazed that a young, under-thirty, woman like Faye would want to be a minister.

"But, Alice," she explains, "in the black community, the church has more power than any other institution. We no longer have our schools. We never did have 'town hall.' All we ever really had was the black church, and thank God it hasn't been integrated out of existence. It is my *church* that sponsors the day-care center I run. There was no other black institution that could take the responsibility.

"My mother can't understand why her daughter wants to be a minister, either. She keeps trying to marry me off again. I believe she thinks if I'm not interested in the men she digs up for me, it must mean I'm gay. Black folks with unmarried daughters are running scared, in this age of women's liberation." She laughs. "I like men; I just don't have time for them right now. But from the way my mother carries on, you'd think she never heard of a woman wanting to be independent."

I am disappointed at this news of my aunt. When I was a child, my aunts (including Faye's mother) were the most independent people I knew. They were nine strong girls who grew up in the second decade of this century on my grandfather's farm. With the help of their three brothers, they had run it. At family reunions they would reminisce about the old days when each of them had been able to fish and hunt and trap, to shoot "straight as a man," and to defend themselves with their own fists. After telling of a typical day's work on the farm, during which she had done everything from rounding up cattle on horseback to helping slaughter pigs, my favorite aunt would add: "And then I'd come in the house, bathe, put on my *red* dress, put a little *red* rouge on my lips, put a dusting of talcum down my bosom, do up my hair, and wait for my 'fella' to come calling."

My aunts had liked to brag about their healthy bodies, their strong muscles, the amount they could cook and eat and work, and their refusal ever to back down from an equal fight out of fear. Unlike many women who were told throughout their adolescence they must marry, I was never told by my mother or any one of her sisters it was something I need even think about. It is because of them that I know women can do anything, and that one's sexuality is not affected by one's work.

"Well," says Faye, "they haven't done anything independent for thirty years. They wanted to sit down in fine houses like white women in the movies. They wanted husbands around to 'protect' them. (Though 'protecting' them has driven most of their husbands, including my daddy, nuts.) Now they just want grandchildren, like everybody else."

I say nothing. I am thinking of the aunts I wished to be like: I still see them standing in overgrown fields shooting hawks, killing snakes, not knowing what it meant to be afraid of mice.

Joe Harris

Faye has stopped the car in a quiet suburban neighborhood. We walk up the driveway to the door of a modest brick house surrounded by trees. A large German shepherd greets Faye by bounding forward and attempting to lick her face. This is the home of Joe Harris, a very old and close friend, whom I have not seen for two years. I am eager to talk to him about his return from Boston to live in the South, since living in the South is something he once swore never to do. Joe comes to the door and lets us in, restraining the dog, Uhuru, by holding his collar. *"Sit, Uhuru!"* he says sharply, pulling out kitchen chairs for us. His wife, Mabel, is at the stove, cooking something that does not smell ethnic—when I am with relatives or old friends I become hungry for specific kinds of food: fried chicken, pork chops, chitterlings, greens, cornbread—I am disappointed that none of these seems to be cooking.

Joe is nearly six feet tall and his muscular body is showing signs of flab. He has nut-brown skin, an aquiline nose, and straightened black hair that curls over his shoulders in the manner of Errol Flynn.

"I *hated* Boston," he tells me. "Black people in Boston have so little unity they won't even get together for a riot."

He asks his wife to hand him a beer. She is black-skinned, curvaceous, and silent.

"Mabel doesn't agree with me," Joe says, sipping his beer, "but that's okay. I love it here. I love the climate, everything. In Boston I was always sick. Had to stay off work all the time because of colds, my tonsils, the flu. Here it doesn't get that cold. In my job as manager of a night club I don't have to be out in all kinds of weather changing tires the way I had to do in Boston. Changing tires was the only kind of job somebody with my education could get."

I know Joe as well as I know my own brothers. We grew up near each other, attended the same school. He was one of the smartest students ever to attend the local schools in Eatonton, Georgia, our hometown. According to his IQ test results he was gifted. But he could not be disciplined. He was eventually expelled from school in the eleventh grade for slapping a teacher and threatening to slap our school principal.

"If I had a college education," he says, "I could really do well here." He thinks back to our high-school days: "I couldn't take school because when I wore my hair long, like an Afro, in 1954 and '55, the teachers bugged me about it. And I couldn't stand Mr. McGlockton [our principal] because he wasn't a man. He let the white folks in town run him. And through him, us. They wouldn't even call him 'Mr.' or 'Dr.'; they called him 'Professor.' "

I had liked Mr. McGlockton. It was true, I said to Joe now, that he was humiliated by whites in town who hated to see any black person with an education or a position of importance, but he had been a kind, gentle man who always made time to talk to the students. I assumed he was *better* than the people who humiliated him, not worse.

This rather generous rationalization (as he sees it) does not impress Joe Harris, who wanted a hero, and got, he thinks, a coward.

"Except," he says sadly, drinking his beer, "those crackers would never have called him 'Mr.' back then, no matter what. That being the case, I should have stuck it out in school, gone off to college somewhere, become a lawyer, and come back home to kick asses. But it's too late now."

His two sons come in. They are bright-eyed, curious eight- and nine-year-olds. "Where've you two little niggers been?" asks Joe.

Hearing this, I remember why I have not seen Joe in such a long time. It is because he calls people nigger. Once, in fact, he called my daughter that. We argued, bitterly. I felt I could never forgive him.

"I've cut down a lot," he says apologetically, "on my use of that word. You know, before you mentioned it to me that time, I didn't realize anybody'd be offended by it."

"Not simply offended," I say, *"hurt.* Whenever I hear a black person I love using that word I feel as if I'm being killed."

Faye has been listening intently. "I still use 'nigger' a lot," she says, "and I just assumed there was nothing negative about it any more. After all, Red Foxx uses it on national television all the time."

"I've told Joe not to call our kids that," says Joe's wife, Mabel. "I keep telling him that just because they're 'niggers' to white people they shouldn't be 'niggers' to him, too."

"I'm preparing them," says Joe.

"You are preparing them to *be.* 'niggers'?" I ask.

He makes a gesture that means I do not understand.

Faye continues: "But then something happened that made me know I *had* been meaning negative things about the person I called 'nigger,' no matter how many positive adjectives I put in front of it. I met a young man, younger than me—I *do* think there's a lot to be said for the younger generation—who was so wise and so fine, I mean, where his head was, and his tenderness toward me and his respect for all black people, that I just had to tell my best friend about him, so I called her and I said, 'Girl, let me tell you about this fine nig—' and I just couldn't finish. I couldn't call him that. Because no matter how I prettied it up, *he just wasn't a nigger.*"

"I hate Red Foxx's show anyway," says Mabel, finally sitting down, 'not just for his stupid nigger and Puerto Rican jokes, but for how he treats 'Aunt Esther.' "

(Aunt Esther is a character on Red Foxx's "Sanford and Son." She is tall, angular, and black, and is called "gorilla" with stunning regularity.)

"Everybody's laughing at Aunt Esther," says Mabel, "but they know she looks just like them or some of their relatives. We forget white people have been calling us 'gorillas' for years. They probably think they're right, now that they see us on TV doing it to ourselves."

I am reminded that on a recent American Airlines flight from San Francisco to New York I watched an NFL football short starring a famous black running back. The opening shot was of several monkeys dressed in scarves and raincoats, waving large pocketbooks, jumping up and down, "cheering" in the stands. After some footage showing the famous star doing his famous running, the closing shot was of his wife and two other black women, dressed almost identically to the monkeys, jumping up and down cheering the famous star, their pocketbooks in the air. The persons who made this film were making a visual derogatory statement; one I could not immediately protest, except to *ache* to rip the screen out of the plane, at thirty-five thousand feet. When I arrived in New York, at Kennedy Airport, I learned La Guardia Airport had been bombed. And I thought: Where there are insults to the dignity of people, acts of retaliatory violence endanger the lives of all of us. Each of us pays in fear and anxiety—if not in actual loss of life—and it is a high price.

Joe Harris talks about his garden, his trees, his unlittered quiet street. "I can go for days, even weeks," he says happily, "without seeing a white person. I buy gas for my car from a black man. I shop, and I see only black faces. Black night clubs here are owned by black people, *and they're nice*, nothing flashy or tacky, like in Boston. Liquor stores are owned by black people. I bought my house from a black realtor. . . . All I get from white folks is my electricity and my telephone.

"In Boston a poor man can work his ass off, and never own anything but dirt and roaches."

"And the children's education?"

"Well"—he frowns—"that's about the same here as in Boston. When they integrate the schools in this country what they integrate is teachers. In my children's classes all the children are black, the teachers white. Our oldest boy is just as rebellious as I was. He has a hard time accepting discipline from a white teacher."

While Joe has graciously gone out to buy me a barbecue sandwich, I ask Mabel why she isn't as satisfied with life in the South as Joe.

"Things *are* nicer here," she says, "but I don't make friends easily. All my friends are in Boston. Of course," she adds, "you have to live where you *can* live. And if leaving people you care about *hurts*, you're just expected to suffer."

And I think, Yes, two hundred years ago you might have tried to escape to Canada, no matter what the slaves who'd already settled there wrote you of the murderous cold.

Taylor Reese

I have asked Taylor Reese to come by Joe's house so I can ask him how it feels to be a success.

"I don't know *how* it feels," he says.

He is the realtor from whom Joe Harris bought his house. He is also from our hometown. Rumor had it several years ago that he was becoming rich selling real estate in and around Atlanta. Living lavishly. Getting fat.

"Nobody's buying houses much in this recession," he says, "it's been rough just keeping the business open."

He has brought his young son with him, and I am immediately attracted to the child, who, at four years old, reminds me of his father years ago. The same deep-brown skin, the same laughing hazel eyes.

I say: "You could have been my child."

He says: "Uh-*uh!*"

I fell in love with Taylor Reese when I was six years old. When I was fourteen and he sixteen we began going steady. Later we became engaged. Our relationship lasted for more than six years, throughout high school and well into my freshman year at college. The last time I saw Taylor was in 1965. I was in

Atlanta on my way farther south to work for a summer in the Movement; he was married and about to become a father. He was not very political then, and I found it hard to relate to him.

Now I discover he *is* political, but I don't want to talk about it. Or about selling houses, success, or the recession. I want to know if he is happy. I want to know if he is the same person I used to love. That he is still good-looking, though not as thin, I can see, and his after shave, as I tell him, is delicious.

"I dream about you," I say.

He smiles, whispers (because Joe and Mabel are in the next room), "We always have fantasies about making love with our old lovers."

I smile back, though that is not what I meant.

"You were my best friend for nearly seven years; we went through things together only best friends go through. I've always wanted to tell you how good I thought you were. . . ."

"Oh, yeah? Good at what?"

"Not *at* anything in particular . . ."

He pretends to be crestfallen. We laugh.

"But just good. I mean, you were loyal, you were gentle, you were thoughtful, loving. *Good.* The older I get, the more I can appreciate that. The more shameful it seems that people who once loved each other are urged to forget it. I want to know all about you. I would like to know your children. I want to know your wife. I want to know all that you've become."

Looking at him, father, husband, businessman, *grown-up*, I remember things I never, now, think about. Our junior-senior prom, our Saturday-night dates, *every single Saturday night for all those years.* How, slowly, we grew apart, attached ourselves to other people, without trying to maintain what had been a great friendship.

I do not tell him this, but my dreams about him are rarely

erotic. He is simply, occasionally, *in* my dreams; perpetually slim, perpetually seventeen. Whether I am picking daisies or facing a firing squad.

"You remain mysterious to me," I tell him. "Because I knew you so well, and now I don't know you at all." Perhaps it is the writer in me that is frustrated, hating loose ends of such personal significance.

"I haven't changed," he says, and I am moved by the casual tenderness with which he caresses the cheek of his son, who stands behind him clinging to one leg. That gesture of nurturing affection, I recognize.

Jackson, Mississippi, January 17, 1976

I have a friend who hates neighborhoods. I hope I will always live in one. When my husband and I moved to Jackson to live in 1967 we were often afraid our house would be attacked. (Our interracial marriage was considered dangerous as well as illegal in Mississippi, though a U.S. Supreme Court ruling three months before we arrived struck down the statute forbidding it. And my husband, as "yet another Jew lawyer from New York," was welcomed only by the black community he served.) We bought a dog and a rifle, but we depended on our neighbors. If they saw a car full of strange white people cruising our street they called us, or stood on their porches until the car disappeared. When I drive past our old house on Rockdale Street I feel as if I'm coming home.

"I got your room all ready for you, soon as you called," Lorene says. Lorene and her family live in the house next door to where we used to live. She works as a nurse's aide at a local hospital. Her husband, Thomas, used to own a small neighborhood grocery store, but now it is not clear what he does. I suspect he is out of work, but he is not the kind of person to offer that particular information. Thomas and Lorene remind me of people I knew growing up in the country: completely accessible and dependable, generous beyond all understanding, so black and yet so unconscious of blackness as an ideology that to visit them is to take a mental rest.

They have three small children, two of them born during the year and a half since we moved away. Thomas is holding the baby, watching television, and attempting to repair a broken toy at the same time. Like most of the people I've talked to, he intends to vote for Jimmy Carter for President. There is a curious pride in the fact that Carter is a Southerner. "A decent, *intelligent* white one, for a change," everyone says. Though Thomas likes him simply because he raises peanuts, on the theory that "a man who raises peanuts *for money* can't help but do the country good."

"I was in New York City once," he says in a slow, deeply accented voice. "Couldn't make sense out of it. The sun rose in the north to me the whole time I was there." He puts the baby in his walker and tosses the broken toy behind his reclining chair. "I drove through Brooklyn one time by mistake. It looked like Korea during war. How in the world do you live there?"

"In my usual country style," I laugh. "With a big flower garden, a smoky fireplace, and a very slow mailman."

Living in Brooklyn (though I commute to Manhattan two or three times a week) is remarkably like living in Mississippi, in fact. My Civil Rights–lawyer husband was suing racist real-estate dealers in Jackson before we left. He is now filing identical suits in Brooklyn. And, again, what makes life bearable, even happy occasionally, is the proximity of our neighbors, a multi-ethnic conglomerate of peacemakers in the war-torn city of New York. I lapse into the usual brownstoner's paean to my neighbor's rose gardens, the way they sweep their sidewalks, the way, in Brooklyn, anything is an excuse to plant another tree. My wonder that the people on my street, who have long since become my friends (willing to look after my house or my child on a moment's notice), are so civil and generous and *clean* they are nobody's idea of what New Yorkers are like.

"Yes," says Lorene, "but what's the *worse* thing that's happened to you since you moved to New York?"

And she's right to be skeptical, because something horrible has indeed happened. I approach her question, as they say here, from the long way.

"You know how, growing up in the South you might be afraid, for good reason, of white people, but you're never afraid of blacks?"

I remember a good illustration of this lack of fear: "When I was a little girl, some black convicts were cutting a road near our house, and one of them used to come up to the porch and ask for water. Back then convicts wore those suits like black-and-white-striped pajamas, so he really should have looked strange to us, but he didn't. We'd give him water, dinner, anything we had, and then we'd ask to walk back to the road with him. We'd go strolling up the path with this convict who was in prison for killing a man, and never once were we afraid. We believed him innocent, even if he was guilty."

"You're sometimes scared of other black people in New York, aren't you?" asks Lorene.

"For the first time in my life." (Of course I have lived in the city before; once, on the lower East Side in a building that had no door. But I was too young then to be afraid of anything.)

For a long time we do not speak; we watch the children playing, struggling over a toy.

"I guess that takes some getting used to," says Thomas.

But I'll never be used to it. The bond of black kinship—so sturdy, so resilient—has finally been broken in the cities of the North. There is no mutual caring, no trust. Even the rhetoric of revolutionary peoplehood is hissed out threateningly. The endearment "sister" is easily replaced with "bitch." My fear is part grief, and if I were ever attacked or robbed by another black person I doubt I'd recover. This thought itself scares me. There is also the knowledge that just as I'm afraid of them, because I no longer know what behavior to expect, they're afraid of me. Of all the vile things that have happened to us in America, this fear of each other is to me the most unbearable, the most humiliating.

"It's the drugs," says Lorene.

"Those little nasty spaces they have to live in," says Thomas.

"All those from the South," says Lorene, "probably miss their gardens."

"Miss going fishing."

"Miss trees."

"Miss having people smile at them out of true affection."

This is the most quaintly put reason, and perhaps it is the truest of all.

Mrs. Cornelius

I walk half a block down the street to the first place my six-year-old daughter went to school. It is a neat brick house with trees and swings in the yard.

"How *is* my Rebecca?" her former teacher, Mrs. Cornelius, asks.

She is stout and black-skinned and warm, and is exactly the sort of person I wanted my daughter's first teacher to be. The nursery school is a large, spotless room added to the house four years ago, and I gaze at the small chairs and tables almost with longing. In Brooklyn my daughter attends a fine public school, with loving teachers and friendly classmates, but it is not the same.

"*Your* Rebecca is fine," I tell her. And we chat about the

changes in the school since we moved away. But I have really come to thank her for what she and her school meant to me and my child.

"When I was four years old," I tell her, "my mother could no longer take me to the fields with her when she went to work. She asked Mrs. Reynolds, the teacher in the local primary school, if she could accept me in her first-grade class. I started the very next day. Though I was the youngest person in the class I was made to feel entirely comfortable. Mrs. Reynolds taught me that school is a wonderful place, full of people who care about you and your family, and understand you and your ways, and love you for what you are.

"When Rebecca was only one, you took her in, because being home all day with her while trying to write a novel was driving me crazy, and it will be because of you, when she grows up, that she will know the meaning of supportive affection and generosity, even from strangers."

Mrs. Cornelius pooh-poohs the assertion that her school is the best I expect Rebecca to know, wherever she is in her life, because it was here that the culture and the curriculum matched serenely, where Rebecca learned to sing "Ain't Gonna Let Nobody Turn Me 'Round" as readily as "You Are My Sunshine," where she could hear the story of Harriet Tubman read to her and see Harriet herself in her teacher's face.

Boston, Massachusetts, January 25, 1976
"The schools in Boston are back where they were when black folks stepped off the boat. Or were dragged, let me say. If all this racial furor keeps up, I'm sending my child south to school."

Martha is a large cinnamon-colored woman with a pleasant voice and large, beautiful eyes. She is disabled and on welfare. She cannot leave the state. Her daughter, Doris, is fifteen, and the local schools have left her with terrible grammar and no easy comprehension of what a sentence is.

Martha is from Georgia, and has lived in Boston for nearly ten years.

"I always thought Boston was the best," she says. "The best place for schools, for hospitals, for intelligent, nonracist people. Well, another dream down the drain. Next to Boston today, Mississippi looks good."

I too have always loved Boston. I used to spend summers here, working and going to the beach. Many of my relatives live in Dorchester, a predominantly black section of the city. My brothers came to the city penniless, worked hard at dirty jobs nobody else wanted, until they could afford to buy nice homes on pleasant streets. Now, though their homes are still in good shape, the neighborhoods around them are in a shambles. Because of massive unemployment in the black community, and the consequent inability to pay mortgages, houses have been abandoned by the dozen, vandals have broken out windows, torn out the plumbing, set fire to whatever they couldn't steal. Driving up once familiar Blue Hill Avenue to visit them I discovered I no longer knew where I was. Whole blocks are boarded up, trash clots the street corners, once-lovely homes have the look of having been assaulted: paint peels, doors fall off hinges, windows are stuffed with rags. The people on the street looked *conquered.*

Martha worries if her daughter spends an unguarded five minutes in the street. Police protection of residents is a joke. In short, Boston could not care less about its poor black citizens: it has segregated them into a ghetto and it is only when they attempt to send their children outside the ghetto to school that they receive any attention at all.

"But you brought Doris north to escape the South," I say.

"And I'll send her south to escape the North."

I wonder if America will ever have a place for poor people. It appears they are doomed to be eternal transients.

"When I leave here," says my brother, a "Bostonite" for nearly twenty years, now looking forward to the freedom of retirement, "I intend to miss it like a toothache."

He, too, is going back south, back to the country.

"I want peace," he says. "Cleanliness and space around me. And just some time to be myself, before I die."

It is an old dream, but no less unfulfilled for all its age.

1977

MY FATHER'S COUNTRY

IS THE POOR

The drab, monotonous postwar architecture of Helsinki concealed the tremendous vibrancy of the youth who were gathering there from all over the world.

In the brief two weeks of the festival, there were spectacular cultural programs, mass political rallies, and countless seminars on the struggle in Africa, Latin America, Asia, the Middle East. . . .

The cultural presentation given by the Cuban delegation was the most impressive event of the festival. Not that they performed in the most polished, sophisticated manner, but because their performance conveyed a fiercely compelling spirit of revolution. They were the youth of a revolution that was not yet three years old. With the U.S. delegation as audience, the Cubans satirized the way wealthy American capitalists had invaded their country and robbed them of all traces of sovereignty. They presented their attack on the invaders in plays, songs, and dances. During those days, long before Women's Liberation had been placed on the agenda, we watched the Cuban militia women zealously defending their people's victory.

It is not easy to describe the strength and enthusiasm of the Cubans. One event, however, illustrates their infectious dynamism and the impact they had on us all. At the end of their show, the Cubans did not simply let the curtain fall. Their "performance," after all, had been much more than a mere show. It had been life and reality. Had they drawn the curtain and bowed to applause, it would have been as if their commitment was simply "art." The Cubans continued their dancing, doing a spirited conga right off the stage and into the audience. Those of us openly enthralled by the Cubans, their revolution, and the triumphant beat of the drums rose spontaneously to join their conga line. And the rest—the timid ones, perhaps even the agents— were pulled bodily by the Cubans into the dance. Before we knew it we were doing this dance—a dance brought into Cuban culture by slaves dancing in a line of chains—all through the building and on into the streets. Puzzled Finns looked on in disbelief at hundreds of young people of all colors, oblivious to traffic, flowing down the streets of Helsinki.

—*Angela Davis, writing on the*
1962 World Youth Peace Festival in Helsinki,
ANGELA DAVIS: AN AUTOBIOGRAPHY

Perhaps I saw Angela Davis at the festival. Perhaps we met. She was not ANGELA DAVIS then. Impressed by the Cubans, I too joined the conga line and danced my way through the chilly Helsinki streets. This was my first trip abroad, financed by remarkably generous women of Atlanta's black churches, who supported me and another young woman from Spelman College in our desire to see the world from another continent and demonstrate—after the United States resumed nuclear testing in 1961—our commitment to world peace.

Although in 1962 Angela Davis and I were both eighteen years old, her political autobiography proves she was far more politically mature than I. She appears to have grasped the international nature of oppression while I could barely see beyond the struggle of black people in the small towns of Georgia. Indeed, I was so ignorant of history and politics that when I left the festival, went to Moscow and was taken on a stroll across Red Square, I could not fathom for the longest time *who* the Russians were queuing up to view in Lenin's tomb.

And yet, I knew enough to know I wanted the world to survive (though, ironically, I was myself at this time illogically suicidal). I wanted peace and the abolition of the possibility of nuclear war. And I believed my *job* at that point (being powerless to do much else) was to begin to see other peoples not as strangers but as kin.

My sense of the Cubans' spiritedness stayed with me. One of them gave me a copy of Fidel Castro's *History Will Absolve Me*, which I read in a tiny, wood-paneled compartment of a Russian train winding its way across the spectacular Crimea, and I read and cried, cried and read, as I recognized the essence of a struggle already familiar to me. In this passionate defense of the Cuban people's right to revolt against tyranny, I could not help but hear the voices of Nat Turner, Harriet Tubman, Sojourner Truth, Frederick Douglass, Malcolm X, and, especially, Martin Luther King, Jr., whose 1963 "Letter from a Birmingham Jail" would so closely resemble it.

By making their revolution, the Cubans proved that oppression needn't last always. Three years after the beginning of the revolution, they had also begun to kick out of their country the greedy and antisharing. Which is to say, they had begun "to overcome." This was profoundly important to me. I think part of my "illogical" despair had been due to my sense of political powerlessness, caused to some extent by a lack of living models. I believed poor people could not win. (And, in fact, no matter how many people, poor or otherwise, protested against nuclear testing, the testing—both in the United States and in the Soviet Union—continued.) But here at last was a revolutionary people I could respect, and they made it quite clear they did not intend to lose.

For several years, I tried to get to Cuba. Because the Cuban Revolution had been achieved through armed struggle, I was eager to see the effect on the people of having used violence to liberate themselves. I was, after all, a pacifist and a believer in the use of nonviolent means to effect social change. After the birth of my own child, I had understood fully the evil of waiting interminably for conditions to change at someone else's convenience, but I still needed to know that the use of violence did not necessarily destroy one's humanity. I wanted to confirm the truth of one of my favorite lines from Flannery O'Connor: "Violence is a force that can be used for good or evil, and among the things taken by it is the Kingdom of Heaven." For the poor of Cuba, their own country had become "the Kingdom of Heaven." It was in their own hands, thanks to the Cuban Revolution.

Before the Revolution only 60 percent of those of working age had regular full-time employment.

In the rural population, only 11 percent drank milk, only 4 percent ate meat, only 2 percent ate eggs.

Forty-four percent had never gone to school.

> Eighty percent of the inhabitants of Havana did not
> have enough to eat.
> —*Ernesto Cardenal,*
> IN CUBA

Today, there is work for everyone in Cuba. Everyone has enough
to eat. Every Cuban child goes to school, as do many adults.
Illiteracy has virtually disappeared.

Many Americans who visit Cuba complain that life there
is hard. And it is. But they do not seem adequately impressed
by the fact that poverty has been eliminated, or that nearly all
the people can read: that a 300,000-copy printing of a new book
can be sold out in days. They do not seem awed by a country
that provides free medical care to all its citizens, and labors daily
to provide decent housing for everyone. They do not say—as I
feel—that a hard life shared equally by all is preferable to a life
of ease and plenty enjoyed by a few. Standing in line for hours
to receive one's daily bread cannot be so outrageous if it means
every person *will receive bread,* and no one will go to bed hungry
at night.

I went to Cuba with a group of African-American artists who
were selected by the editors of the *Black Scholar* and the Cuban
Institute for Friendship Among Peoples. We were there for two
weeks—not nearly long enough to comprehend all the things we
saw. What follows are fragments of my experience, offered with
an acute awareness that my view of Cuba is neither definitive
nor complete.

I am sitting in the Pavilion dining room of the Hotel Habana
Libre, which, before the revolution, was the Havana Hilton. It
is full of people who, twenty years ago, would not have been
allowed through the front door. It is as if, in New York, everyone

oné saw on the Lexington Avenue IRT during rush hour was accustomed to spending the weekend in the Palm Court of the Plaza. I am talking to Black Panther exile Huey Newton and his wife, Gwen. He is saying:

"If I come back to America talking like Eldridge [Cleaver], I hope black and progressive people renounce and reject me."

I assure him we will.

When the Newtons came to Cuba two years ago, they asked to live "like the people." They were sent to Santa Clara, "a very small, country town," says Newton, but a good symbol of how the revolution has changed habits and attitudes in Cuba. He tells me about the Santa Clara park, in which, before the revolution, black people could not walk. And of how this park —now used by all the people—represents the fall of racist institutions throughout the island.

Unable to live "like the people" on rationed food that invariably ran out before the end of the week (and unable to get the knack of wringing the necks of their own live chickens), the urban-raised Newtons moved eventually to their present suite (two small adjoining rooms, for the family of four) in the Habana Libre. Like the majority of exiles and guests of the Cuban government, they use a special identification card that allows them to eat in the hotel restaurant and to order up quantities of strong Cuban cigarettes and light and dark rum.

The resemblance of Huey Newton to some large human cat is striking. One feels his bright brown eyes would glow in the dark. His manner is quick, graceful, lithe, and of a sinewy gentleness.

Before mentioning the chameleonic Cleaver, now a "born again" TV Christian, Newton was speaking of his father, who died shortly after Newton arrived in Cuba.

Now he says, apologetically, "You would probably not approve of him."

I realize he is wary of me because I am a feminist. It pains me to assume Newton is not. But, thinking how much easier it is to approve of dead people than of live ones, I shrug. "I'm prepared to like him," I say, puffing on a cigarillo, and hoisting my glass of rum. "Give me his case."

"We lived on a farm in Louisiana and he did not want my mother to work. He told the white bossman, 'When you send Miss Ann out in the fields to work, *I'll* send out *my* wife.'"

This did not seem impossible to comprehend. We were eating delicious stewed rabbit, like my father used to make. I smiled to think of myself eating rabbit in a fancy Havana restaurant, talking to Huey Newton about whether I approved of his sharecropper father or not. It was a moment.

"The *problem*," said Gwen, "was that the choice of not working was not made by your mother."

"You mean she *wanted* to work?" I asked.

"Well, yeah, I guess so," said Huey.

Suddenly I remembered Louisiana, certainly one of the ugliest American states. Flat, hot, with houses miles apart. Black women and white women might go crazy there from boredom.

"Well," I said, "I guess I don't approve of your father. I understand, but don't approve. Your father's concern was for his own pride, his rebellion against the white man. It wasn't about your mother."

Earlier we had been together in their suite. Their two children made a brief appearance. I had brought the family gifts of magazines, books, T-shirt iron-ons for the children. Gwen is a stunning woman, with large, serene black eyes and hair that stands by itself. She and Huey seem to be the only blacks in Havana wearing the Afro hair style. The Cubans apparently consider long hair an expression of antisocial behavior. This is incredible, considering that "longhairs" won the revolution.

Before I left the United States I had heard ugly rumors about Newton. That he'd been a pimp, and had murdered a young black woman prostitute because she called him a punk; that he'd pistol-whipped his tailor (!), and other such charges.

To my indirect questions, he responds that he was vilified and framed, probably by the FBI, and that he fled to Cuba to save his life. He will be returning to the United States, however, because he is both homesick and innocent.

To dissipate the tension that accumulates around this exchange, we talk about trivia: an ideal way to spend an afternoon with exiles who miss their country and who don't speak the language of the country they're in. We discuss movie stars. (He knows some personally, I know none.) Gwen encourages Huey to explain to me the meaning of his favorite movie: it is a Japanese classic called *The Forty Outcasts*. His eyes become brilliant as he describes the story: it is apparently about the sacrifices involved in maintaining one's honor in a society of men whose rules for membership are patently absurd.

Our best poets
write poetry full of holes:

The women who love women, never tell.
The men who love men write of wombs.
The genius who loves both is rendered mute
by the complexity of choice.
The black father of white children suffers in silence.
The mother of the dope fiend is ashamed to reveal her
shame.

The poetry is full of holes, I say.

They will not give you life,
but pseudo-life
where all halves can be made to fit.

Is it because they know that even Cuba
that liberated country
would tolerate anything
that helped the Revolution
except a gay discoverer of a cure for cancer
or a Jehovah's Witness
whose musing paradisical agronomy
would provide milk and honey
dirt cheap
for this Promised Land?
—*ruminations of the author*

And the story of the Cuban writer who was living abroad
and came home when the Revolution triumphed. The Revolution became the center of his life. He worked as a
journalist with great enthusiasm, with great euphoria, writing propaganda for the Revolution. But they found out that
he was a homosexual. They didn't want to wound him by
any accusation, and they didn't fire him from his job. They
just said that he could go on drawing his pay but that he
must stop going to the office. He understood why they told
him this and became deeply depressed. He was rejected by
the Revolution he loved so much. He left Cuba and committed suicide in Rome.
—*Ernesto Cardenal,*

IN CUBA

.   .   .

We are sitting in a bus outside the Moncada Barracks (now part museum, part school); it was here, in 1953, that the Cuban insurrectionists, led by Fidel Castro, attempted to seize the weapons that would have meant control of the surrounding Oriente Province. They were defeated, temporarily. Fidel fled to the mountains: others were tortured, murdered, or jailed—as Fidel was—after capture.

The Dramatist in our group declaims dramatically that it is a matter of record that half the city of San Francisco is homosexual. She declares further her intention, because of this threat to her and her children, to move. We are ten black American artists—painters, poets, musicians, novelists. I feel a sad bitterness in the air. Some of us say, with disgust, "Move!" It is not that we are gay; it is probably that we have known the pain of moving into neighborhoods where we were not wanted.

When I heard that Jehovah's Witnesses are banned in Cuba and considered counterrevolutionary, I did not feel deeply disturbed, though it meant that some of my relatives, as recent converts to this religion, would be unwelcome there. Cuba's government-sanctioned dislike of homosexuals, however, seemed to me unfair and dangerous. An affront to human liberty and a mockery of the most profoundly revolutionary statement in the Cuban *Family Code:* "All children are equal." Surely homosexuals are born as well as made? One assumes a Jehovah's Witness chooses her or his religion. But if a child is born a homosexual what is to be done about it?

"Tell us," we ask our hosts, "just what is it about homosexuals that threatens the revolution?"

"We do not bother them, as you do in New York," they reply. "You'll never hear of homosexuals being beaten up in the street."

"But you do not like them."

"We do not *condone* their actions. We do not *approve* of

them. In Cuba, because of poverty, before the revolution, the Cuban family was nearly destroyed. We believe we must strengthen it."

"So homosexuals are seen as a threat to the family?"

"We believe homosexuality is an aberration in nature—and that the more corrupt the society becomes, the weaker the family structure, the more homosexuality perpetuates itself."

"What are the legal sanctions against homosexuals?"

"They are not permitted to teach," says one of our interpreters. "And they cannot become doctors. They are not allowed to hold positions in which they can influence youth."

This is all to our Dramatist's liking. She nods her approval. The rest of us are silent. It is their revolution, after all. Perhaps some of us are chilled, thinking of gay friends back home who would not feel as free as we do, in Free Cuba.

What Cuba teaches is that revolution is not a flash in the pan of injustice. It is, as Fidel says, "a process." It takes years and years and generations to build a just society. The overthrow of a repressive government is only the beginning of that struggle.

Everywhere we go, we stress the fact that we are cultural *workers,* not tourists; that we have come to Cuba to learn, but also to teach. We do not want simply to see films, we want to discuss them with film makers. We don't want simply to visit museums, we want to see art schools. We want to share our poetry and music and painting with the poets, musicians, and painters of Cuba. We are permitted to do this, and spend long afternoons with writers (there is a scarcity of women writers, and we are offered no plausible reasons why this is so), film makers, and musicians. We can see that great efforts have been made to have Cuban art reflect the masses of Cuban people, that the African heritage is given equal time with the Spanish, and that the "dominant culture" is recognized as being a synthesis of the two.

All of this is developing. It is by no means complete. The status of the arts is analogous to the development of the rest of the country in direction and change. For example: during our first days in Cuba we were dismayed that the inevitable refreshment of rum and sweets offered us was presented by a black waiter; invariably an older person, male or female. What was this? we indignantly asked our Cuban hosts. Though we realized the occupation of waiter is not in itself demeaning, the consistent use of blacks to fill it *is*. We were told what should perhaps have been obvious: that before the revolution, blacks were disproportionately employed in menial jobs, in which many remained. Before the revolution, they would have been destined to remain in these jobs until they died. Now, everyone, including the black waiters, studies constantly in order to improve their positions. Education is free, and once having prepared and been tested for a higher position, they could take it. But the main thing, our hosts pointed out, was that the revolution made it virtually impossible for any group to be relegated forever to a servitude of any kind.

When we saw Cuban child-care centers and high schools, we could see that this was true. No distinctions are made between black, brown, and white, or between male and female. All learn to speak languages (including Russian and English), to make computers, to swim, to study math, the dance, music, science, and geography. In their trim school uniforms, it is impossible to tell a child's background. Color remains, but beyond color there is a shared *Cuban-ness*.

Watching young black Cubans is exhilarating but, frankly, I also felt bereft. Unlike black Americans, who have never felt at ease with being Americans, black Cubans raised in the revolution take no special pride in being black. They take great pride in being Cuban. Nor do they appear able to feel, viscerally, what racism is. The more we insisted on calling ourselves *black* Americans and spoke of *black* culture, the more confused and distant they grew.

Young white Cubans seem equally unaware of themselves as white. (Though older white Cubans certainly retain the racism they grew up with, the revolution does not permit them to display it, except by attitude. The only people who treated us with the arrogance that in this country one considers racist were some of the senior members of the Union of Cuban Writers and of the Institute of Cuban Films. They seemed annoyed that North American blacks dared to question anything about Cuba —including the absence of women in film-making and writing. Nor did they appear attentive to our carefully documented presentation of the experience of black actors in North American films. It was good to feel that these men represent attitudes that belong to Cuba's past and not to its present or future.)

At the Lenin school outside Havana, an institution for especially bright pupils, I came face to face with my own prejudice. Our group was taken on a tour of the school, given a glimpse of its large outdoor swimming pools and sports area, and shown photographs of its surrounding cedar fields. (In Cuba, all students, even first graders, work as well as study in an educational plan that is almost exactly like that begun at Tuskegee Institute in the late 1880s by Booker T. Washington. Young children raise lettuce; older children raise trees and citrus fruits.) Then we were entertained by what I perceived (with North American eyes, seeing narrowly) as an "integrated" group. Such a group! Black, brown, white, yellow, pink, gold complexions. And such music! Mellow, rhythmic, soulful, lovingly presented. When the group of teen-agers finished, we surged forward to thank them. They were happy, open, expectant. Cuban and human from the blackest to the whitest. And then *we* presented ourselves as "black" Americans (they presented themselves, un-self-consciously and without words, as Cubans, of course), and their faces changed. For the first time they seemed aware of color differences *among themselves—and were embarrassed for us.* And I realized that as I had sat listening to them, I had separated them, mentally, into black and white and "mixed," and that I had assumed certain things on the basis of my own perverted categorization. And now I saw that these young Cubans did not see themselves as I saw them at all. They were, like their music, well blended into their culture and did not need to separate on the basis of color, or to present any definition of themselves at all.

"Of course they know what racism is," their headmaster explained. "They study it in their schoolbooks."

Eldridge Cleaver makes much of racism in Cuba, and it is useless to claim it does not exist. But the older Cubans, in whom racism is endemic, will be dead someday. Young Cubans will not have the social structures that *allow* racism to flourish. *That* is revolution. Not instant eradication of habits learned over a lifetime, but the abolition of everything that would foster those habits, and the creation instead of new structures that prevent them from returning.

A week before I flew to Cuba, I began to dream about my father. For several nights he appeared in a pose I recognized but could not place: standing by the side of a road in front of a filling station, his hat in his hands, watching me as I moved farther and farther away from him.

It was not unusual for me to dream about my father: he died in the winter of 1973, but my dreams of him before were solely about an absence of something I observed, sometimes in his eyes.

My father, near his death, was a gaunt, coffee-colored man, with a fine large nose and immense dark and intelligent eyes. All his life he worked for other people; rough, unpleasant labor that forced him (along with a wife and eight children) to subsist on as little as three hundred dollars a year. My father, then, was a poor man exploited by the rural middle-class rich, like millions of peasants the world over. But as a child I was not aware of any others. I thought it was my father's own peculiar failing that we were poor.

My excitement over finally going to Cuba did not divert my interest from the new dream I was having of my father. Each night it came: him at the side of a Georgia highway, large eyes full of—what? Me moving farther and farther away.

I thought of my father's face as I boarded a Cubana airplane in Mexico City, and again when I was escorted off the unmoved plane and it and my luggage were thoroughly searched by Cuban flight personnel. Three weeks before my trip, a Cuban airliner carrying seventy-three passengers had been blown up over the Caribbean—the CIA held responsible by the Cubans, who believed this barbaric act was the United States's response to the Cuban military presence in Angola. Was the fear I felt suddenly surfacing the reason I dreamed of my father? Was he trying to tell me now, as he often had in life, that my curiosity about other people and places could endanger my life?

But the flight, four hours behind schedule, finally lifted us to Havana. And there, waiting for me on the patio of a lovely old mansion liberated from someone who had to have been shamelessly rich, was my father.

The same dark, coffee-colored skin, the same large nose, the same vibrant and intelligent eyes.

My father's name in Havana was Pablo Díaz, and he spoke in Spanish, which I do not understand. His resemblance to my father—even the timbre of his voice—was so striking, however, that when he opened his mouth and Spanish came out, I glanced about me to locate the source of the trick.

Before the Cuban Revolution, Pablo Díaz had been, like my father, a man who might have belonged to any country, or to none, so poor was he. So unlikely it would have been for anyone in the government to wonder or care what he wanted of life, what he thought, what he observed. He had cut cane, done the "Hey, *boy!*" jobs of the big cities (Havana and New York), and had joined the revolution early—an option my father never had. From the anonymity he shared with my father, Pablo Díaz had fought his way to the other side of existence; and it is from his lips that many visitors to Cuba learn the history of the Cuban struggle.

As an official spokesperson for the Cuban Institute for Friendship Among Peoples (ICAP), this black man, telling the Cuban story to whoever comes, increases my respect for the Cuban Revolution. Señor Díaz talked to us about the revolution for three hours, his cadence as steady as a *griot*'s; every turning in his people's progress he knew by heart.

He spoke of the black *mambises* of the 1800s; of Jose Martí, the "father" of Cuba; of Antonio Maceo, "the bronze titan"; of the attack in 1953 on the Moncada Barracks; the exile in Mexico of the revolutionists; the fighting in the Sierra Maestra; the abdication of the tyrant Batista; the triumph of the revolution; and of Che, Camilo, and Fidel.

Helping to throw off his own oppressors obviously had given him a pride in himself that nothing else could, and, as he talked, I saw in his eyes a quality my own father's eyes had sometimes lacked: the absolute assurance that he was a man whose words—because he had helped destroy a way of life he despised—would always be heard, with respect, by his children.

There is no story, beyond this, of Pablo Díaz. I saw him

twice during my two weeks in Cuba. I told him he reminded me of my father. He replied: "You honor me." In a photograph I have of us posing with our Cuban/African-American group, I see that his hand is resting on my shoulder, and I am easy under it, and smiling.

> The hotel was still in deep silence; it seemed that nobody had waked up. The only sounds came from two maids who were cleaning near the kitchen, but they must have been shouting to each other because I could hear everything they said. One told the other that she had a very beautiful poem. Or rather that she had two. And one of them she had sent to her mamma on Mother's Day. The other maid talked about her classes in the hotel and that she was taking down a dictation on the United States. They said something about their Ancient History class, and that they were taking a "History of Cuba up to '57." One of them said the arithmetic and algebra classes were the dullest ones, but the other said she liked them. I watched them go off with their pails leaving the red terrace floor shining with water.
> —*Ernesto Cardenal,*
> IN CUBA

The transformation of Pablo Díaz from peasant to official historian deeply impressed me. I envied his children, all the children of Cuba, whose parents are encouraged and permitted to continue to grow, to develop, to change, to "keep up with" their children. To become *compañeros* as well as parents. A society in which there is respectful communication between generations is not likely, easily, to fail. Considering these thoughts, I recalled the incident that is the source of the dream I was having about my father. It is a story about economics, about politics, about class. Still, it is a very simple story, and happens somewhere in the world every day.

When I left my hometown in Georgia at seventeen and went off to college, it was virtually the end of my always tenuous relationship with my father. This brilliant man—great at mathematics, unbeatable at storytelling, but unschooled beyond the primary grades—found the manners of his suddenly middle-class (by virtue of being at a college) daughter a barrier to easy contact, if not actually frightening. I found it painful to expose my thoughts in language that to him obscured more than it revealed. This separation, which neither of us wanted, is what poverty engenders. It is what injustice means.

My father stood outside the bus that day, his hat—an old gray fedora—in his hands; helpless as I left the only world he would ever know. Unlike Pablo Díaz, there was no metamorphosis possible for him. So we never spoke of this parting, or of the pain in his beautiful eyes as the bus left him there by the side of that lonely Georgia highway, and I moved—blinded by tears of guilt and relief—ever farther and farther away; until, by the time of his death, all I understood, *truly*, of my father's life, was how few of its possibilities he had realized, how relatively little of its probable grandeur I had known.

With a bleeding human eye in his hand, a sergeant and several other men went to the cell where our comrades Melba Hernández and Haydée Santamaría were held. Addressing the latter and showing her the eye, they said: "This eye belonged to your brother. If you will not testify what he refused to testify, we will tear out the other." She, who loved her valiant brother [Abel Santamaría] above all things, replied, full of dignity: "If you tore out an eye and he did not testify falsely, much less will I."

Later they came back and burned her arms with lit cigarettes until at last, full of disrespect, they told her: "You

no longer have a fiancé because we have killed him too."
But, still imperturbable, she answered: "He is not dead,
because to die for one's country is to live forever."
—*Fidel Castro,*

HISTORY WILL ABSOLVE ME

Since my return from Cuba, I have been asked about my sense
of Cuban women. Generally speaking, women appear to be well
integrated into Cuba's revolutionary society. There are women
doctors, laborers, heads of publishing companies, and so on, as
well as teachers, nurses, and directors of child-care centers. With
Fidel Castro frequently verbalizing the conviction that the revolution cannot be called complete until women share full opportunities and responsibilities, Cubans—both male and female—
actively combat centuries of Spanish/African *machismo.* The
equality of men and women is stressed throughout the Cuban
Family Code, which contains the laws that regulate family life.
The following articles are from Section I of the *Code,* listed
under "Relations Between Husband and Wife":

Article 24. Marriage is established with equal rights and
duties for both parties.

Article 25. Spouses must live together, be loyal, consider-
ate, respectful, and mutually helpful to each other.

The rights and duties that this code establishes for the
couple will remain in effect as long as the marriage is not
legally ended, even if the parties do not live together for any
well-founded reason.

Article 26. Both parties must care for the family they
have created and each must cooperate with the other in the
education, upbringing, and guidance of the children according to the principles of socialist morality. They must
participate, to the extent of their capacity or possibilities,

in the running of the home and cooperate so that it will develop in the best possible way.

Article 27. The parties must help meet the needs of the family they have created with their marriage, each according to his or her ability and financial status. However, if one of them only contributes by working at home and caring for the children, the other must contribute to this support alone, without prejudice to his duty of cooperating in the above-mentioned work and care.

Article 28. Both parties have the right to practice their profession or skill, and it is their duty to help each other and to cooperate in this direction and to study or improve their knowledge. However, they must always see to it that home life is organized in such a way that these activities are coordinated with the fulfillment of the obligations posed by this code.

Cuban women with whom I had personal contact were, in almost every instance, like women I already knew at home, so that by the time I left Cuba, it seemed entirely natural to be happy to see them each morning, and to be pleased that they appeared to feel the same. One of these women who, in her patience and gentleness, was an inspiration to our group was Magalys, a young woman in her twenties who acted as our interpreter. What I managed to learn about Magalys is not, I think, unique to her: she is married, her husband works as an adjuster of salaries all over the island and is, therefore, frequently away from home for long periods. This does not appear to bother Magalys: she accepts these separations as part of marriage in a revolutionary country and is busy studying, taking exams in mathematics (presumably for a different kind of occupation than the one she now has as interpreter and guide for English-speaking groups). A lovely, delicately made woman of brown skin and warm brown eyes, she is from time to time distressed because we black North Americans want to claim her as one of us, exclusively, whereas she has been brought up to believe she belongs to the world.

On a different (possibly irrelevant) level altogether, I was disturbed by the Cuban use of make-up (the first heavily made-up woman I noticed was a curvaceous young soldier in army fatigues who also had her hair in curlers) and have still to resolve my own feelings about, for example, a revolutionary woman who dyes her hair blond—as Haydée Santamaría (who was with the rebels at the Moncada Barracks as well as in the Sierra Maestra) did for several years—or who otherwise (through hair straighteners and whatnot) endeavors to look like someone other than herself.

At first glance, it is actually *cheering* to see that women revolutionaries also paint their faces and process their hair, but then one wonders: if a revolution fails to make one comfortable with what one is (Fidel, one notices, has not tampered with *his* looks or his style of dress, and has, since the revolution began, even ceased to shave), can one assume that, on a personal level, it is a success at all?

On the other hand, it is possible that a revolution frees women who are part of it to do with themselves whatever they like. Presumably, now that everyone can afford make-up, everyone may wear it. This interpretation appeals to me, probably because I sometimes paint *my* face, and I would not like to endure a speech about why I do it. But does this apply to Cuban women who pattern themselves—in dress and make-up—on European models almost exclusively? In a country with such a large black and brown and gold population, this is a question that at some point the revolution might address: can equality be said to be realized if a gorgeous black woman *still* aspires to lighter skin and straight hair, or if a luscious white woman who is brunette longs for blond hair, blue eyes, and a skinny figure?

A Cuban film we were shown exemplifies, to me, the danger of perpetuating stereotypic models of beauty. In this film, *The New School,* now being shown in the United States, hundreds of students are on display. It is hard to tell, after the first several frames, that one is looking at youngsters in a Caribbean country: they seem almost entirely Nordic. If this is the image of itself that Cuba is sending out to the rest of the world, one can only wonder what is the true if subconscious *ideal* image Cubans have of themselves. (Fortunately, most Cuban films do not have this problem, and are excellent examples of how a richly multiracial, multicultural society can be reflected unselfconsciously in popular art.)

We all had strict instructions to be, above all, humane in the struggle. Never was a group of armed men more generous to the adversary. From the very first, we took numerous prisoners—eventually nearly 20—and there was one moment when three of our men—Ramiro Valdes, Jose Suarez, and Jesus Montane—managed to enter a barrack and hold nearly 50 soldiers prisoners for a short time. Those soldiers have testified before the court, and all without exception have acknowledged that we treated them with absolute respect, without even offending them by the use of an unpleasant word. Apropos of this, I want to give the prosecutor my heartfelt thanks for one thing in the trial of my comrades: when he made his report he was fair enough to acknowledge as an incontestable fact that we maintained a high spirit of chivalry throughout the struggle.
—*Fidel Castro,*
HISTORY WILL ABSOLVE ME

I have also been asked about Cuba's political prisoners, none of whom I was privileged to see, though no one that we asked in Cuba denied their existence. I cannot believe, as my gay and lesbian friends fear, that the man who wrote *History Will Absolve Me,* one of the great human-rights documents of our century, orders homosexuals tortured or shot, or that he jails all the people who disagree with his politics. The people's love of Fidel seems genuine and nearly universal. In any case, I cannot, furthermore, take comfort in the fact that the United States tortures and destroys political prisoners, for to do so would be to evade the question of whether imprisonment of politicals is right.

The Cubans seem to feel that the imprisonment of certain people is justified because of their activity against the revolution. They point out also that many of the imprisoned stole food and housing and education from the people, or murdered and terror-ized the people under the Batista regime. Since I do not know the facts, I can only recount their presentation of them.

My own bias, when considering a country like Cuba, is to think almost entirely of the gains of the formerly dispossessed. I can be brought to tears by the sight of braces on the teeth of formerly poor children who, through bad diet and no dental care before the revolution, might have been robbed forever of the careless pleasure of smiling. Seeing healthy bodies at play or hearing the intelligent voices of well-educated human beings—whose parents and grandparents languished for centuries in pov-erty and ignorance—can nearly wipe out my powers of serious scrutiny beyond these facts. To criticize anything at all seems presumptuous, even absurd.

Perhaps it is because Cuba has struggled so persistently to alleviate the burdens of the dispossessed that I believe Cubans will become ever more sensitive to those in their society who are dispossessed now in the revolution: homosexuals, Jehovah's Witnesses, women *as we really are,* political prisoners who are perhaps innocent of everything but "wrong" thought. After all, it is but a short distance from understanding that, just as a life of mere survival is insufficient for the flourishing of the spirit, the spirit is an insufficient support for human life if it lacks a full expression of its *essence.*

Finally, I believe in the combination of compassion, intelligence, and work that characterizes the Cuban people. In spite of everything that threatens to make them less than free to be *themselves,* I believe, with them, that they will continue to win.

1977

. . . .

RECORDING THE SEASONS

Here we have watched
a thousand seasons
come and go.
And unmarked graves atangled
in the brush
turn our own legs to trees
vertical forever between earth
and sun.
Here we are not quick to disavow
the pull of field and wood
and stream;
we are not quick to turn
upon our dreams.

I was writing about Mississippi, the whole South. Yet, on the
morning we left our home there for good I was so tired of it that,

at the end of our street, when the car stopped for a final farewell, I could not, would not, look back. I did not expect ever to set foot in Mississippi again.

But it was not Mississippi's fault that I was exhausted by it. I had come there in the first place to "tirelessly observe it," as I wrote in my journal in 1966. To kill the fear it engendered in my imagination as a place where black life was terrifyingly hard, pitifully cheap. Mississippi had simply continued its evolution into newer versions of itself long after my eyes had begun to close.

I wrote to an old friend who had partially financed my earlier trip to Mississippi that I was going to live there for a while because "the stories are knee-deep." And it was true. The first two years passed in a fever to get everything down—in poems, stories, the novel I was writing, essays—that I observed. It was a period of constant revelation, when mysteries not understood during my Southern childhood came naked to me to be embraced. I grew to adulthood in Mississippi.

And yet, the cost was not minor. Always a rather moody, periodically depressed person, after two years in Mississippi I became—as I had occasionally been as a young adult—suicidal. I also found motherhood onerous, a threat to my writing. The habits of a lifetime—of easy mobility, of wandering and day-dreams—must be, if not abandoned, at least drastically rearranged. And all the while there was the fear that my young husband would not return from one of his trips to visit his clients in the Mississippi backwoods.

It was the last of our seven years in Mississippi that made me wish never to see it again. For in that year the threat of self-destruction plagued me as it never had before. I no longer feared for my husband's safety. In fact, such is American media curiosity, he had become a celebrity to the same extent that he had earlier been "an outside agitator" and a pariah. Since the

Jackson school-desegregation cases were his, our daughter and I could watch him at least once or twice a week being interviewed on TV. Nor did I fear any longer for my own safety with or without my husband's company. In the beginning, going to the movies was agony for us. For several years we were the only interracial, married, home-owning couple in Mississippi. Our presence at the ticket booth caused an angry silence. But even this had ceased to be true that last year. More than any other place in this country, the large cities, at least in Mississippi, learned how not to misbehave in public. And the young are everywhere interested in their own pleasures, and those pleasures, in Mississippi, have become less and less attached to the humiliation of other people.

I believe that part of my depression came out of anguish that I was not more violent than I was. For years I fantasized sneaking into various oppressors' houses perhaps disguised as a maid and dropping unplugged hand grenades in their laps. Yet, though I considered these people, who attacked and murdered our children, called us chimpanzees from their judges' benches, and made life a daily ordeal for us, the Hitlers of our time, I did not act out the fantasy. No one else, black, has lived out this fantasy—though I believe this particular one and others like it are rampant among us.

The burden of a nonviolent, pacifist philosophy in a violent, nonpacifist society caused me to feel, almost always, as if I had not done enough.* When I was working well and the poems and stories grew, I had no time to think of this. When the writing went badly, I questioned the value of writing at all. It did not

---

*Whenever I am referred to as an "activist" or, worse, "a 'veteran' of the Civil Rights Movement," I cringe at the inappropriateness. The true activists and veterans—the young people in SNCC (who remain some of the people I have most admired), Mrs. Hudson, Fannie Lou Hamer, Mel Leventhal, Dr. King—did things for freedom of which I merely dreamed.

seem equal to the goals of many of the people who came to visit us during that time.

And yet, many of the "revolutionaries" who visited us, mainly to criticize the Mississippi Movement, were clearly absurd. Typical of the scholarly type of revolutionary was the young man from Harvard Law School who, while consuming quantities of cheese and wine at our house, referred to my husband, repeatedly, as "the honky" and even suggested he would start the revolution in our living room, by killing him. It is amazing to me now that we didn't simply throw this young man out, along with the black "militant" woman, also a law student, who came with him, but was rarely allowed to say anything. We were so hospitable and understanding our hearts nearly burst.

Only later in the evening were we repaid for this misdirected behavior. As night crept closer and the darkness stirred our young guests' racial memories—all of them horrible—of Mississippi, the young "revolutionist" became too afraid to venture out of doors alone. His "honky" host was required to call one of his black law partners to escort him back to his hotel through the sleeping city.

I laughed bitterly at this even then. Yet it bothered me. Only now does it seem merely pathetic.

My salvation that last year was a black woman psychiatrist who had also grown up in the South. Though she encouraged me to talk about whether or not I had loved and/or understood my father, I became increasingly aware that I was holding myself responsible for the condition of black people in America. Unable to murder the oppressors, I sat in a book-lined study and wrote about lives that persisted in seeming quite extraordinary to me, whatever their subjects' situations.

In short, I could see that I felt Art was not enough and that my art, in particular, would probably change nothing. And yet

I felt it was the privilege of my life to observe and "save" for the future some extraordinary lives.

Many times over the past fifteen years, I have wondered how black people managed to keep going through periods of "benign neglect." Those periods that comprise most of our history in these United States. With the major Civil Rights battles televised, the most militant of black leaders photographed for the covers of *Newsweek* and *Time*, and my own sense of having come of age at the most visible of all times for black people in America, it had often seemed to me incredible that my parents and their parents and their parents before them had acted out the drama of their lives with none to observe what they did but themselves. I pitied them their obscurity, and could not imagine a period in my lifetime that could be similar to theirs. How naïve I was not to suspect that those hidden lives, generations old, were the constant reality of the race and that they would continue—without benefit of TV or newsprint exposure—to be its great strength. I should have known the truth of a popular saying among people in the black movement who chose not to become its stars and instead remained paranoid about interviews and persistently camera shy: "The revolution, when it comes, will not be televised."

(The person who had the greatest impact on me, the person I considered the greatest revolutionary, I never saw.)

Writing this now, in New York City, it is impossible not to feel that black people who are poor are lost completely in the American political and economic system, and that black people and white people who are not have been turned to stone. Our moral leaders have been murdered, our children worship power and drugs, our official leadership is frequently a joke, usually merely oppressive. Our chosen and most respected soul singer —part of whose unspoken duty is to remind us who we are— has become a blonde.

Fifteen years of struggle would seem to have returned many of us to the aspirations of the fifties—security, social obliviousness, improbable colors of skin and hair. And yet, there is a reality deeper than what we see, and the consciousness of a people cannot be photographed.

But to some extent, it can be written.

1976

PART
THREE

MOTHEROOT

Creation often
needs two hearts
one to root
and one to flower
One to sustain
in time of drouth
and hold fast
against winds of pain
the fragile bloom
that in the glory
of its hour
affirms a heart
unsung, unseen.

—Marilou Awiakta,
ABIDING APPALACHIA

IN SEARCH OF OUR MOTHERS' GARDENS

I described her own nature and temperament. Told how they needed a larger life for their expression. . . . I pointed out that in lieu of proper channels, her emotions had over-flowed into paths that dissipated them. I talked, beautifully I thought, about an art that would be born, an art that would open the way for women the likes of her. I asked her to hope, and build up an inner life against the coming of that day. . . . I sang, with a strange quiver in my voice, a promise song.
—*Jean Toomer,* "*Avey,*"
CANE

The poet speaking to a prostitute who falls asleep while he's talking—

When the poet Jean Toomer walked through the South in the early twenties, he discovered a curious thing: black women whose spirituality was so intense, so deep, so *unconscious*, that they were themselves unaware of the richness they held. They stumbled blindly through their lives: creatures so abused and mutilated in body, so dimmed and confused by pain, that they considered themselves unworthy even of hope. In the selfless abstractions their bodies became to the men who used them, they became more than "sexual objects," more even than mere women: they became "Saints." Instead of being perceived as whole persons, their bodies became shrines: what was thought to be their minds became temples suitable for worship. These crazy Saints stared out at the world, wildly, like lunatics—or quietly, like suicides; and the "God" that was in their gaze was as mute as a great stone.

Who were these Saints? These crazy, loony, pitiful women?

Some of them, without a doubt, were our mothers and grandmothers.

In the still heat of the post-Reconstruction South, this is how they seemed to Jean Toomer: exquisite butterflies trapped in an evil honey, toiling away their lives in an era, a century, that did not acknowledge them, except as "the *mule* of the world." They dreamed dreams that no one knew—not even themselves, in any coherent fashion—and saw visions no one could understand. They wandered or sat about the countryside crooning lullabies to ghosts, and drawing the mother of Christ in charcoal on courthouse walls.

They forced their minds to desert their bodies and their striving spirits sought to rise, like frail whirlwinds from the hard red clay. And when those frail whirlwinds fell, in scattered particles, upon the ground, no one mourned. Instead, men lit candles to celebrate the emptiness that remained, as people do who enter a beautiful but vacant space to resurrect a God.

Our mothers and grandmothers, some of them: moving to music not yet written. And they waited.

They waited for a day when the unknown thing that was in them would be made known; but guessed, somehow in their darkness, that on the day of their revelation they would be long dead. Therefore to Toomer they walked, and even ran, in slow motion. For they were going nowhere immediate, and the future was not yet within their grasp. And men took our mothers and grandmothers, "but got no pleasure from it." So complex was their passion and their calm.

To Toomer, they lay vacant and fallow as autumn fields, with harvest time never in sight: and he saw them enter loveless marriages, without joy; and become prostitutes, without resistance; and become mothers of children, without fulfillment.

For these grandmothers and mothers of ours were not Saints, but Artists; driven to a numb and bleeding madness by the springs of creativity in them for which there was no release. They were Creators, who lived lives of spiritual waste, because they were so rich in spirituality—which is the basis of Art—that the strain of enduring their unused and unwanted talent drove them insane. Throwing away this spirituality was their pathetic attempt to lighten the soul to a weight their work-worn, sexually abused bodies could bear.

What did it mean for a black woman to be an artist in our grandmothers' time? In our great-grandmothers' day? It is a question with an answer cruel enough to stop the blood.

Did you have a genius of a great-great-grandmother who died under some ignorant and depraved white overseer's lash? Or was she required to bake biscuits for a lazy backwater tramp, when she cried out in her soul to paint watercolors of sunsets, or the rain falling on the green and peaceful pasturelands? Or was her body broken and forced to bear children (who were more often than not sold away from her)—eight, ten, fifteen, twenty children—when her one joy was the thought of modeling heroic figures of rebellion, in stone or clay?

How was the creativity of the black woman kept alive, year after year and century after century, when for most of the years black people have been in America, it was a punishable crime for a black person to read or write? And the freedom to paint, to sculpt, to expand the mind with action did not exist. Consider, if you can bear to imagine it, what might have been the result if singing, too, had been forbidden by law. Listen to the voices of Bessie Smith, Billie Holiday, Nina Simone, Roberta Flack, and Aretha Franklin, among others, and imagine those voices muzzled for life. Then you may begin to comprehend the lives of our "crazy," "Sainted" mothers and grandmothers. The agony of the lives of women who might have been Poets, Novelists, Essayists, and Short-Story Writers (over a period of centuries), who died with their real gifts stifled within them.

And, if this were the end of the story, we would have cause to cry out in my paraphrase of Okot p'Bitek's great poem:

> O, my clanswomen
> Let us all cry together!
> Come,
> Let us mourn the death of our mother,
> The death of a Queen
> The ash that was produced
> By a great fire!
> O, this homestead is utterly dead
> Close the gates
> With *lacari* thorns,
> For our mother
> The creator of the Stool is lost!
> And all the young women
> Have perished in the wilderness!

But this is not the end of the story, for all the young women —our mothers and grandmothers, *ourselves*—have not perished in the wilderness. And if we ask ourselves why, and search for and find the answer, we will know beyond all efforts to erase it from our minds, just exactly who, and of what, we black American women are.

One example, perhaps the most pathetic, most misunderstood one, can provide a backdrop for our mothers' work: Phillis Wheatley, a slave in the 1700s.

Virginia Woolf, in her book *A Room of One's Own*, wrote that in order for a woman to write fiction she must have two things, certainly: a room of her own (with key and lock) and enough money to support herself.

What then are we to make of Phillis Wheatley, a slave, who owned not even herself? This sickly, frail black girl who required a servant of her own at times—her health was so precarious— and who, had she been white, would have been easily considered the intellectual superior of all the women and most of the men in the society of her day.

Virginia Woolf wrote further, speaking of course not of our Phillis, that "any woman born with a great gift in the sixteenth century [insert "eighteenth century," insert "black woman," insert "born or made a slave"] would certainly have gone crazed, shot herself, or ended her days in some lonely cottage outside the village, half witch, half wizard [insert "Saint"], feared and mocked at. For it needs little skill and psychology to be sure that a highly gifted girl who had tried to use her gift for poetry would have been so thwarted and hindered by contrary instincts [add "chains, guns, the lash, the ownership of one's body by someone else, submission to an alien religion"], that she must have lost her health and sanity to a certainty."

The key words, as they relate to Phillis, are "contrary instincts." For when we read the poetry of Phillis Wheatley—as when we read the novels of Nella Larsen or the oddly false-sounding autobiography of that freest of all black women writers, Zora Hurston—evidence of "contrary instincts" is everywhere. Her loyalties were completely divided, as was, without question, her mind.

But how could this be otherwise? Captured at seven, a slave of wealthy, doting whites who instilled in her the "savagery" of the Africa they "rescued" her from . . . one wonders if she was even able to remember her homeland as she had known it, or as it really was.

Yet, because she did try to use her gift for poetry in a world that made her a slave, she was "so thwarted and hindered by . . . contrary instincts, that she . . . lost her health. . . ." In the last years of her brief life, burdened not only with the need to express her gift but also with a penniless, friendless "freedom" and several small children for whom she was forced to do strenuous work to feed, she lost her health, certainly. Suffering from malnutrition and neglect and who knows what mental agonies, Phillis Wheatley died.

So torn by "contrary instincts" was black, kidnapped, enslaved Phillis that her description of "the Goddess"—as she poetically called the Liberty she did not have—is ironically, cruelly humorous. And, in fact, has held Phillis up to ridicule for more than a century. It is usually read prior to hanging Phillis's memory as that of a fool. She wrote:

The Goddess comes, she moves divinely fair,
Olive and laurel binds her *golden* hair.
Wherever shines this native of the skies,
Unnumber'd charms and recent graces rise. [My italics]

It is obvious that Phillis, the slave, combed the "Goddess's" hair every morning; prior, perhaps, to bringing in the milk, or fixing her mistress's lunch. She took her imagery from the one thing she saw elevated above all others.

With the benefit of hindsight we ask, "How could she?"

But at last, Phillis, we understand. No more snickering when your stiff, struggling, ambivalent lines are forced on us. We know now that you were not an idiot or a traitor; only a sickly little black girl, snatched from your home and country and made a slave; a woman who still struggled to sing the song that was your gift, although in a land of barbarians who praised you for your bewildered tongue. It is not so much what you sang, as that you kept alive, in so many of our ancestors, *the notion of song.*

Black women are called, in the folklore that so aptly identifies one's status in society, "the *mule* of the world," because we have been handed the burdens that everyone else—*everyone* else—refused to carry. We have also been called "Matriarchs," "Superwomen," and "Mean and Evil Bitches." Not to mention "Castraters" and "Sapphire's Mama." When we have pleaded for understanding, our character has been distorted; when we have asked for simple caring, we have been handed empty inspirational appellations, then stuck in the farthest corner. When we have asked for love, we have been given children. In short, even our plainer gifts, our labors of fidelity and love, have been knocked down our throats. To be an artist and a black woman, even today, lowers our status in many respects, rather than raises it: and yet, artists we will be.

Therefore we must fearlessly pull out of ourselves and look at and identify with our lives the living creativity some of our great-grandmothers were not allowed to know. I stress *some* of them because it is well known that the majority of our great-grandmothers knew, even without "knowing" it, the reality of their spirituality, even if they didn't recognize it beyond what happened in the singing at church—and they never had any intention of giving it up.

How they did it—those millions of black women who were not Phillis Wheatley, or Lucy Terry or Frances Harper or Zora Hurston or Nella Larsen or Bessie Smith; or Elizabeth Catlett, or Katherine Dunham, either—brings me to the title of this essay, "In Search of Our Mothers' Gardens," which is a personal account that is yet shared, in its theme and its meaning, by all of us. I found, while thinking about the far-reaching world of the creative black woman, that often the truest answer to a question that really matters can be found very close.

In the late 1920s my mother ran away from home to marry my father. Marriage, if not running away, was expected of seventeen-year-old girls. By the time she was twenty, she had two children and was pregnant with a third. Five children later, I was born. And this is how I came to know my mother: she seemed a large, soft, loving-eyed woman who was rarely impatient in our home. Her quick, violent temper was on view only a few times a year, when she battled with the white landlord who had the misfortune to suggest to her that her children did not need to go to school.

She made all the clothes we wore, even my brothers' overalls. She made all the towels and sheets we used. She spent the summers canning vegetables and fruits. She spent the winter evenings making quilts enough to cover all our beds.

During the "working" day, she labored beside—not behind —my father in the fields. Her day began before sunup, and did not end until late at night. There was never a moment for her to sit down, undisturbed, to unravel her own private thoughts; never a time free from interruption—by work or the noisy inquiries of her many children. And yet, it is to my mother—and all our mothers who were not famous—that I went in search of the secret of what has fed that muzzled and often mutilated, but vibrant, creative spirit that the black woman has inherited, and that pops out in wild and unlikely places to this day.

But when, you will ask, did my overworked mother have time to know or care about feeding the creative spirit?

The answer is so simple that many of us have spent years discovering it. We have constantly looked high, when we should have looked high—and low.

For example: in the Smithsonian Institution in Washington, D.C., there hangs a quilt unlike any other in the world. In fanciful, inspired, and yet simple and identifiable figures, it portrays the story of the Crucifixion. It is considered rare, beyond price. Though it follows no known pattern of quilt-making, and though it is made of bits and pieces of worthless rags, it is obviously the work of a person of powerful imagination and deep spiritual feeling. Below this quilt I saw a note that says it was made by "an anonymous Black woman in Alabama, a hundred years ago."

If we could locate this "anonymous" black woman from Alabama, she would turn out to be one of our grandmothers—an artist who left her mark in the only materials she could afford, and in the only medium her position in society allowed her to use.

As Virginia Woolf wrote further, in *A Room of One's Own:*

Yet genius of a sort must have existed among women as it must have existed among the working class. [Change this to "slaves" and "the wives and daughters of sharecroppers."] Now and again an Emily Brontë or a Robert Burns [change this to "a Zora Hurston or a Richard Wright"] blazes out and proves its presence. But certainly it never got itself on to paper. When, however, one reads of a witch being ducked, of a woman possessed by devils [or "Sainthood"], of a wise woman selling herbs [our root workers], or even a very remarkable man who had a mother, then I think we are on the track of a lost novelist, a suppressed poet, of some mute and inglorious Jane Austen. . . . Indeed, I would venture to guess that Anon, who wrote so many poems without signing them, was often a woman. . . .

And so our mothers and grandmothers have, more often than not anonymously, handed on the creative spark, the seed of the flower they themselves never hoped to see: or like a sealed letter they could not plainly read.

And so it is, certainly, with my own mother. Unlike "Ma" Rainey's songs, which retained their creator's name even while blasting forth from Bessie Smith's mouth, no song or poem will bear my mother's name. Yet so many of the stories that I write, that we all write, are my mother's stories. Only recently did I fully realize this: that through years of listening to my mother's stories of her life, I have absorbed not only the stories themselves, but something of the manner in which she spoke, something of the urgency that involves the knowledge that her stories —like her life—must be recorded. It is probably for this reason that so much of what I have written is about characters whose counterparts in real life are so much older than I am.

But the telling of these stories, which came from my mother's lips as naturally as breathing, was not the only way my mother showed herself as an artist. For stories, too, were subject to being distracted, to dying without conclusion. Dinners must be started, and cotton must be gathered before the big rains. The artist that was and is my mother showed itself to me only after many years. This is what I finally noticed:

Like Mem, a character in *The Third Life of Grange Cope-land*, my mother adorned with flowers whatever shabby house we were forced to live in. And not just your typical straggly country stand of zinnias, either. She planted ambitious gardens —and still does—with over fifty different varieties of plants that bloom profusely from early March until late November. Before she left home for the fields, she watered her flowers, chopped up the grass, and laid out new beds. When she returned from the fields she might divide clumps of bulbs, dig a cold pit, uproot and replant roses, or prune branches from her taller bushes or trees—until night came and it was too dark to see.

Whatever she planted grew as if by magic, and her fame as a grower of flowers spread over three counties. Because of her creativity with her flowers, even my memories of poverty are seen through a screen of blooms—sunflowers, petunias, roses, dahlias, forsythia, spirea, delphiniums, verbena . . . and on and on.

And I remember people coming to my mother's yard to be given cuttings from her flowers; I hear again the praise showered on her because whatever rocky soil she landed on, she turned into a garden. A garden so brilliant with colors, so original in its design, so magnificent with life and creativity, that to this day people drive by our house in Georgia—perfect strangers and imperfect strangers—and ask to stand or walk among my mother's art.

I notice that it is only when my mother is working in her flowers that she is radiant, almost to the point of being invisible —except as Creator: hand and eye. She is involved in work her soul must have. Ordering the universe in the image of her personal conception of Beauty.

Her face, as she prepares the Art that is her gift, is a legacy of respect she leaves to me, for all that illuminates and cherishes life. She has handed down respect for the possibilities—and the will to grasp them.

For her, so hindered and intruded upon in so many ways, being an artist has still been a daily part of her life. This ability to hold on, even in very simple ways, is work black women have done for a very long time.

This poem is not enough, but it is something, for the woman who literally covered the holes in our walls with sunflowers:

> They were women then
> My mama's generation
> Husky of voice—Stout of
> Step
> With fists as well as
> Hands
> How they battered down
> Doors
> And ironed
> Starched white
> Shirts
> How they led
> Armies
> Headragged Generals
> Across mined
> Fields
> Booby-trapped
> Kitchens
> To discover books
> Desks
> A place for us
> How they knew what we
> *Must* know

Without knowing a page
Of it
Themselves.

Guided by my heritage of a love of beauty and a respect for strength—in search of my mother's garden, I found my own.

And perhaps in Africa over two hundred years ago, there was just such a mother; perhaps she painted vivid and daring decorations in oranges and yellows and greens on the walls of her hut; perhaps she sang—in a voice like Roberta Flack's—*sweetly* over the compounds of her village; perhaps she wove the most stunning mats or told the most ingenious stories of all the village storytellers. Perhaps she was herself a poet—though only her daughter's name is signed to the poems that we know.

Perhaps Phillis Wheatley's mother was also an artist.

Perhaps in more than Phillis Wheatley's biological life is her mother's signature made clear.

1974

. . . .

FROM AN INTERVIEW

I have always been a solitary person, and since I was eight years old (and victim of a traumatic accident that blinded and scarred one eye*), I have daydreamed—not of fairy tales—but of falling on swords, of putting guns to my heart or head, and of slashing my wrists with a razor. For a long time I thought I was very ugly and disfigured. This made me shy and timid, and I often reacted to insults and slights that were not intended. I discovered the cruelty (legendary) of children, and of relatives, and could not recognize it as the curiosity it was.

I believe, though, that it was from this period—from my solitary, lonely position, the position of an outcast—that I began really to see people and things, really to notice relationships and to learn to be patient enough to care about how they turned out.

---

*See "Beauty: When the Other Dancer Is the Self."

I no longer felt like the little girl I was. I felt old, and because I felt I was unpleasant to look at, filled with shame. I retreated into solitude, and read stories and began to write poems.

But it was not until my last year in college that I realized, nearly, the consequences of my daydreams. That year I made myself acquainted with every philosopher's position on suicide, because by that time it did not seem frightening or even odd—but only inevitable. Nietzsche and Camus made the most sense, and were neither maudlin nor pious. God's displeasure didn't seem to matter much to them, and I had reached the same conclusion. But in addition to finding such dispassionate commentary from them—although both hinted at the cowardice involved, and that bothered me—I had been to Africa during the summer, and returned to school healthy and brown, and loaded down with sculptures and orange fabric—and pregnant.

I felt at the mercy of everything, including my own body, which I had learned to accept as a kind of casing over what I considered my real self. As long as it functioned properly I dressed it, pampered it, led it into acceptable arms, and forgot about it. But now it refused to function properly. I was so sick I could not even bear the smell of fresh air. And I had no money, and I was, essentially—as I had been since grade school—alone. I felt there was no way out, and I was not romantic enough to believe in maternal instincts alone as a means of survival; in any case, I did not seem to possess those instincts. But I knew no one who knew about the secret, scary thing abortion was. And so, when all my efforts at finding an abortionist failed, I planned to kill myself, or—as I thought of it then—to "give myself a little rest." I stopped going down the hill to meals because I vomited incessantly, even when nothing came up but yellow, bitter bile. I lay on my bed in a cold sweat, my head spinning.

While I was lying there, I thought of my mother, to whom abortion is a sin; her face appeared framed in the window across from me, her head wreathed in sunflowers and giant elephant-ears (my mother's flowers love her; they grow as tall as she wants); I thought of my father, that suspecting, once-fat, slowly shrinking man, who had not helped me at all since I was twelve years old, when he bought me a pair of ugly saddle oxfords I refused to wear. I thought of my sisters, who had their own problems (when approached with the problem I had, one sister never replied, the other told me—in forty-five minutes of long-distance carefully enunciated language—that I was a slut). I thought of the people at my high-school graduation who had managed to collect seventy-five dollars, to send me to college. I thought of my sister's check for a hundred dollars that she gave me for finishing high school at the head of my class: a check I never cashed, because I knew it would bounce.

I think it was at this point that I allowed myself exactly two self-pitying tears; I had wasted so much, how dared I? But I hated myself for crying, so I stopped, comforted by knowing I would not have to cry—or see anyone else cry—again.

I did not eat or sleep for three days. My mind refused, at times, to think about my problem at all—it jumped ahead to the solution. I prayed to—but I don't know Who or What I prayed to, or even if I did. Perhaps I prayed to God a while, and then to the Great Void a while. When I thought of my family, and when—on the third day—I began to see their faces around the walls, I realized they would be shocked and hurt to learn of my death, but I felt they would not care deeply at all, when they discovered I was pregnant. Essentially, they would believe I was evil. They would be ashamed of me.

For three days I lay on the bed with a razor blade under my pillow. My secret was known to three friends only—all inexperienced (except verbally), and helpless. They came often to cheer me up, to bring me up to date on things as frivolous as classes. I was touched by their kindness, and loved them. But each time they left, I took out my razor blade and pressed it deep into my arm. I practiced a slicing motion. So that when there was no longer any hope, I would be able to cut my wrists quickly, and (I hoped) painlessly.

In those three days, I said good-bye to the world (this seemed like a high-flown sentiment, even then, but everything was beginning to be unreal); I realized how much I loved it, and how hard it would be not to see the sunrise every morning, the snow, the sky, the trees, the rocks, the faces of people, all so different (and it was during this period that all things began to flow together; the face of one of my friends revealed itself to be the friendly, gentle face of a lion, and I asked her one day if I could touch her face and stroke her mane. I felt her face and hair, and she really was a lion; I began to feel the possibility of someone as worthless as myself attaining wisdom). But I found, as I had found on the porch of a building in Liberty County, Georgia—when rocks and bottles bounced off me as I sat looking up at the stars—that I was not afraid of death. In a way, I began looking forward to it. I felt tired. Most of the poems on suicide in *Once* come from my feelings during this period of waiting.

On the last day for miracles, one of my friends telephoned to say someone had given her a telephone number. I called from school, hoping for nothing, and made an appointment. I went to see the doctor and he put me to sleep. When I woke up, my friend was standing over me holding a red rose. She was a blonde, gray-eyed girl, who loved horses and tennis, and she said nothing as she handed me back my life. That moment is engraved on my mind—her smile, sad and pained and frightfully young—as she tried so hard to stand by me and be my friend. She drove me back to school and tucked me in. My other friend, brown, a wisp of blue and scarlet, with hair like thunder, brought me food.

That week I wrote without stopping (except to eat and go to the toilet) almost all of the poems in *Once*—with the exception of one or two, perhaps, and these I do not remember.

I wrote them all in a tiny blue notebook that I can no longer find—the African ones first, because the vitality and color and friendships in Africa rushed over me in dreams the first night I slept. I had not thought about Africa (except to talk about it) since I returned. All the sculptures and weavings I had given away, because they seemed to emit an odor that made me more nauseated than the smell of fresh air. Then I wrote the suicide poems, because I felt I understood the part played in suicide by circumstances and fatigue. I also began to understand how alone woman is, because of her body. Then I wrote the love poems (love real and love imagined), and tried to reconcile myself to all things human. "Johann" is the most extreme example of this need to love even the most unfamiliar, the most fearful. For, actually, when I traveled in Germany I was in a constant state of terror, and no amount of flattery from handsome young German men could shake it. Then I wrote the poems of struggle in the South. The picketing, the marching, all the things that had been buried, because when I thought about them the pain caused a paralysis of intellectual and moral confusion. The anger and humiliation I had suffered were always in conflict with the elation, the exaltation, the *joy* I felt when I could leave each vicious encounter or confrontation whole, and not—like the people before me—spewing obscenities or throwing bricks. For, during those encounters, I had begun to comprehend what it meant to be lost.

Each morning, the poems finished during the night were stuffed under Muriel Rukeyser's door—her classroom was an old gardener's cottage in the middle of the campus. Then I would hurry back to my room to write some more. I didn't care what she did with the poems. I only knew I wanted someone to read them as if they were new leaves sprouting from an old tree. The same energy that impelled me to write them carried them to her door.

This was the winter of 1965, and my last three months in college. I was twenty-one years old, although *Once* was not published till three years later, when I was twenty-four. (Muriel Rukeyser gave the poems to her agent, who gave them to Hiram Haydn at Harcourt Brace Jovanovich—who said right away that he wanted them; so I cannot claim to have had a hard time publishing, yet). By the time *Once* was published, it no longer seemed important—I was surprised when it went, almost immediately, into a second printing—that is, the book itself did not seem to me important; only the writing of the poems, which clarified for me how very much I loved being alive. It was this feeling of gladness that carried over into my first published short story, "To Hell with Dying," about an old man saved from death countless times by the love of his neighbor's children. I was the children, and the old man.

I have gone into this memory because I think it might be important for other women to share. I don't enjoy contemplating it; I wish it had never happened. But if it had not, I firmly believe I would never have survived to be a writer. I know I would not have survived at all.

Since that time, it seems to me that all of my poems—and I write groups of poems rather than singles—are written when I have successfully pulled myself out of a completely numbing despair, and stand again in the sunlight. Writing poems is my way of celebrating with the world that I have not committed suicide the evening before.

Langston Hughes wrote in his autobiography that when he was sad, he wrote his best poems. When he was happy, he didn't write anything. This is true of me, where poems are concerned. When I am happy (or neither happy nor sad), I write essays, short stories, and novels. Poems—even happy ones—emerge from an accumulation of sadness. . . .

The writing of my poetry is never consciously planned; although I become aware that there are certain emotions I would like to explore. Perhaps my unconscious begins working on poems from these emotions long before I am aware of it. I have learned to wait patiently (sometimes refusing good lines, images, when they come to me, for fear they are not lasting), until a poem is ready to present itself—*all* of itself, if possible. I sometimes feel the urge to write poems way in advance of ever sitting down to write. There is a definite restlessness, a kind of feverish excitement that is tinged with dread. The dread is because after writing each batch of poems I am always convinced that I will never write poems again. I become aware that I am controlled by them, not the other way around. I put off writing as long as I can. Then I lock myself in my study, write lines and lines and lines, then put them away, underneath other papers, without looking at them for a long time. I am afraid that if I read them too soon they will turn into trash; or, worse, something so topical and transient as to have no meaning—not even to me—after a few weeks. (This is how my later poetry-writing differs from the way I wrote *Once*.) I also attempt, in this way, to guard against the human tendency to try to make poetry carry the weight of half-truths, of cleverness. I realize that while I am writing po-etry, I am so high as to feel invisible, and in that condition it is possible to write anything.

I am preoccupied with the spiritual survival, the survival *whole* of my people. But beyond that, I am committed to exploring the oppressions, the insanities, the loyalties, and the triumphs of black women. In *The Third Life of Grange Copeland*, ostensibly about a man and his son, it is the women and how they are treated that colors everything. In my new book, *In Love & Trouble: Stories of Black Women,* thirteen women—mad, raging, loving, resentful, hateful, strong, ugly, weak, pitiful, and magnificent—try to live with the loyalty to black men that characterizes all of their lives. For me, black women are the most fascinating creations in the world.

Next to them, I place the old people—male and female— who persist in their beauty in spite of everything. How do they do this, knowing what they do? Having lived what they have lived? It is a mystery, and so it lures me into their lives. My grandfather, at eighty-five, never been out of Georgia, looks at me with the glad eyes of a three-year-old. The pressures on his life have been unspeakable. How can he look at me in this way? "Your eyes are widely open flowers. / Only their centers are darkly clenched / To conceal Mysteries / That lure me to a keener blooming / Than I know. / And promise a secret / I must have." All of my "love poems" apply to old, young, man, woman, child, and growing things. . . .

It is possible that white male writers are more conscious of their own evil (which, after all, has been documented for several centuries—in words and in the ruin of the land, the earth) than black male writers, who, along with black and white women, have seen themselves as the recipients of that evil and therefore on the side of Christ, of the oppressed, of the innocent.

The white women writers that I admire—Kate Chopin, the Brontës, Simone de Beauvoir, and Doris Lessing—are well aware of their own oppression and search incessantly for a kind of salvation. Their characters can always envision a solution, an evolution to higher consciousness on the part of society, even when society itself cannot. Even when society is in the process of killing them for their vision. Generally, too, they are more tolerant of mystery than is Ahab, who wishes to dominate, rather than be on equal terms with, the whale.

If there is one thing African-Americans and Native Americans have retained of their African and ancient American heritage, it is probably the belief that everything is inhabited by spirit. This belief encourages knowledge perceived intuitively. It does not surprise me, personally, that scientists now are discovering that trees, plants, flowers, have feelings . . . emotions, that they shrink when yelled at; that they faint when an evil person is about who might hurt them.

One thing I try to have in my life and my fiction is an awareness of and openness to mystery, which, to me, is deeper than any politics, race, or geographical location. In the poems I read, a sense of mystery, a deepening of it, is what I look for —because that is what I respond to. I have been influenced— especially in the poems in *Once*—by Zen epigrams and Japanese haiku. I think my respect for short forms comes from this. I was delighted to learn that in three or four lines a poet can express mystery, evoke beauty and pleasure, paint a picture—and not dissect or analyze in any way. The insects, the fish, the birds, and the apple blossoms in haiku are still whole. They have not been turned into something else. They are allowed their own majesty, instead of being used to emphasize the majesty of people; usually the majesty of the poets writing.

I believe in change: change personal, and change in society. I have experienced a revolution (unfinished, without question, but one whose new order is everywhere on view) in the South. And I grew up—until I refused to go—in the Methodist church, which taught me that Paul *will* sometimes change on the way to Damascus, and that Moses—that beloved old man—went through so many changes he made God mad. So Grange Copeland was *expected* to change. He was fortunate enough to be touched by love of something beyond himself. Brownfield did not change, because he was not prepared to give his life for anything, or *to* anything. He was the kind of man who could never understand Jesus (or Che or King or Malcolm or Medgar) except as the white man's tool. He could find nothing of value within himself and he did not have the courage to imagine a life without the existence of white people to act as a foil. To become what he hated was his inevitable destiny.

A bit more about the "Southern Revolution." When I left Eatonton, Georgia, to go off to Spelman College in Atlanta (where I stayed, uneasily, for two and a half years), I deliberately sat in the front section of the Greyhound bus. A white woman complained to the driver. He—big and red and ugly—ordered me to move. I moved. But in those seconds of moving, everything changed. I was eager to bring an end to the South that permitted my humiliation. During my sophomore year I stood on the grass in front of Trevor-Arnett Library at Atlanta University and I listened to the young leaders of SNCC. John Lewis was there, and so was Julian Bond, thin, well starched and ironed in light-colored jeans; he looked (with his cropped hair that still tried to curl) like a poet (which he was). Everyone was beautiful, because everyone (and I now think of Ruby Doris Robinson, who has since died) was conquering fear by holding the hands of the persons next to them. In those days, in Atlanta, springtime turned the air green. I've never known this to happen in any other place I've been—not even in Uganda, where green, on hills, plants, trees, begins to dominate the imagination. It was as if the air turned into a kind of water—and the short walk from Spelman to Morehouse was like walking through a green sea. Then, of course, the cherry trees—cut down, now, I think—that were always blooming away while we—young and bursting with fear and determination to change our world—thought, beyond our fervid singing, of death. It was not surprising, considering the intertwined thoughts of beauty and death, that the majority of the people in and around SNCC at that time were lovers of Camus.

Random memories of that period: Myself, moving like someone headed for the guillotine, with (as my marching mate) a beautiful girl who spoke French and came to Spelman from Tuskegee, Alabama ("Chic Freedom's Reflection" in *Once*), whose sense of style was unfaltering, in the worst of circumstances. She was the only really black-skinned girl at Spelman who would turn up dressed in stark white from head to toe—because she knew, instinctively, that white made an already beautiful black girl look like the answer to everybody's prayer. Myself, marching about in front of a restaurant, seeing—inside —the tables set up with clean napkins and glasses of water, the owner standing in front of us barring the door, a Jewish man who went mad on the spot, and fell to the floor. Myself, dressed in a pink faille dress, with my African roommate, my first real girl friend, walking up the broad white steps of a broad white church. And men (white) in blue suits and bow ties materializing on the steps above with ax handles in their hands ("The Welcome Table" in *In Love & Trouble*). We turned and left. It was a bright, sunny day. Myself, sitting on a porch in Liberty County, Georgia, at night, after picketing the jailhouse (where a local black schoolteacher was held) and holding in my arms the bleeding head of a little girl—where is she now?—maybe eight or ten years old, but small, who had been cut by a broken bottle wielded by one of the mob in front of us. In this memory there is a white girl I grew to respect because she never flinched and never closed her eyes, no matter what the mob—where are they now?—threw. Later, in New York, she tried to get me to experiment with LSD with her, and the only reason I never did was because on the night we planned to try it I had a bad cold. I believe the reason she never closed her eyes was because she couldn't believe what she was seeing. We tried to keep in touch —but, because I had never had very much (not even a house that didn't leak), I was always conscious of the need to be secure; because she came from an eleven-room house in the suburbs of Philadelphia and, I assume, never had worried about material security, our deepest feelings began to miss each other. I identified her as someone who could afford to play poor for a while (her poverty interrupted occasionally by trips abroad), and she probably identified me as one of those inflexible black women black men constantly complain about: the kind who interrupt light-hearted romance by saying, "Yes, well . . . but what are the children going to eat?"

The point is that less than ten years after all these things I walk about Georgia (and Mississippi) eating, sleeping, loving, singing, burying the dead—the way men and women are supposed to do in a place that is the only "home" they've ever known. There is only one "For Coloreds" sign left in Eatonton, and it is on a black man's barbershop. He is merely outdated. Booster, if you read this, *change* your sign!

I see the work that I have done already as a foundation. That being so, I suppose I knew when I started *The Third Life of Grange Copeland* that it would have to cover several generations, and over half a century of growth and upheaval. It begins around 1900 and ends in the sixties. But my first draft (which was never used, not even one line, in the final version) began with Ruth as a Civil Rights lawyer in Georgia going to rescue her father, Brownfield Copeland, from a drunken accident, and to have a confrontation with him. In that version she is married —also to a lawyer—and they are both committed to insuring freedom for black people in the South. In Georgia, specifically. There was lots of love-making and courage in that version. But it was too recent, too superficial—everything seemed a product of the immediate present. And I believe nothing ever is.

So, I brought in the grandfather. Because all along I wanted to explore the relationship between parents and children, specifically between daughters and their fathers (this is most interesting, I've always felt; for example, in "The Child Who Favored Daughter" in *In Love & Trouble*, the father cuts off the breasts of his daughter because she falls in love with a white boy; why this, unless there is sexual jealousy?), and I wanted to learn, myself, how it happens that the hatred a child can have for a parent becomes inflexible. And I wanted to explore the relationship between men and women, and why women are always condemned for doing what men do as an expression of their masculinity. Why are women so easily "tramps" and "traitors" when men are heroes for engaging in the same activity? Why do women stand for this?

My new novel will be about several women who came of age during the sixties and were active (or not active) in the Movement in the South. I am exploring their backgrounds, familial and sibling connections, their marriages, affairs, and political persuasions, as they grow toward a fuller realization (and recognition) of themselves.

Since I put together my course on black women writers, which was taught first at Wellesley College and later at the University of Massachusetts, I have felt the need for real critical and biographical work on these writers. As a beginning, I am writing a long personal essay on my own discovery of these writers (designed, primarily, for lectures), and hope soon to visit the birthplace and home of Zora Neale Hurston, Eatonville, Florida. I am so involved with my own writing that I don't think there will be time for me to attempt the long, scholarly involvement that all these writers require. I am hopeful, however, that as their books are reissued and used in classrooms across the country, someone will do this. If no one does (or if no one does it to my satisfaction), I feel it is my duty (such is the fervor of love) to do it myself.

I read all of the Russian writers I could find in my sophomore year in college. I read them as if they were a delicious cake. I couldn't get enough: Tolstoy, especially his short stories, and the novels *The Kreutzer Sonata* and *Resurrection*, which taught me the importance of diving through politics and social forecasts to dig into the essential spirit of individual persons, because otherwise characters, no matter what political or current social issue they stand for, will not live), and Dostoevsky, who found his truths where everyone else seemed afraid to look, and Turgenev, Gorky, and Gogol, who made me think that Russia must have something floating about in the air that writers breathe from the time they are born. The only thing that began to bother me, many years later, was that I could find almost nothing written by a Russian woman writer.

Unless poetry has mystery, many meanings, and some ambiguities (necessary for mystery) I am not interested in it. Outside of Basho and Shiki and other Japanese haiku poets, I read and was impressed by the poetry of Li Po, the Chinese poet, Emily Dickinson, E. E. Cummings (deeply), and Robert Graves, especially his poems in *Man Does, Woman Is*—which is surely a male-chauvinist title, but I did not think about that then. I liked Graves because he took it as given that passionate love between man and woman does not necessarily last forever. He enjoyed the moment, and didn't bother about the future. My poem "The Man in the Yellow Terry" is very much influenced by Graves.

I also loved Ovid and Catullus. During the whole period of discovering haiku and the sensual poems of Ovid, the poems of E. E. Cummings and William Carlos Williams, my feet did not touch the ground. I ate, I slept, I studied other things (like European history) without ever doing more than giving it serious thought. It could not change me from one moment to the next, as poetry could.

I wish I had been familiar with the poems of Gwendolyn Brooks when I was in college. I stumbled upon them later. If there was ever a *born* poet, I think it is Brooks. Her natural way of looking at anything, of commenting on anything, comes out as a vision, in language that is peculiar to her. It is clear that she is a poet from the way your whole spiritual past begins to float around in your throat when you are reading, just as it is clear from the first line of *Cane* that Jean Toomer is a poet, blessed with a soul that is surprised by nothing. It is not unusual to weep when reading Brooks, just as when reading Toomer's "Song of the Sun" it is not unusual to comprehend—in a flash—what a dozen books on black people's history fail to illuminate. I have embarrassed my classes occasionally by standing in front of them in tears as Toomer's poem about "some genius from the South" flew through my body like a swarm of golden butterflies on their way toward a destructive sun. Like Du Bois, Toomer was capable of comprehending the black soul. It is not "soul" that *can* become a cliché, but something to be illuminated rather than explained.

The poetry of Arna Bontemps has strange effects on me too. He is a great poet, even if he is not recognized as such until after his death. Or is never acknowledged. The passion and compassion in his poem "A Black Man Talks of Reaping" shook the room I was sitting in the first time I read it. The ceiling began to revolve and a breeze—all the way from Alabama—blew through the room. A tide of spiritual good health tingled the bottoms of my toes. I changed. Became someone the same, but different. I understood, at last, what the transference of energy was.

It is impossible to list all of the influences on one's work. How can you even remember the indelible impression upon you of a certain look on your mother's face? But random influences are the following.

Music, which is the art I most envy.

Then there's travel—which really made me love the world, its vastness, and variety. How moved I was to know that there is no center of the universe. Entebbe, Uganda, or Bratislava, Czechoslovakia, exist no matter what we are doing here. Some writers—Camara Laye, and the man who wrote *One Hundred Years of Solitude* (Gabriel García Márquez)—have illumined this fact brilliantly in their fiction. Which brings me to African writers I *hope* to be influenced by: Okot p'Bitek has written my favorite modern poem, "Song of Lawino." I am crazy about *The Concubine* by Elechi Ahmadi (a perfect story, I think), *The Radiance of the King,* by Camara Laye, and *Maru,* by Bessie Head. These writers do not seem afraid of fantasy, of myth and mystery. Their work deepens one's comprehension of life by going beyond the bounds of realism. They are like musicians: at one with their cultures and their historical subconscious.

Flannery O'Connor has also influenced my work. To me, she is the best of the white Southern writers, including Faulkner. For one thing, she practiced economy. She also knew that the question of race was really only the first question on a long list. This is hard for just about everybody to accept, we've been trying to answer it for so long.

I did not read *Cane* until 1967, but it has been reverberating in me to an astonishing degree. *I love it passionately;* could not possibly exist without it. *Cane* and *Their Eyes Were Watching God* are probably my favorite books by black American writers. Jean Toomer has a very feminine sensibility (or, phrased another way, he is both feminine and masculine in his perceptions), unlike most black male writers. He loved women.

Like Toomer, Zora Neale Hurston was never afraid to let her characters be themselves, funny talk and all. She was incapable of being embarrassed by anything black people did, and so was able to write about everything with freedom and fluency. My feeling is that Zora Neale Hurston is probably one of the most misunderstood, least appreciated writers of this century. Which is a pity. She is great. A writer of courage, and incredible humor, with poetry in every line.

When I started teaching my course in black women writers at Wellesley (the first one, I think, ever), I was worried that Zora's use of black English of the twenties would throw some of the students off. It didn't. They loved it. They said it was like reading Thomas Hardy, only better. In that same course I taught Nella Larsen, Frances Watkins Harper (poetry and novel), Dorothy West, Ann Petry, Paule Marshall, among others. Also Kate Chopin and Virginia Woolf—not because they were black, obviously, but because they were women and wrote, as the black women did, on the condition of humankind from the perspective of women. It is interesting to read Woolf's *A Room of One's Own* while reading the poetry of Phillis Wheatley, to read Larsen's *Quicksand* along with *The Awakening*. The deep-throated voice of Sojourner Truth tends to drift across the room while you're reading. If you're not a feminist already, you become one.

There are two reasons why the black woman writer is not taken as seriously as the black male writer. One is that she's a woman. Critics seem unusually ill-equipped to discuss and analyze the works of black women intelligently. Generally, they do not even make the attempt; they prefer, rather, to talk about the lives of black women writers, not about what they write. And, since black women writers are not, it would seem, very likable—until recently they were the least willing worshipers of male supremacy—comments about them tend to be cruel.

In Nathan Huggins's very readable book *Harlem Renaissance*, he hardly refers to Zora Neale Hurston's work, except negatively. He quotes from Wallace Thurman's novel *Infants of the Spring* at length, giving us the words of a character, "Sweetie Mae Carr," who is allegedly based on Zora Neale Hurston. Sweetie Mae is a writer noted more "for her ribald wit and personal effervescence than for any actual literary work. She was a great favorite among those whites who went in for Negro prodigies." Huggins goes on for several pages, never quoting Zora Neale Hurston herself, but, rather, the opinions of others about her character. He does say that she was "a master of dialect," but adds that "her greatest weakness was carelessness or indifference to her art."

Having taught Zora Neale Hurston, and, of course, having read her work myself, I am stunned. Personally, I do not care if Zora Hurston was fond of her white women friends. When she was a child in Florida, working for nickels and dimes, two white women helped her escape. Perhaps this explains it. But even if it doesn't, so what? Her work, far from being done carelessly, is done (especially in *Their Eyes Were Watching God*) almost too perfectly. She took the trouble to capture the beauty of rural black expression. She saw poetry where other writers merely saw failure to cope with English. She was so at ease with her blackness it never occurred to her that she should act one way among blacks and another among whites (as her more "sophisticated" black critics apparently did).

It seems to me that black writing has suffered because even black critics have assumed that a book that deals with the relationships between members of a black family—or between a man and a woman—is less important than one that has white people as primary antagonists. The consequences of this is that many of our books by "major" writers (always male) tell us little about the culture, history, or future, imagination, fantasies, and so on, of black people, and a lot about isolated (often improbable) or limited encounters with a nonspecific white world. Where is the book by an American black person (aside from *Cane*) that equals Elechi Ahmadi's *The Concubine*, for example? A book that exposes the *subconscious* of a people, because the people's dreams, imaginings, rituals, legends are known to be important, are known to contain the accumulated collective reality of the people themselves. Or *The Radiance of the King*, where the white person is shown to be the outsider he is, because the culture he enters in Africa *itself* expells him. Without malice, but as nature expells what does not suit. The white man is mysterious, a force to be reckoned with, but he is not glorified to such an extent that the Africans turn their attention away from themselves and their own imagination and culture. Which is what often happens with "protest literature." The superficial becomes—for a time—the deepest reality, and replaces the still waters of the collective subconscious.

When my own novel was published, a leading black monthly admitted (the editor did) that the book itself was never read; but the magazine ran an item stating that a *white* reviewer had praised the book (which was, in itself, an indication that the book was no good—so went the logic) and then hinted that the reviewer had liked my book because of my life style. When I wrote to the editor to complain, he wrote me a small sermon on the importance of my "image," of what is "good" for others to see. Needless to say, what others "see" of me is the least of my worries, and I assume that "others" are intelligent enough to recover from whatever shocks my presence or life choices might cause.

Women writers are supposed to be intimidated by male disapprobation. What they write is not important enough to be read. How they live, however, their "image," they owe to the race. Read the reason Zora Neale Hurston gave for giving up her writing. See what "image" the Negro press gave her, innocent as she was. I no longer read articles or reviews unless they are totally about the work. I trust that someday a generation of men and women will arise who will forgive me for such wrong as I do not agree I do, and will read my work because it is a true account of my feelings, my perception, and my imagination, and because it will reveal something to them of their own selves. They will also be free to toss it—and me—out of a high window. They can do what they like. . . .

When I take the time to try to figure out what I am doing in my writing, where it is headed, and so on, I almost never can come up with anything. This is because it seems to me that my poetry is quite different from my novels (*The Third Life of Grange Copeland* and the one I am working on now); for example, *Once* is what I think of as a "happy" book, full of the spirit of an optimist who loves the world and all the sensations of caring in it; it doesn't matter that it began in sadness; *The Third Life of Grange Copeland*, though sometimes humorous and celebrative of life, is a grave book in which the characters see the world as almost entirely menacing. The optimism that closes the book makes it different from most of my short stories, and the political and personal content of my essays makes them different—again—from everything else. So I would not, as some critics have done, categorize my work as "gothic." I would not categorize it at all. Eudora Welty, in explaining why she rebels against being labeled "gothic," says that to her "gothic" conjures up the supernatural, and that she feels what she writes has "something to do with real life." I agree with her.

I like those of my short stories that show the plastic, shaping, almost painting quality of words. In "Roselily" and "The Child Who Favors Daughter" the prose is poetry, or, prose and poetry run together to add a new dimension to the language. But the most that I would say about where I am trying to go is this: I am trying to arrive at that place where black music already is; to arrive at that unself-conscious sense of collective oneness; that naturalness, that (even when anguished) grace.

The writer—like the musician or painter—must be free to explore, otherwise she or he will never discover what is needed (by everyone) to be known. This means, very often, finding oneself considered "unacceptable" by masses of people who think that the writer's obligation is not to explore or to challenge, but to second the masses' motions, whatever they are. Yet the gift of loneliness is sometimes a radical vision of society or one's people that has not previously been taken into account. Toomer was, I think, a lonely, wandering man, accustomed to being tolerated and misunderstood—a man who made choices many abhorred—and yet, *Cane* is a great reward; though Toomer himself probably never realized it.

The same is true of Zora Neale Hurston. She is probably more honest in her fieldwork and her fiction than she is in her autobiography, because she was hesitant to reveal how different she really was. It is interesting to contemplate what would have been the result and impact on black women—since 1937—if they had read and taken to heart *Their Eyes Were Watching God*. Would they still be as dependent on material things—fine cars, furs, big houses, pots and jars of face creams—as they are today? Or would they, learning from Janie that materialism is the dragrope of the soul, have become a nation of women immune (to the extent that is possible in a blatantly consumerist society like ours) to the accumulation of things, and aware, to their core, that love, fulfillment as women, peace of mind, should logically come before, not after, selling one's soul for a golden stool on which to sit. Sit and be bored.

Hurston's book, though seemingly apolitical, is, in fact, one of the most radical novels (without being a tract) we have.

Although I am constantly involved, internally, with religious questions—and I seem to have spent all of my life rebelling against the church and other people's interpretations of what religion is—the truth is probably that I don't believe there is a God, although I would like to believe it. Certainly I don't believe there is a God beyond nature. The world is God. Man is God. So is a leaf or a snake . . . So, when Grange Copeland refuses to pray at the end of the book, he is refusing to be a hypocrite. All his life he has hated the church and taken every opportunity to ridicule it. He has taught his granddaughter, Ruth, this same humorous contempt. He does, however, appreciate the humanity of man-womankind as a God worth embracing. To him, the greatest value a person can attain is full humanity, which is a state of oneness with all things, and a willingness to die (or to live) so that the best that has been produced can continue to live in someone else. He "rocked himself in his own arms to a final sleep" because he understood that man is alone—in his life as in his death—without any God but himself (and the world).

Like many, I waver in my convictions about God, from time to time. In my poetry I seem to be for; in my fiction, against.

I am intrigued by the religion of the Black Muslims. By what conversion means to black women, specifically, and what the religion itself means in terms of the black American past: our history, our "race memories," our absorption of Christianity, our *changing* of Christianity to fit our needs. What will the new rituals mean? How will this new religion imprint itself on the collective consciousness of the converts? Can women be free in such a religion? Is such a religion, in fact, an anachronism? So far I have dealt with this interest in two stories, "Roselily," about a young woman who marries a young Muslim because he offers her respect and security, and "Everyday Use," a story that shows respect for the "militance" and progressive agricultural programs of the Muslims, but at the same time shows skepticism about a young man who claims attachment to the Muslims because he admires the rhetoric. It allows him to acknowledge his contempt for whites, which is all he believes the group is about.

In other stories, I am interested in Christianity as an imperialist tool used against Africa ("Diary of an African Nun") and in voodoo used as a weapon against oppression ("The Revenge of Hannah Kemhuff"). I see all of these as religious questions.

The poem "Revolutionary Petunias" did not have a name when I sat down to write it. I wanted to create a person who engaged in a final struggle with her oppressor, and won, but who, in every other way, was "incorrect." Sammy Lou in the poem is everything she should not be: her name is Sammy Lou, for example; she is a farmer's wife; she works in the fields. She goes to church. The walls of her house contain no signs of her blackness—though that in itself reveals it; anyone walking into that empty house would know Sammy Lou is black. She is so incredibly "incorrect" that she is only amused when the various poets and folk singers rush to immortalize her heroism in verse and song. She did not think of her killing of her oppressor in that way. She thought—and I picture her as tall, lean, black, with short, badly straightened hair and crooked teeth—that killing is never heroic. Her reaction, after killing this cracker-person, would be to look up at the sky and not pray or ask forgiveness but to say—as if talking to an old friend—"Lord, you know my heart. I never wanted to have to kill nobody. But I couldn't hold out to the last, like Job. I had done took more than I could stand."

Sammy Lou is so "incorrect" she names her children after Presidents and their wives: she names one of them after the founder of the Methodist church. To her, this does not mean a limitation of her blackness; it means she feels she is so black she can absorb—and change—all things, since everybody knows that a black-skinned Jackie Kennedy still bears resemblance only to her own great-aunt, Sadie Mae Johnson.

But the most "incorrect" thing about Sammy Lou is that she loves flowers. Even on her way to the electric chair she reminds her children to water them. This is crucial, for I have heard it said by one of our cultural visionaries that whenever you hear a black person talking about the beauties of nature, that person is not a black person at all, but a Negro. This is meant as a put-down, and it is. It puts down all of the black folks in Georgia, Alabama, Mississippi, Texas, Louisiana—in fact, it covers just about everybody's mama. Sammy Lou, of course, is so "incorrect" she does not even know how ridiculous she is for loving to see flowers blooming around her unbearably ugly gray house. To be "correct" she should consider it her duty to let ugliness reign. Which is what "incorrect" people like Sammy Lou refuse to do.

Actually, the poem was to claim (as Toomer claimed the people he wrote about in *Cane*, who were all as "incorrect" as possible) the most "incorrect" black person I could, and to honor her as my own—on a level with, if not above, the most venerated saints of the black revolution. It seems our fate to be incorrect (look where we live, for example), and in our incorrectness stand.

Although Sammy Lou is more a rebel than a revolutionary (since you need more than one for a revolution) I named the poem "Revolutionary Petunias" because she is not—when you view her kind of person historically—isolated. She is part of an ongoing revolution. Any black revolution, instead of calling her "incorrect," will have to honor her single act of rebellion.

Another reason I named the poem "Revolutionary Petunias" is that I like petunias and like to raise them because you just put them in any kind of soil and they bloom their heads off—exactly, it seemed to me, like black people tend to do. (Look at the blues and jazz musicians, the blind singers from places like Turnip, Mississippi, the poets and writers and all-around blooming people you know, who—from all visible evidence—achieved their blooming by eating the air for bread and drinking muddy water for hope.) Then I thought, too, of the petunias my mother gave me when my daughter was born, and of the story (almost a parable) she told me about them. Thirty-seven years ago, my mother and father were coming home from somewhere in their wagon—my mother was pregnant with one of my older brothers at the time—and they passed a deserted house where one lavender petunia was left, just blooming away in the yard (probably to keep itself company)—and my mother said Stop! let me go and get that petunia bush. And my father, grumbling, stopped, and she got it, and they went home, and she set it out in a big stump in the yard. It never wilted, just bloomed and bloomed. Every time the family moved (say twelve times) she took her petunia—and thirty-seven years later she brought me a piece of that same petunia bush. It had never died. Each winter it lay dormant and dead-looking, but each spring it came back, livelier than before.

What underscored the importance of this story for me is this: modern petunias do not live forever. They die each winter and the next spring you have to buy new ones.

In a way, the whole book is a celebration of people who will not cram themselves into any ideological or racial mold. They are all shouting Stop! I want to go get that petunia!

Because of this they are made to suffer. They are told that they do not belong, that they are not wanted, that their art is not needed, that nobody who is "correct" could love what they love. Their answer is resistance, without much commentary; just a steady knowing that they stand at a point where—with one slip of the character—they might be lost, and the bloom they are after wither in the winter of self-contempt. They do not measure themselves against black people or white people; if anything, they learn to walk and talk in the presence of Du Bois, Hurston, Hughes, Toomer, Attaway, Wright, and others—and when they bite into their pillows at night these spirits comfort them. They are aware that the visions that created them were all about a future where all people—and flowers too—can bloom. They require that in the midst of the bloodiest battles or revolution this thought not be forgotten.

When I married my husband there was a law that said I could not. When we moved to Mississippi three years after the lynching of Cheney, Schwerner, and Goodman, it was a punishable crime for a black person and a white person of opposite sex to inhabit the same house. But I felt then—as I do now—that in order to be able to live at all in America I must be unafraid to live anywhere in it, and I must be able to live in the fashion and with whom I choose. Otherwise, I'd just as soon leave. If society (black or white) says, Then you must be isolated, an outcast, then I will be a hermit. Friends and relatives may desert me, but the dead—Douglass, Du Bois, Hansberry, Toomer, and the rest—are a captive audience. . . . These feelings went into two poems, "Be Nobody's Darling" and "While Love Is Unfashionable."

"For My Sister Molly Who in the Fifties" is a pretty real poem. It really is about one of my sisters, a brilliant, studious girl who became one of those Negro wonders—who collected scholarships like trading stamps and wandered all over the world. (Our hometown didn't even have a high school when she came along.) When she came to visit us in Georgia it was—at first—like having Christmas all during her vacation. She loved to read and tell stories; she taught me African songs and dances; she cooked fanciful dishes that looked like anything but plain old sharecropper food. I loved her so much it came as a great shock—and a shock I don't expect to recover from—to learn she was ashamed of us. We were so poor, so dusty and sunburnt. We talked wrong. We didn't know how to dress, or use the right eating utensils. And so, she drifted away, and I did not understand it. Only later did I realize that sometimes (perhaps) it becomes too painful to bear: seeing your home and family—shabby and seemingly without hope—through the eyes of your new friends and strangers. She had felt—for her own mental health—that the gap that separated us from the rest of the world was too wide for her to keep trying to bridge. She understood how delicate she was.

I started out writing this poem in great anger; hurt, really. I thought I could write a magnificently vicious poem. Yet, even in the first draft, it did not turn out that way, which is one of the great things about poetry. What you really feel, underneath everything else, will present itself. Your job is not to twist that feeling. So that although being with her now is too painful with memories for either of us to be comfortable, I still retain (as I hope she does), in memories beyond the bad ones, my picture of a sister I loved, "Who walked among the flowers and brought them inside the house, who smelled as good as they, and looked as bright."

This poem (and my sister received the first draft, which is hers alone, and the way I wish her to relate to the poem) went through fifty drafts (at least) and I worked on it, off and on, for five years. This has never happened before or since. I do not know what to say about the way it is constructed other than to say that as I wrote it the lines and words went, on the paper, to a place comparable to where they lived in my head.

I suppose, actually, that my tremendous response to the poems of William Carlos Williams, Cummings, and Basho convinced me that poetry is more like music—in my case, improvi-

sational jazz, where each person blows the note that she hears
—than like a cathedral, with every stone in a specific, predeter-
mined place. Whether lines are long or short depends on what
the poem itself requires. Like people, some poems are fat and
some are thin. Personally, I prefer the short, thin ones, which
are always like painting the eye in a tiger (as Muriel Rukeyser
once explained it). You wait until the energy and vision are just
right, then you write the poem. If you try to write it before it
is ready to be written you find yourself adding stripes instead of
eyes. Too many stripes and the tiger herself disappears. You will
paint a photograph (which is what is wrong with "Burial")
instead of creating a new way of seeing.

The poems that fail will always haunt you. I am haunted
by "Ballad of the Brown Girl" and "Johann" in *Once*, and I
expect to be haunted by "Nothing Is Right" in *Revolutionary
Petunias*. The first two are dishonest, and the third is trite.

The poem "The Girl Who Died #2" was written after I
learned of the suicide of a student at the college I attended. I
learned, from the dead girl's rather guilty-sounding "brothers
and sisters," that she had been hounded constantly because she
was so "incorrect"; she thought she could be a black hippie. To
top that, they tried to make her feel like a traitor because she
refused to limit her interest to black men. Anyway, she was a
beautiful girl. I was shown a photograph of her by one of her few
black friends. She was a little brown-skinned girl from Texas,
away from home for the first time, trying to live a life she could
live with. She tried to kill herself two or three times before, but
I guess the brothers and sisters didn't think it "correct" to
respond with love or attention, since everybody knows it is
"incorrect" to even think of suicide if you are a black person.
And, of course, black people do not commit suicide. Only colored people and Negroes commit suicide. (See "The Old War-
rior Terror": Warriors, you know, always die on the battlefield.)

I said, when I saw the photograph, that I wished I had been there for her to talk to. When the school invited me to join the Board of Trustees, it was her face that convinced me. I know nothing about boards and never really trusted them; but I can listen to problems pretty well. . . . I believe in listening—to a person, the sea, the wind, the trees, but especially to young black women whose rocky road I am still traveling.

1973

A LETTER TO THE EDITOR OF MS.

I realized at the National Black Feminist Organization conference that it had been much too long since I sat in a room full of black women and, unafraid of being made to feel peculiar, spoke about things that matter to me. We sat together and talked and knew no one would think, or say, "Your thoughts are dangerous to black unity and a threat to black men." Instead, all the women understood that we gathered together to assure understanding among black women, and that understanding among women is not a threat to anyone who intends to treat women fairly. So the air was clear and rang with earnest voices freed at last to speak to ears that would not automatically begin to close. And then to hear Shirley Chisholm speak: to feel all of history compressed into a few minutes and to sing "We love Shirley!"—a rousing indication of our caring that we could not give to Sojourner Truth or Harriet Tubman or Mary McLeod Bethune. To see her so small, so impeccable in dress, in speech, and in logic, and so very black, and to think of her running for President of this country, which has, in every single age, tried to destroy her. It was as if, truly, the faces of those other women were just beneath the skin of Shirley Chisholm's face. And later, at the same general meeting, being one among and with all those black women, I thought of all the questions about us I have been asking myself.

For four or five years I have been watching the faces of young black men and women as they emerge from the movie houses of this city, their faces straight from Southern black homes and families, which means *upright, Christian, striving* homes with mothers and fathers who are shown respect. I've watched them, innocence and determination to grow mingling in their bodies, respond to images of black women and men they never have seen before. Watched them stagger, slink, or strut away from the Sweetback flicks . . . a doomed look on the faces of the young women, a cruelty or a look of disgust beginning behind the innocence on the faces of the young men. And I have asked myself: Who will stop this slinging of mud on the character of the black woman? Who will encourage the tenderness that seeks to blossom in young black men? Who will stand up and say, "Black women, at least, have had enough!" And I began to feel, at the conference, that, yes, there are black women who will do that.

And I looked again at Shirley Chisholm's face (which I had never seen before except on television) and was glad she has kept a record of her political and social struggles, because our great women die, often in poverty and under the weight of slander, and are soon forgotten. And I thought of how little we have studied any of our ancestors, but how close to zero has been our study of those who were female . . . and I have asked myself: Who will secure from neglect and slander those women who have kept our image as black women clean and strong for us? And at the conference, I met women who are eager to do this job.

And of course I thought of Frederick Douglass. And knew that *his* newspaper would have been pleased to cover our conference, because we are black and we are women and because we intend to be as free as anyone. He understood that it is not incumbent upon the slave to make sure her or his uprising is appropriate or "correct." It is the nature of the oppressed to rise against oppression. Period. Women who wanted their rights did not frighten him, politically or socially, because he knew his own rights were not diminished by theirs. I'm sure he would have sent someone from his newspaper to see what things—abortion, sterilization, welfare rights, women in the black movement, black women in the arts, and so forth—we were talking about. I don't think he would have understood—any more than I do —why no representatives from black magazines and newspapers came. Are not black women black news?

And then, when I came home, I stood looking at a picture of Frederick Douglass I have on my wall. And I asked myself: Where is your picture of Harriet Tubman, the General? Where is your drawing of Sojourner Truth? And I thought that if black women would only start asking questions like that, they'd soon —all of them—have to begin reclaiming their mothers and grandmothers—and what an enrichment that would be!

When we look back over our history it is clear that we have neglected to save just those people who could help us most. Because no matter what anyone says, it is the black woman's words that have the most meaning for us, her daughters, because she, like us, has experienced life not only as a black person, but as a woman; and it was *different* being Frederick Douglass than being Harriet Tubman—or Sojourner Truth, who only "looked like a man," but bore children and saw them sold into slavery.

I thought of the black women writers and poets whose books—even today—go out of print while other works about all of us, less valuable if more "profitable," survive to insult us with their half-perceived, half-rendered "truths." How simple a thing it seems to me that to know ourselves as we are, we must know our mothers' names. Yet, we do not know them. Or if we do, it is only the names we know and not the lives.

And I thought of the mountain of work black women must do. We must work as if we are the last generation capable of work—for it is true that the view we have of the significance of the past will undoubtedly die with us, and future generations will have to stumble in the dark, over ground we should have covered.

Someone claimed, rhetorically, that we are the only "true queens of the universe." I do not want to be a queen, because queens are oppressive, but even so the thought came to me that any true queen knows the names, words, and actions of the other queens of her lineage and is very sharp about her herstory. I think we might waive the wearing of a crown until we have at least seriously begun our work.

I thought about friends of mine whose views do not differ very much from mine, but who decided not to come to the conference because of fear. Fear of criticism from other black people (who, I assume, consider silence a sign of solidarity), and fear of the presence of lesbians. The criticism will no doubt be forthcoming, but what can one do about that? Nothing, but continue to work. As for the lesbians—a black lesbian would undoubtedly be a black woman. That seems simple enough. In any case, I only met other black women, my sisters, and valuable beyond measuring, every one of them.

And we talked and we discussed and we sang for Shirley

Chisholm and clapped for Eleanor Holmes Norton and tried to follow Margaret Sloan's lyrics and cheered Flo Kennedy's anecdotes. And we laughed a lot and argued some. *And had a very good time.*

1974

BREAKING CHAINS AND
ENCOURAGING LIFE

Four stories:

1. At two o'clock in the morning when I was living in
Brooklyn, I received a call from a black woman who had
recently invited me to read at her school. I had, in fact,
spent the night in the house she shared with her third-
world woman, nonblack lover, and had had an enjoyable
time.

Among the preliminaries of this conversation was the
news that she and her lover had broken up, and did I know
I was beautiful and did I know my eyes were sad?

She had heard I intended to move to San Francisco. She
intended to do the same. In fact, intended to "haunt" me.
To "camp" on my doorstep.

I could not advise that, I said.

Well, in that case, she had been reading my work, and

teaching it, and decided I myself was not in it. She implied this was fraud.

And another thing, why do you write so patronizingly about lesbians?

What?

Well, I think you misrepresent black women. I know more about black women than you'll ever know. I think . . .

I don't give a damn what you think, I said. And hung up.

2. I am speaking to a class of thirty on feminist aesthetics. A white woman says: I would love to work with black and third-world women, but I'm a separatist.

A what?

Well, black and third-world women always seem connected to some man. Since I am a separatist, this means I can't work with them. What do you suggest I do?

Personally I'm not giving up Stevie Wonder and John Lennon, no matter what, I reply, but you should do whatever you want to do, which obviously is not to work with black and third-world women.

My daughter, sitting beside me, looks up from her Rosa Guy novel. Mom, she whispers, shocked, there's only one other black woman in here. She knows my motto is "Never be the only one, except, possibly, in your home."

This lone black woman, no doubt angered at her isolated position in the class, annoyed that both of us, in such a "separatist" environment can count only as diversion and entertainment, attacks me bitterly, as if to obliterate the pain of her own presence.

3. A lesbian friend who tried on two occasions to "pull me out of the closet" before accepting the friendship I offer,

tells me there is a developing split in black lesbian ranks.

Oh, yeah?

Yeah. Between black-women-identified women and white-women-identified black women.

And who judges?

Well, there are these black women with white women lovers and they bring 'em to meetings and it's just disruptive. We only have so much time and money to spend getting our own shit together, and we end up wasting it discussing them.

Her present though outgoing lover is a white woman. She met me while I was in an interracial marriage.

We sigh.

Two thoughts come to mind. A swaggering one first: Black women are notorious for loving anybody they want to love and some of those they don't. And, less swaggering: Black women love those who love them.

4. I am doing meditation at a center in Oakland. A new black woman acquaintance, who I hope will become a friend, carries me off to her house afterward.

She says: Have you seen *Conditions: Five, The Black Women's Issue?*

No, I haven't, I say with excitement, where is it?

I have it, she says.

Great, I say. Don't let me leave without looking at it.

You'll be disappointed, she says.

Why? I ask.

The writing is *terrible.*

Really?

And it's put together poorly.

Oh, no!

And it's full of lesbians.

Hummmm. Well, don't forget to show it to me.

But she does forget, still saying as I leave an hour later: You'll be disappointed.

. . .

> *If I hadn't helped my sister*
> *They'd have put those chains on me!*
> *—Niobeth Tsaba,*
> SONG OF A SISTER'S FREEDOM

One of the most exciting and healthiest things to happen lately in the black community is the coming out of black lesbians. *Conditions: Five. The Black Women's Issue* (which also includes work by many nonlesbians) reflects this with power, intelligence, and style. There are poems, essays, book reviews (of Shange's *Nappy Edges*, Wallace's *Black Macho and the Myth of the Superwoman*, and Lorde's *The Black Unicorn*) excerpts from journals, and part of a novel in progress. Reading the collection is not unlike seeing women breaking chains with their bare hands.

"This bullshit should not be encouraged," a black male student and critic declared in a 1975 review of Ann Allen Shockley's lesbian novel, *Loving Her*, which appeared in the now defunct *Black World* magazine. One is struck by the use of patriarchal intimidation in this remark, and, since the critic is presumably much younger than Shockley (a librarian for many years at Fisk University), it is surprisingly disrespectful of her life. For surely black women have earned the right to write about anything they please; and to denigrate this right reveals an antipathy to us so vast that all recorded history cannot, apparently, limit it. To say that a black lesbian is writing "bullshit" because she expresses her own perception of existence is as presumptuous as the belief that lesbianism will disappear if black people refuse to "encourage" it.

In an invaluable essay in *Conditions: Five* called "The Black Lesbian in American Literature: An Overview" Shockley writes: "Until recently there has been almost nothing written by or about the black lesbian in American literature—a void signifying that the black lesbian was a nonentity in imagination as well as reality. This unique black woman, analogous to Ralph Ellison's *Invisible Man*, was seen but not seen because of what the eyes did not wish to behold."

The "eyes did not wish to behold" women loving women in a primary or sexual way, and so, Shockley writes, even black women writers who might at least have written novels, stories, or even reviews of lesbian work, opted instead to write nothing, or to join those who in various often subtle ways agreed that "this bullshit should not be encouraged." She shows how negatively black lesbians are presented in the work of several contemporary black women authors, and how such depiction reinforces antilesbian stereotypes already prevalent in the black community.

"It is my belief," writes Shockley, "that those black female writers who could have written well and perceptively enough to warrant publication chose instead to write about black women in a heterosexual milieu. *The preference was motivated by the fear of being labeled a lesbian, even if in some cases they were not*" (my italics).

And because of this, and I think Shockley's belief is largely true, many black women writers, whose responsibility is to the truth and to our children (who may, for all we know, *be* gay or lesbian, as we too may be or become: we're born but we aren't dead), have backed down, have said, by their silence or negative, stereotypical portrayals of black lesbians: "This bullshit should not be encouraged."

And yet, as Audre Lorde says in the poem quoted by Gloria Hull at the opening of *Conditions: Five:*

> Whether we speak or not,
> The machine will crush us to bits—
> and we will also be afraid
>
> Your silence
> will not
> protect you

Barbara Smith and Lorraine Bethel make this observation chillingly real in their introduction. As they were compiling materials for this volume in New Haven and Boston, *between January 29 and May 28, 1979, twelve black women were systematically sought out and brutally murdered* in Boston's third-world communities. "While we were working to create a place for celebration of Black women's lives, our sisters were dying. The sadness, fear, and anger as well as the unforeseen need to do political work around the murders affected every aspect of our lives including work on *Conditions: Five.* The murder of Black women right where we lived also made crystal clear the . . . need for such a publication and for a Black feminist movement absolutely opposed to violence against us and the taking of our lives on any and all levels."

One of the most remarkable pieces in *Conditions: Five* is an excerpt from Beverly Smith's journal that was almost lost to us. It describes her attendance, "masquerading as a nice, straight, middle-class Black 'girl,'" at the stuffy, upper-middle-class wedding of her close friend "J——."

She is irretrievably lost to me and I to her. She's getting married and since I'm a dyke I am anathema to her. She's made her feelings on homosexuality clear on several occasions. (I no longer use the terms homosexual or homosexuality to refer to lesbians.)

Two last things and then I'll stop. Last night I was on the second floor after going to the bathroom (I must have gone four times, I was hiding and trying to maintain my sanity). I went into a bedroom where J—— and others of her bridesmaids and Susan (the wife of a friend of H——'s) were talking. J—— was talking about what still needed to be done and about her feelings concerning the wedding. Mostly anxieties over whether everything would go well. But at one point she said something to the effect that "It seems strange. We've been together all our lives [her three friends] and after tomorrow we won't be." Her friends assured her that they'd still be a part of her life. Ha! I know better. She'll be H——'s chattel from now on. It occurred to me that celebrating a marriage is like celebrating being sold into slavery. Yes, I'm overgeneralizing (I'm only 90-95% right); but in this case I feel sure.

One piece of evidence for the above. At the rehearsal yesterday J—— was on the fourth floor shouting to someone. H—— yelled up to her, "J——, don't shout!" J—— replied, defending herself, and H—— interrupted her by saying sharply, "J——!" as if he were reprimanding a child or a dog. I was sick. This is the essence. He will try to make her into his slave, his child, in short, his wife.

The only people Smith feels drawn to at the wedding are the servants catering the affair.

Directly after her own wedding some years earlier, Smith burned all the journals she had written, "partly because I felt I had no safe place for them away from my husband and partly because one of my duties in that marriage was to forget who I was before it." For *four* years she kept unpublished her notes on J——'s wedding, a crucial piece of black women's experience, until the support of other black feminists and lesbians permitted her to deal with it.

Reading Smith's biting, often arch account of the wedding ("Did I mention that this is frightfully badly organized? Everything in chaos. But I have no doubt it will come off. Unfortunately.") I think of another New England dyke (who may have fainted at the word, for all I know), Angelina Weld Grimké (1880–1958), who, sadly, according to Gloria Hull's moving essay "Under the Days: The Buried Life and Poetry of Angelina Weld Grimké," was never able publicly to affirm her love of women, not even, often, to the women themselves. And who, though considered a good "minor" poet by male critics who were as patronizing then as they are now, published very little, and what she did publish was mutilated by her attempts to camouflage the truth.

The question . . . is: What did it mean to be a Black *lesbian*/poet in America at the beginning of the Twentieth century? First, it meant that you wrote (or half wrote)—in isolation—a lot which you did not show and knew you could not publish. It meant that when you did write to be printed, you did so in shackles—chained between the real experience you wanted to say and the conventions that would not give you voice. It meant that you fashioned a few race and nature poems, transliterated lyrics, and double-tongued verses which—sometimes (racism being what it is)—got published. It meant, finally, that you stopped writing altogether, dying, no doubt, with your real gifts stifled within—and leaving behind (in a precious few cases) the little to survive of your true self in fugitive pieces.

And for what?

So that, fifty years later, a young black man can say, with much of the black community echoing his hostility to the priceless expressions of a black woman's life: "This bullshit should not be encouraged."

Grimké wrote:

> The days fall upon me;
>
> . . .
>
> They cover me
> They crush,
> They smother.
> Who will ever find me
> Under the days?

Grimké's life was indeed a buried one. She was smothered by "the days" that did not encourage her, and "had no spirit left to leave us." Unlike her contemporary Alice Dunbar-Nelson, poet and journalist, wife of Paul Lawrence Dunbar and lover of women and men, who managed to affirm her complete self in unpublished material she contrived to leave behind, Grimké was defeated. Flattened. Crushed. "She is a lesson," says Hull, "whose meaning each person will interpret as they see fit and are able. What she means to me, is that we must work, write, live so that who and what she was never has to mean the same."

In Shockley's essay on the absence of black lesbians in American literature, she quotes Muhammed Ali's response to a female reporter for the *Amsterdam News* who asked him to comment on the ERA and the equalizing of economic opportunities. Ali replied: ". . . some professions shouldn't be open to women because they can't handle certain jobs, like construction work. Lesbians, maybe, but not women."

A black woman, perhaps (let us say) our daughter, needs to work. Has to work. Wants to work. Wants to work at construction. She reads Ali's words and knows all her community will respect and believe what he says. Our daughter's spirit is torn. If she takes the job her head is bent, her shoulders hunched against the assaults of ignorance. If she does not take the job, she starves, goes on welfare, or is easily defeated by a world that prefers broken black spirits anyway.

In this one comment Ali undermines our daughter's belief in the wholeness of her maternal ancestors (were not our slave great-grandmothers, to whom modern-day construction work would doubtless seem easy, women?), threatens her present existence, and narrows her future. As surely as if he clamped a chain on her body, he has clamped a chain on her spirit. And by our silence, our fear of being labeled lesbian, we help hold it there. *And this is inexcusable.* Because we know, whatever else we don't know and are afraid to guess, black lesbians *are* black women. It is in our power to say that the days of intimidating black women with impunity are over.

I was once criticized because I wrote that Zora Neale Hurston's critics said she "must have been" bisexual, she had such tremendous drive. "I've never seen that in print," the person criticizing said. I replied that our oral tradition, which works as well as ever, kills successful black women off at house parties. For black women, malicious gossip (elevated to the status of "news" in the sad examples of Hurston and Nella Larsen) *is* the criticism that damages our lives and our work, which, because we are women, is rarely considered on its own terms.

During the sixties my own work was often dismissed by

black reviewers "because of my life style," a euphemism for my interracial marriage. At black literature conferences it would be examined fleetingly, if at all, in light of this "traitorous" union, by critics who were themselves frequently interracially married and who, moreover, hung on every word from Richard Wright, Jean Toomer, Langston Hughes, James Baldwin, John A. Williams, and LeRoi Jones (to name a few), all of whom were at some time in their lives interracially connected, either legally or in more than casual ways. Clearly it was not interracialism itself that bothered the critics, but that I, a black woman, had dared to exercise the same prerogative as they. While it is fine for black men to embrace other black men, black women, white women and white men in intimate relationships, the black woman, to be accepted *as a black woman,* must prefer being alone to the risk of enjoying "the wrong choice." Now that I am no longer married, the value of my work is questioned because of my "politics." This means, I think, what the first dismissal meant: that I am a black woman. Something is always wrong with us. To those who feel this, "lesbianism" is simply another, perhaps more extreme, version of "something wrong with us." After all, it is passé to say we're too black, or too loud, or that our kinky hair clashes with pastel interiors. And to say we're too bourgeois or work too closely with whitefolks raises eyebrows if it comes from black professors at Harvard or Yale. The charge of "emotionalism" occasionally bandied in our direction today merely replaces an earlier charge of *un* emotionalism, hard-heartedness, and frigid bitchiness.

Luckily, we have a fighting tradition. Ida B. Wells wrote many years ago that "a Winchester rifle should have a place of honor in every black home," which the murdered black women in Boston should have known. But in any case, if we are writers, we have our typewriters, and if we are not writers, we have our tongues. Like black men and women who refused to be the exceptional "pet" Negro for whites, and who instead said they were "niggers" too (the original "crime" of "niggers" and lesbians is that they prefer themselves), perhaps black women writers and nonwriters should say, simply, whenever black lesbians are being put down, held up, messed over, and generally told their lives should not be encouraged, *We are all lesbians.* For surely it is better to be thought a lesbian, and to say and write your life exactly as you experience it, than to be a token "pet" black woman for those whose contempt for our autonomous existence makes them a menace to human life.

Conditions: Five represents a continuation of the struggle for self-definition and affirmation that is the essence of what "African-American" means in this country. It is because black lesbians *are* black women out of this tradition that the chain will never be accepted as a natural garment.

1980

.   .   .   .

IF THE PRESENT LOOKS LIKE THE PAST,
WHAT DOES THE FUTURE LOOK LIKE?

Dear————,

After our talk of all the things hoped gone forever but now "back with the wind"—the KKK, obscene national "leadership," "good hair"—I thought somewhat uneasily of something I had said in reply to your question about Color. You may recall that we were speaking of the hostility many black black women feel toward light-skinned black women, and you said, "Well, I'm light. It's not my fault. And I'm not going to apologize for it." I said apology for one's color is not what anyone is asking. What black black women would be interested in, I think, is a consciously heightened awareness on the part of light black women that they are capable, often quite unconsciously, of inflicting pain upon them; and that unless the question of Colorism—in my definition, prejudicial or preferential treatment of same-race people based solely on their color—is addressed in our communities and definitely in our black "sisterhoods" we cannot, as a people, progress. For colorism, like colonialism, sexism, and racism, impedes us.

What bothers me is my statement that I myself, halfway between light and dark—a definite brown—must align myself with black black women; that not to do so is to spit in our black mother's face. Meaning the primordial, the Edenic, the Goddess, Mother Africa. For now I recall meeting your actual mother, who looks white, as did your grandmother, whose picture you once showed me, and whose beautiful old clothes you sometimes wear. For you, the idea of alignment with black black women solely on the basis of color must seem ridiculous *and* colorist, and I have come to agree with you.

Still, I think there is probably as much difference between the life of a black black woman and a "high yellow" black woman as between a "high yellow" woman and a white woman. And I am worried, constantly, about the hatred the black black woman encounters within black society. To me, the black black woman is our essential mother—the blacker she is the more us she is—and to see the hatred that is turned on her is enough to make me despair, almost entirely, of our future as a people.

Ironically, much of what I've learned about color I've learned because I have a mixed-race child. Because she is lighter-skinned, straighter-haired than I, her life—in this racist, colorist society—is infinitely easier. And so I understand the subtle programming I, my mother, and my grandmother before me fell victim to. Escape the pain, the ridicule, escape the jokes, the lack of attention, respect, dates, even a job, any way you can. And if you can't escape, help your children to escape. Don't let them suffer as you have done. And yet, what have we been escaping to? Freedom used to be the only answer to that question. But for some of our parents it is as if freedom and whiteness were the same destination, and that presents a problem for any person of color who does not wish to disappear.

Thinking about color, thinking about you, me, my daughter and mother, I thought of a story that illustrates some of what I've just said. It begins in the South, when I was in my late teens, and ends in a coffee shop in New Mexico some twelve years later.

Doreena, who figures prominantly in the story, haunts me, even today, and I find myself worried about her, and wondering how she is. She was, when I knew her, a brilliant, elegant, and very very black girl. To look at Doreena was as Mari Evans says in one of her poems "to be restored." For she was "pure." Genes untampered with. Totally "unimproved" by infusions of white or Indian blood. She was beautiful. However, the word "beautiful" itself was never used to describe black women in those days. They might be called "handsome" in a pinch. "Her skin is black *but* she is sure nuff pretty," someone might have thought, but not sung. Stevie Wonder's lyrics, though in our time backward in this one instance ("but" rather than "and"), would have been considered revolutionary in the fifties and early sixties. "Beautiful" was for white women and black women who look like you. Medium browns like me might evoke "good-looking" or "fine." A necessary act of liberation within myself was to acknowledge the beauty of black black women, but I was always aware I was swimming against the tide.

In any case, Doreena was rejected by a very light-skinned young man whom she had been dating for some time, with an eye toward marriage. His parents said she was too dark and would not look right in their cream-colored family. And she did what many black black women do when rejected because of their color, she flung herself into the purest, blackest arms she could find. Those of a West Indian. (She might, instead, have gone the other "traditional" way: into the arms of a "real" white person, thumbing her nose at the "fakes.")

Well, there went our sister Doreena. Off into a sexist,

patriarchial, provincial culture she didn't understand, one felt fairly sure.

And what of the young man? Let us call him Hypolytus. Hypolytus married a Finn. (Memo to his parents.) And, at a coffee shop in New Mexico where he and I spent an hour over lunch, he told me the following tale: He and his Finnish wife had divorced rather soon. For one thing, she insisted on living in Finland; a move he had definitely not expected, since he was of the "Whither thou goest . . ." school, but ascribing this commitment only to women, of course; and he had recently visited her and their daughter there. While there, he took the daughter shopping. And it was the various shopkeepers of Helsinki—used to American tourists—who translated for him and the child, because she did not speak English and his scant knowledge of Finnish had lapsed.

I think it was hearing this story, and feeling so deeply that our brother Hypolytus had been tricked by society and his parents that caused me to examine color oppression in my own experience and my own life. I remembered ———, who was asked by the light-skinned girls who shared one end of our college dormitory to move somewhere else, because she was so dark; the men who came to call on them found her blackness "inharmonious." I remembered being literally pushed off the sidewalk outside the Dom in New York, by young black men who wanted to speak to the white women I was with. Perhaps it is no accident that my best friend during this period was a black black woman from Africa who was never approached by black men for dates. She dated instead a white seminary student from Texas, while my fiancé was an Irish Jew from New England.

This essay is for you. You are younger than I, so I think of you as a younger sister who will take all that your older sisters have learned even further. A sister I do not wish to lose to the entreaties of parents or grandparents standing behind you whispering "lighten up" or "darken up" the race. Nor do I, a dark woman, intend to give you up. When we walk down a street together and those who hate their black mothers admire only you (really your skin color and hair) we will not let this divide us, but will think instead with pity of their ignorance and sure end in self-eradication. For no one can hate their source and survive, as has been said.

The woman whose statement precedes the essay was my teacher in high school. A woman of courage, great love of us, and soul. It can only be good for us as a people to attempt to deal with the pain and alienation she reveals to us here.

> In Sisterhood,
> Alice

.   .   .

A Consciousness Raising Paper for Black Black Women and Whiter Black Women Who Wish to Struggle Together Over the "Dirty Little 'Secret'" of Color in African-American Life

Equally important, however [to "What it is, brother?"], is "What it is, sister?" No one dares to utter the plight of her reality, not even my black sisters themselves. But what it is, is the great cannon of cruel racism directed toward the black black woman by the black middle class. The black middle class has for generations excluded the black black woman from the mainstream of black middle-class society, and it has, by its discrimination against her, induced in itself a divisive cancer that has chopped the black race in this country into polarized sections; consequently the black middle class has devoured its own soul and is doomed, a large number of black working class people believe, to extinction.

What it is, is an insanity that has helped whites turn blacks on themselves and that has caused the black middle class to claw itself into a form of psychic annihilation.

Thus the black working class is beginning to ask itself the questions: "What is a people that props itself up on the color of its skin? And what is a people that excludes the womb-source of its own genetic heritage?" For certainly every Afro-American is descended from a black black woman. What then can be the destiny of a people that pampers and cherishes the blood of the white slaveholder who maimed and degraded their female ancestor? What can be the future of a class of descendants of slaves that implicitly gives slaveholders greater honor than the African women they enslaved? What can be the end of a class that pretends to honor blackness while secretly despising working class blackskinned women whose faces reveal no trace of white blood?

— *Trellie Jeffers,*
"*The Black Black Woman and*
the Black Middle Class,"
THE BLACK SCHOLAR

For many years I pondered Jeffers's statement, then turned to black literature, because it is so very instructive, to see whether it had support. I began with three nineteenth-century novels by black women, as background, and this is what I found.

In the first novel one character says to another: "But if you'd seed them putty white hands of hern you'd never think she kept her own house, let 'lone anybody else's.

"My! but she's putty. Beautiful long hair comes way down

her back: putty blue eyes, an' jez ez white as anybody in dis place. . . ."

In the second novel, it goes like this:

"Meg Randal opened wide a pair of lovely dark eyes and raised two small, white hands in surprise.

"Ethel sat down and took one of Meg's perfect little hands in her own. Meg's hand was her one source of pride, and it would almost seem as if she were justified in this pride. Such a delicate, white, slender, dimpled hand it was!"

In the third novel:

"Her dress was plain black, with white chiffon at the neck and wrists, and on her breast a large bunch of 'Jack' roses was fastened. . . . Tall and fair, with hair of a golden cast, aquiline nose, rosebud mouth, soft brown eyes veiled by long, dark lashes which swept her cheek, just now covered with a delicate rose flush, she burst upon them—a combination of 'queen rose and lily in one.' "

The novels quoted from are: *Iola LeRoy, Or Shadows Uplifted,* by Frances Ellen Watkins Harper, published in 1895; *Megda,* by Emma Dunham Kelly, published in 1891; and *Contending Forces,* by Pauline E. Hopkins, published in 1900.

Photographs of the novelists show them to be identifiably "colored" if not literally black. Why are their black heroines depicted as white—and non-working class? After all, Frances Watkins Harper—the most notable of these writers—did not spend most of her time with white-skinned, middle-class black women; instead, she worked as a lecturer and teacher among the black- and brown-skinned freed people during Reconstruction, in the briefly "liberated" South.

She wrote of the women:

I know of girls from sixteen to twenty-two who iron till midnight that they may come to school in the day. Some of our scholars, aged about nineteen, living about thirty miles off, rented land, ploughed, planted, and then sold their cotton, in order to come to us. A woman near me, urged her husband to go in debt five hundred dollars for a home, as titles to the land they had built on were insecure, and she said to me, "We have five years to pay it in, and I shall begin today to do it, if life be spared. I will make a hundred dollars at washing, for I have done it." Yet they have seven little children to feed, clothe and educate. In the field the women receive the same wages as the men, and are often preferred, clearing the land, hoeing, or picking cotton, with equal ability.

No "queen rose and lily in one" here. No "delicate white hands." Brown hands, and black hands, all—if not because of genetics, then because of the work. Yet no nineteenth-century black novelist, female or male, wrote novels about these women.

Indeed, the very first novel by an African-American to be published, *Clotelle, Or The Colored Heroine*, by William Wells Brown, 1867, in the very first paragraph, not only offers black womanhood as indistinguishable, physically, from white, but also slanders, generally, the black woman's character:

For many years the South has been noted for its beautiful Quadroon [one-fourth black and capable of passing as white] women. Bottles of ink, and reams of paper, have been used to portray the "finely-cut and well-moulded features," the "splendid forms, the fascinating smiles," and "accomplished manners" of these impassioned and voluptuous daughters of the two races — the unlawful product of the crime of human bondage. When we take into consideration the fact that no safeguard was ever thrown around virtue, and no inducement held out to slave-women to be pure and chaste, we will not be surprised when told that immorality pervades the domestic circle in the cities and towns of the South to an extent unknown in the Northern States. Many a planter's wife has dragged out a miserable existence, with an aching heart, at seeing her place in her husband's affections usurped by the unadorned beauty and captivating smiles of her waiting maid. *Indeed, the greater portion of the colored women, in the days of slavery, had no greater aspiration than that of becoming the finely-dressed mistress of some white man* [my italics].

Notice how adroitly Brown places the responsibility for rape, child abuse, incest, and other "immoralities" squarely on the shoulders of the persons least responsible for them, being enslaved and powerless; whom he sets up for this calumny by describing them as "voluptuous" and "impassioned."

It is unlikely that a raped, enslaved servant to a planter's wife assumed, because of this rape, that she had "usurped" the wife's place in the rapist's "affections." Brown obviously intended blacks to feel proud of the insulting "attentions" of the rapist and victorious because of the suffering of the wife. In fact, Brown would have us believe the enslaved woman was as powerful as the enslaver, since with her smile she "captivate[d]," i.e. captured, him, just as he captured her with his gun and his laws.

Nor does Brown consider the millions of raped, enslaved African women who had no likelihood whatsoever of becoming "finely-dressed," or ever attaining "mistress" status.

"Bottles of ink, reams of paper . . ." he says. But who were these writers? They were, in the seventeenth, eighteenth, and nineteenth centuries, with few exceptions, white men, writing out their own sadistic fantasies about black women, and describing—in lurid detail—their own perverse sexual preferences where enslaved women were concerned. These feverishly imagined "quadroon" women were not real, and had more to do with the way white men *chose* to perceive black women than the way black men perceived them or black women perceived themselves.

And yet, Brown, our first black novelist,* in this, our first black novel, gives us scene after scene and crisis after crisis in which pale, fragile blondes and brunettes—burdened by the weight of their alleged "color"—grapple with the tedium of slave life—always involved with some faithless white man or other, and rarely doing anything resembling ordinary slave work.

The three black women novelists of the nineteenth century turned away from their own *selves* in depicting "black woman-hood," and followed a black man's interpretation of white male writers' fantasies. Consequently, as late as 1929 it was unheard of for a very dark-skinned woman to appear in a novel unless it was clear she was to be recognized as a problem or a joke. As is the case of Emma Lou in Wallace Thurman's *The Blacker the Berry*, published in 1929, which explored the very real trials of a black black woman in a white and a color-struck black society.

"She should have been a boy, then color of skin wouldn't have mattered so much, for wasn't her mother always saying that a black boy would get along, but that a black girl would never know anything but sorrow and disappointment?"

The heroine of this novel thinks of her black color as something unnatural, even demonic. Yet for millions of quite contented women, here and in Africa, black skin is the most natural, *un*demonic thing in the world.

---

*The recent discovery of Harriet E. Wilson's 1859 novel, *Our Nig*, which predates Brown's novel by several years, makes her our first known black novelist. Her story is also, interestingly, about the life of a woman of biracial parents: the mother white, the father black. However, possession of a lighter skin fails to exalt her condition as a black indentured servant in a hostile white, middle-class Northern household before the Civil War.

Some readers consider Charles Chesnutt's story "The Wife of His Youth," 1899, an example of a nineteenth-century effort at writing realistically about a black black woman. But this story, of a near-white former slave who falls in love with a woman younger and whiter-looking than he, and whose plans for marriage with her are thwarted by the appearance of an earlier wife, older and blacker than he, proves the point. "The wife of his youth" is perceived by the narrator and others in the tale as both a problem *and* a joke. Though he acknowledges this earlier wife before his present friends, our hero's racial philosophy is summed up neatly, by Chesnutt, in this way:

> "I have no race prejudice," he would say, "but we people of mixed blood are ground between the upper and the nether millstone. Our fate lies between absorption by the white race *and extinction in the black* [my italics]. The one doesn't want us yet, but may take us in time. The other would welcome us, but it would be for us a backward step. 'With malice towards none, with charity for all,' we must do the best we can for ourselves and those who are to follow. Self-preservation is the first law of nature."

Fortunately, "the wife of his youth" is too old to bear children to represent this "extinction," this "backward" step.

It is interesting to note the changes wrought in the male hero of William Wells Brown's novel over the course of its several versions. In the first version he is white-skinned, even as Brown was himself (his father was white, his mother "mulatta") and capable of passing. In the final version he is black-skinned, though with *straight* black hair. The heroine, however, remains fair, and never becomes darker than a "dark" European.

Viz. ". . . there was nothing in the appearance of Clotelle

to indicate that a drop of African blood coursed through her veins, except, perhaps, the slight wave of her hair, and the scarcely perceptible brunettish tinge upon the countenance. She passed as a rebel lady. . . ."

One reason the novels of nineteenth-century black authors abound with white-skinned women characters is that most readers of novels in the nineteenth century were white people: white people who then, as, more often than not, now, could identify human feeling, humanness, only if it came in a white or near-white body. And although black men could be depicted as literally black and still be considered men (since dark *is* masculine to the Euro-American mind), the black-skinned woman, being dark and female, must perforce be whitened, since "fairness" was and is the standard of Euro-American femininity.

Of course in the nineteenth century, few of the former slaves could read at all, having been denied literacy under penalty of law, and certainly could not hope to struggle through a novel, however true it might have been to their experience. It is understandable that writers wrote to the capacities of the audience at hand. Yet their depictions of themselves and black people as whiter than we are has led to a crippling of the imagination and of truth itself for which we pay dearly—in anger, hurt, envy, and misunderstanding—to this day.

Fortunately, for us, there came a black woman writer who did not view her black women characters through the eyes of men, black or white, and it is in her work—coming after Brown, Watkins, Kelly, and Hopkins in the nineteenth century, and after Fauset, Larsen, and Toomer in the 1920s (writers who still depicted black women as fair-skinned, if not actually *white-skinned*; and in other ways atypical)—that black women begin to emerge naturally in all the colors in which they exist, predominantly brown and black, and culturally African-American. Though Janie Crawford, Zora Neale Hurston's best-known heroine, is described as being light of skin and feathery of hair, as soon as she opens her mouth we know who and what she is, and her hands, though genetically "light," are brown from the labor she shares with other blacks, from whom she is not, in fact, separate, though all three of her husbands attempt to convince her that she is.

Many dark-skinned black women find it hard to identify with Janie Crawford and speak disparagingly of her "mulatto privileges." "Privileges" that stem from being worshiped for her color and hair, and being placed—by her color-struck husbands —above other black women while not being permitted to speak in public because her looks are supposed to say it all.

And, for the black man—if we judge by our literature and too often, unfortunately, by reality—the white-looking woman's looks *do* say it all. But what do these "looks" in fact say? For the dark-skinned black woman it comes as a series of disappointments and embarrassments that the wives of virtually all black leaders (including Marcus Garvey!) appear to have been chosen for the nearness of their complexions to white alone. It is true that Frederick Douglass's first wife was black-skinned, but he managed to hide most of her activity in his life. According to research done by Sylvia Lyons Render, Annie Murray Douglass sewed the very sailor suit Douglass escaped from slavery wearing, yet nowhere does he give her adequate credit for her help. His second wife, the wife he chose in freedom, was white; this marriage continued a pattern that began in the days of slavery, when white was right and the octoroon or quadroon offspring of a raped black or mulatto mother was the next best thing to white. A look at the photographs of the women chosen by our male leaders is, in many ways, chilling if you are a black-skinned woman. (And this "chilling" experience is one that the dark-skinned black woman can hardly escape having in these times of black pictorial history.*) Because it is apparent that though they may have consciously affirmed blackness in the abstract and for others, for themselves light remained right. Only Malcolm X, among our recent male leaders, chose to affirm, by publicly loving and marrying her, a black black woman. And it is this, no less than his "public" politics, that accounts for the respect black people, and especially women, had for him, and this that makes him radical and revolutionary, in a way few of our other black male leaders are.

Black black women are not supposed to notice these things. But to tell the truth (and why shouldn't we? We may be living our last months on earth), this is often *all* we notice. We are told such things are not "serious" and not "political" and mean nothing to the black liberation struggle. And some of us, after all, marry white men; who are we to "complain"? But no black woman pursues and proposes to octoroon or quadroon or white men as a matter of female prerogative; the patriarchal society in

*For instance, a few years ago I was invited to address a conference in Atlanta called "The Southern Woman: From Myth to Modern Times." When I received the brochure I felt sick: on the cover, yes indeed, there was a tiny black woman's head, sandwiched between a white woman's head (on top, of course) and an Asian woman's head (on the bottom). On page three or four, a larger picture of an exquisitely dressed black black woman appeared. In between, however, and completely overwhelming these two, was picture after picture of white women. How could I possibly address such a tokenist crowd? Once in Atlanta, I expressed my feeling to one of the black women on the committee that had invited me (a yellow-skinned, wonderfully funny woman who kept us both in giggles), and she dragged me around the floor of the Atlanta Historical Society, where I was scheduled to speak. Pointing to the same women's pictures on the walls that had been printed in the brochure, she said: "This one is black, and this one; that one, and all those over there." "All those over there" referred to a photograph of the Atlanta Ladies' Auxiliary, circa 1912, all wives of Atlanta's leading black men. Only one of the dozen or so women could pass, in the photograph, for black, and she might have been white, with a tan. I could not resist commenting on the hundred years of struggle that went into "integrating" places like the Atlanta Historical Society, only to be unable, at struggle's end, to tell the difference.

which we live does not permit it. The man chooses; frequently with the same perceptivity with which he chooses a toy.

Every black man in *Their Eyes Were Watching God* lusts after Janie Crawford. They lust after her color and her long hair, never once considering the pain her mother and grandmother (one raped by a white man, one by a black) must have endured to "pass along" these qualities to her. Never once thinking of Janie's isolation because of looks she did not choose, or of her confusion when she realizes that the same men who idolize her looks are capable of totally separating her looks from her self. These were all back-country folk, and they wouldn't have thought of it in these terms, but their true interest in Janie is sadistic and pornographic, just as that of the white men of the time would have been. And I think this is one of the reasons Hurston (with her usual attention to the difference between what black folks said and what they meant) made her character so "fair": to point this out to us.

The first few times I read *Their Eyes* I managed to block the significance of the scene in chapter seventeen in which TeaCake beats Janie. Feminists have often flagged my attention to it, but I always explained it as simply a "mistake" on Hurston's part. In truth, I missed the point entirely of what happened, and what happened provides one of the most important insights in the book.

As the Hurston reader will recall, TeaCake is very jealous of Janie where Mrs. Turner's brother—he of light skin and flyaway hair—is concerned. There is no reason for this, as Janie time and again insists. One reason TeaCake is jealous is because it is so unusual for a woman as light and well-to-do as Janie to be with a man as poor and black as he is. Not because all the light-skinned women chase after and propose to light-skinned men, but because both light- and dark-skinned men chase after and propose to light-skinned women. Since the light-skinned men generally have more education than the blacker men, and better jobs (morticians to this day in the South are generally light-skinned blacks, as are the colored doctors and insurance men), they have the advantage of color, class, and gainful employment, and so, secure the "prizes" light-skinned women represent to them. Like all "prizes" the women are put on display and warned not to get themselves dirty. (Other black black people often being this "dirt.") Their resemblance to the white man's "prize," i.e., the white woman—whom they resemble largely because of rape (and I submit that any sexual intercourse between a free man and a human being he owns or controls is rape)—must be maintained at all times.

Unlike Janie's first two husbands, TeaCake has discovered that his "prize" is as attractive dirty as she is clean and supports her in her determination to dress, speak, and act as she likes. But he must still show his male friends, and the ubiquitous Mrs. Turner, who wishes to bring Janie and her brother together (light belongs to light, in her mind), that his ownership is intact. When Mrs. Turner brings her brother over and introduces him, TeaCake has a "brainstorm." Before the week is over, he has "whipped" Janie.

He whips her not, Hurston writes, "because her behavior justified his jealousy, but it relieved that awful fear inside him. Being able to whip her reassured him in possession. No brutal beating at all. He just slapped her around a bit to show he was boss. Everybody talked about it next day in the fields. It aroused a sort of envy in both men and women. The way he petted and pampered her as if those two or three face slaps had nearly killed her made the women see visions and the helpless way she hung on him made men dream dreams."

An astute reader would realize that this is the real reason TeaCake is killed by Janie in the end. Or, rather, this is the reason Hurston *permits* Janie to kill TeaCake in the end. For all her "helpless" hanging on him, Janie knows she has been publicly humiliated, and though she acts the role of battered wife (from what I read coming out of battered women's shelters, the majority of such batterings end in sex and the total submission —"hanging on helplessly"—of the wife) her developing consciousness of self does not stop at that point. She could hardly enjoy knowing her beating becomes "visions" for other women —who would have to imagine themselves light and long-haired, like Janie, to "enjoy" them—and "dreams," i.e., sexual fantasies, for TeaCake's male friends.

> "TeaCake, you sho is a lucky man," Sop-de-Bottom told him. "Uh person can see every place you hit her. Ah bet she never raised her hand tuh hit yuh back, neither. Take some uh dese ol' rusty black women and dey would fight yuh all night long and next day nobody couldn't tell you ever hit'em. Dat's de reason Ah done quit beating mah women. You can't make no mark on'em at all. *Lawd! wouldn't Ah love tuh whip uh tender woman lak Janie! Ah bet she don't even holler. She jus' cries, eh TeaCake?"* [My italics]
> "Dat's right."
> "See dat! Mah woman would spread her lungs all over Palm Beach County, let alone knock out mah jaw teeth. You don't know dat woman uh mine. She got ninety-nine rows uh jaw teeth and git her good and mad, she'll wade through solid rock up to her hip pockets."
> [To which TeaCake replies:]
> "Mah Janie is uh high time woman and uster things. Ah didn't git her outa de middle uh de road."

What is really being said here?
What is being said is this: that in choosing the "fair,"

white-looking woman, the black man assumes he is choosing a weak woman. A woman he can own, a woman he can beat, can enjoy beating, can *exhibit* as a woman beaten; in short, a "conquered" woman who will not cry out, and will certainly not fight back. And why? Because she is a lady, like the white man's wife, who is also beaten (the slaves knew, the servants knew, the maid always knew because she doctored the bruises) but who has been trained to suffer in silence, even to pretend to enjoy sex better afterward, because her husband obviously does. A masochist.

And who is being rejected? Those women "out of the middle of the road"? Well, Harriet Tubman, for one, Sojourner Truth, Mary McLeod Bethune, Shirley Chisholm. Ruby McCullom, Assata Shakur, Joan Little, and Dessie "Rashida" Woods. You who are black-skinned and fighting and screaming through the solid rock of America up to your hip pockets every day since you arrived, and me, who treasures every ninety-nine rows of my jaw teeth, because they are all I have to chew my way through this world.

That black men choose light and white women is not the women's fault, any more than it was their fault they were chosen as concubines to rich plantation owners during slavery. Nobody seems to choose big, strong, *fighting* light or white women (and these have existed right along with those who could be beaten). Though there used to be a saying among black men that *fat* white women are best because the bigger they are the more whiteness there is to love, this is still in the realm of ownership, of "prize." And any woman who settles for being owned, for being a "prize," is more to be struggled with than blamed.

We are sisters of the same mother, but we have been separated—though put to much the same use—by different fathers. In the novels of Frank Yerby, a wildly successful black writer, you see us: the whiter-skinned black woman placed above the blacker as the white man's mistress or the black man's "love." The blacker woman, when not preparing the whiter woman for sex, marriage, or romance, simply raped. Put to work in the fields. Stuck in the kitchen. Raising everybody's white and yellow and brown and black kids. Or knocking the overseer down, or cutting the master's throat. But never desired or romantically loved, because she does not care for "aesthetic" suffering. Sexual titillation is out, because when you rape her the bruises don't show so readily, and besides, she lets you know she hates your guts, goes for your balls with her knees, and calls you the slime-covered creep you are until you knock her out.

Perhaps one problem has been that so many of our leaders (and writers) have not been black-skinned themselves. Think of Brown, who could pass; Chesnutt, who could and did pass; Toomer, who passed with a vengeance; Hughes, who could pass (when young) as a Mexican; Booker T. Washington, John Hope, James Weldon Johnson, Douglass, Du Bois, Bontemps, Larsen, Wright, Himes, Yerby . . . all very different in appearance from, say, Wallace Thurman, who was drawn to write about a black black woman because he was so black himself, and blackness was a problem for him among other blacks lighter than he, as it was among whites. We can continue to respect and love many of these writers, and treasure what they wrote because we understand *America;* but we must be wary of their depictions of black women because we understand ourselves.

Suppose you have a daughter, and she is black-skinned, and she is enrolled in African-American studies at, for instance, Harvard. She is in an overwhelmingly white setting and required to try to see herself as half a dozen white-looking black women in the nineteenth century, and as at least two dozen white and yellow women in the early twentieth. There will be an occasional black- or brown-skinned woman in the texts, but she will be— well, in Brown's novel, for example, let us take a look. After pages and pages of the tribulations of white-looking Clotelle (and her mother and sister before her), on the last page we encounter a mulatta named (of course) Dinah.

Here is the exchange between Clotelle, the white-looking octoroon, who speaks clear, precise English, and Dinah, who is brown, cannot pass, and talks "black."

"I see that your husband has lost one of his hands: did he lose it in the war?" asks Clotelle.

. "Oh no, missus," said Dinah. "When dey was taken all de men, black and white, to put in de army, dey cotched my ole man too, and took him long wid'em. So you see, he said he'd die afore he'd shoot at de Yanks. So you see, missus, Jimmy jes took and lay his left han' on a log, and chop it off wid de hatchet. Den, you see, dey let him go, an' he come home. You see, missus, my Jimmy is a free man: he was born free, an' he bought me, an' pay fifteen hundred dollars for me."

[Brown continues:]

It was true that Jim had purchased his wife; nor had he forgotten the fact, as was shown a day or two after, while in conversation with her. The woman, like many of her sex [though obviously not like the "missus," Clotelle], was an inveterate scold, and Jim had but one way to govern her tongue. "Shet your mouf, madam, an' hole your tongue," said Jim, after his wife had scolded and sputtered away for some minutes. "Shet your mouf dis minit, I say: You shan't stan' dar, an' talk to me in dat way. I bought you, an' paid my money fer you, an' I ain't gwine ter let you sase me in dat way. Shet your mouf dis minit: ef you don't I'll sell you; fore God I will. Shet up, I say, or I'll sell you." This had the desired effect, and settled Dinah for the day.

Is it this same fear of being "sold" that keeps black women silent, one wonders, imagining—as apparently Brown could not —the horrifying impact of these words on a woman formerly sold only by whites. And yet, our silence has not saved us from being sold, as "Dinah" herself is "sold"—as a "scold" and object of ridicule *and sale* to the readers of Brown's day.

Clotelle, Iola LeRoy, and Megda are actually "sold" as pitilessly as Dinah, though their "sale"—into the structured colorism of the black middle class (which generations later Janie Crawford exposes and escapes)—is camouflaged by the promise of "upward" mobility, i.e., proximity to, imitation of, and eventual merger with (or, as Chesnutt wrote, "absorption into") the white middle class.

No wonder "black" nineteenth-century heroines seem so weak and boring! They are prisoners of a fatal social vision. Their destination—total extinction as blacks within, at most, two generations—is preordained. One imagines their grandchildren saying—as the white grandchildren of American Indians do, while adding another feather to their cowboy hats—"I'm not prejudiced against those people, I'm one-twelfth (Indian) (black) myself."

In his landmark essay "Of the Dawn of Freedom," 1903, W. E. B. Du Bois wrote that "the problem of the twentieth century is the problem of the color-line—the relation of the darker to the lighter races of men in Asia and Africa, in America and the islands of the sea. It was a phase of this problem that caused the Civil War. . . ." This is a true statement, but it is a man's vision. That is to say, it sees clearer across seas than across the table or the street. Particularly it omits what is happening within the family, "the race," at home; a family also capable of *civil* war.

In paraphrase of this statement I would say that the problem of the twenty-first century will still be the problem of the color line, not only "the relation of the darker to the lighter races of men [sic] in Asia and Africa, in America and the islands of the sea," but the relations between the darker and the lighter people of the same races, and of the women who represent both dark and light within each race. It is our "familial" relations with each other in America that we need to scrutinize. And it is the whole family, rather than the dark or the light, that must be affirmed.

Light- and white-skinned black women will lose their only link to rebellion against white America if they cut themselves off from the black black woman. Their children will have no hip pockets in which to keep their weapons, no teeth with which to chew up racist laws. And black black women will lose the full meaning of their history in America (as well as the humor, love, and support of good sisters) if they see light and white black women only as extensions of white and black male oppression, while allowing themselves to be made ashamed of their own strength and fighting spirit: that fighting spirit that is our birthright, and, for some of us, our "rusty black" joy.

As black women, we have been poorly prepared to cherish what should matter most to us. Our models in literature and life have been, for the most part, devastating. Even when we wish it, we are not always able to save ourselves for future generations: not our spiritual selves, not our physical characteristics. (In the past, in our literature—and in life too—the birth of a "golden" child to a dark mother has been perceived as a cause for special celebration. But was it? So much of the mother was obliterated, so much changed, in the child, whose birth as often as not was by her unplanned.) But perhaps we *can* learn something, even from the discouraging models of earlier centuries and our own time. Perhaps black women who are writers in the twenty-first century will present a fuller picture of the multiplicity of oppression—and of struggle. Racism, sexism, classism, and colorism will be very much a part of their consciousness. They will have the wonderful novels of black African women to read—Buchi Emecheta, Ama Ata Aidoo, Bessie Head, and others—as nineteenth-century black women did not. They will have a record of the struggles of our own times. They will not think of other women with envy, hatred, or adulation because they are "prizes." They will not wish to be prizes themselves. How men want them to look, act, speak, dress, acquiesce in beatings and rape will mean nothing whatsoever to them. They will, in fact, spend a lot of time talking to each other, and smiling. Women of all colors will be able to turn their full energies on the restoration of the planet, as they can't now because they're tied up with all this other stuff: divisions, resentments, old hurts, charges and countercharges. And talk about the need for teeth and hip pockets then! Women who are writers in the twenty-first century will undoubtedly praise every one.

In any case, the duty of the writer is not to be tricked, seduced, or goaded into verifying by imitation or even rebuttal, other people's fantasies. In an oppressive society it may well be that *all* fantasies indulged in by the oppressor are destructive to the oppressed. To become involved in them in any way at all is, at the very least, to lose time defining yourself.

To isolate the fantasy we must cleave to reality, to what *we* know, *we* feel, *we* think of life. Trusting our own experience and our own lives; embracing both the dark self and the light.

1982

. . . .

LOOKING TO THE SIDE,

AND BACK

From the time I was two years old, until I was six, my best friend was a little girl exactly my age, whose name was Cassie Mae Terrell. Everyone called her "Sister." Sister Terrell. We *looked* like sisters: with gleaming brown skin and bright dark eyes— with plenty of shining, springy hair, which our mothers decorated with large satin bows. . . . Sister Terrell and I used to spend the night at each other's house, and we would giggle half the night away.

When I was six, Sister and her family moved to New Jersey, and I suffered my first separation trauma. I tried to encourage my father to move to New Jersey, but he wouldn't. For a long time I held him responsible, poor man, for my loss of Sister Terrell—whom I was not to see again for twenty years. And whom I didn't forget for a single year.

Throughout grade school, high school, and college, I had close friends like Sister Terrell. I loved them deeply and loyally

—and always with the fear that they'd be taken away. And in so many cases, they were. When next I saw Sister Terrell, for example, she had been married for years to a man who literally kept her from eating. So that when her family finally went to rescue her, she was so weak and malnourished they had to carry her off in their arms. She was in this condition when I saw her again. Gone the gleaming skin and bright dark eyes. Gone the spring from her plentiful hair—in fact, gone a good bit of the plentiful hair.

One reason I had loved her was that I love, simply *love*, to giggle, and love to *hear* giggling. And Sister Terrell, at five and six, was an incomparable giggler. Her giggle was one of the best sounds I ever heard in the world. How could anyone, for any reason, wish to stop it?

And yet—she giggled no more.

On my desk there is a picture of me when I was six—dauntless eyes, springy hair, optimistic satin bow and all—and I look at it often; I realize I am always trying to keep faith with the child I was. The child I was thought the women in our local church held together the world. Often kind beyond understanding, sometimes shrewish, stubborn, willfully obtuse, but always *there*, with their dimes and quarters, their spotless children and beloved husbands, building up the church, first, and the local school, second, for the benefit of the community. The child that I was rarely saw individualistic behavior, and when I did see it, for a long time I could understand it only as rejection of community, rather than the self-affirmation it very often was.

The men in my immediate community seemed to love and appreciate their wives; and if the wife had more initiative and energy than the husband, this was not held against her. My father loved my mother's spunk and her inability to lie when asked a direct question. He was himself innately easygoing and disinclined to waste any part of life in argument, and with a mind that easily turned any question asked of him into a "story."

This is what I remember; but surely this memory is too good to be entirely true.

While I was in college I became fascinated by the way women I knew remained loyal to men who had long since ceased being loyal to them, or even thought about being loyal to them. Many black women, myself among them, assumed we had a right to be loved and treated well. We did not, fortunately, limit ourselves to any category or group, even if we were inclined to do so. We wanted love, respect, admiration, and moral support. We did not spurn getting these things wherever they could be found. Many black women, however, were reduced to the condition of grumbling after some anonymous black man on the street as he strolled along beside what he loved, respected, admired, and sometimes supported—and it was often not a woman, and very often not black.

Many of these women find themselves hating lesbians because in a sense the lesbian has "gotten away clean." She isn't concerned about *what* black men do; she can even view some of their behavior as amusing, if absurd—and, in fact, frequently and unfortunately, copies it. There is a hatred of women of color who marry or establish relationships with white men because in addition to the very real historical weight such unions must bear, there is just a general resentment of unformulaic joy. A rigidity has set in; the same vital instinct to "preserve the race and culture" from dilution through intermarriage—or, where lesbians are concerned, through extinction—causes a narrowing of the range of choice. The result is that only in great stress—and often deliberately brutal isolation—are a hundred somewhat stunted flowers allowed to bloom; while the one flower that is truly desired (the married, black, heterosexual couple) is often watered with the tears of conformity and compromise—and is, consequently, unhealthy.

In 1973 I was keynote speaker at a symposium at Radcliffe called "The Black Woman: Myths and Realities." It was to that gathering of the *crème de la crème* of black educated women in America (some two hundred) that I delivered a speech I'd written especially for black women, called "In Search of Our Mothers' Gardens." It is largely about the tenacity of the artistic spirit among us, from a historical perspective. Many women wept, they later told me, as I read it, and they gave me, in the words of the *Radcliffe Quarterly,* which later published the essay, "a tumultuous standing ovation."

Later there was a panel discussion and, still high from my speech, I looked forward to an exchange among all of us that would be more than a sharing of history and survivalist emotion.

June Jordan and I were sitting together in the audience. Four or five women were on stage. One was a psychologist, one a well-known actress, one a Civil Rights lawyer. Every one was *some*thing. I was so excited!

·   June and I had often talked between ourselves about the plight of young black women who were killing themselves at an alarming (to us) rate. We thought *this* should be brought before our sisters. In fact, the week before, I had visited Sarah Lawrence (where I was at the time a member-of-the-board-of-trustees impersonator) and had been told in grisly detail of the suicide of one young woman. She had been ridiculed by the black men on campus because she dated white guys (meanwhile, these black guys dated white girls and each other). She couldn't take it. She killed herself. That *same* week, a young Oriental girl had jumped to her death from a window at Radcliffe. And from all sides I had been hearing how impossible it was becoming to be a young woman of color. It appeared that any kind of noncon-formity was not permitted.

What occurred when June and I brought all this up, how-ever, was nothing short of incredible. There was *no* response whatsoever to the increased suicide rate among young women of color. Instead, we were treated to a lecture on the black woman's responsibilities to the black man. I will never forget my sense of horror and betrayal when one of the panelists said to me (and to the rest of that august body of black women gathered there): "The responsibility of the black woman is to support the black man; *whatever* he does."

It occurred to me that my neck could be at that minute under some man's heel, and this woman would stroll by and say, "Right on."

I burst into the loudest tears I've ever shed. And though I soon dried my face, I didn't stop crying inside for . . . Maybe I haven't stopped yet. But that's okay; what I'm crying about is worth it.

But a really fascinating thing happened around my crying: many of the women blamed me for crying! I couldn't believe it. They came over to me, one or two at a time, and said:

"I understand what you are trying to say . . ." (I wasn't *trying*, I muttered through clenched teeth, I *said* it; you just didn't listen.) "but don't let it *get* to you!"

Or: "Why would you let *anyone* make you cry?!"

Not *one* of them *ever* said a word about why young women of color were killing themselves. They could take the black woman as invincible, as she was portrayed to some extent in my speech (what they *heard* was the invincible part), but there was no sympathy for struggle that ended in defeat. Which meant there was no sympathy for struggle itself—only for "winning."

I was reminded of something that had puzzled me about

the response of black people to Movement people in the South. During the seven years I lived in Mississippi, I never knew a Movement person (and I include myself) who wasn't damaged in some way from having to put her or his life, principles, children, on the line over long, stressful periods. And this is only natural. But there was a way in which the black community could not look at this. I remember a young boy who was shot through the neck by racist whites, and almost died. When he recovered, he was the same gentle, sweet boy he'd always been, but he hated white people, which at that time didn't fit in with black people's superior notion of themselves as people who could consistently turn the other cheek. Nobody ever really tried to incorporate the new reality of this boy's life. When they spoke of him it was as if his life stopped just before the shot.

I knew a young girl who "desegregated" the local white high school in her small town. No one, except her teachers, spoke to her *for four years*. There was one white guy—whom she spoke of with contempt—who left love notes in her locker. This girl suffered acute anxiety; so that when she dragged herself home from school every day, she went to bed, and stayed there until the next morning, when she walked off, ramrod straight, to school. Even her parents talked only about the bravery, never about the cost.

It was at the Radcliffe symposium that I saw that black women are more loyal to black men than they are to themselves, a dangerous state of affairs that has its logical end in self-destructive behavior.

But I also learned something else:

The same panelist who would not address the suicide rate of young women of color also took the opportunity to tell me what she thought my "problem" was. Since I spoke so much of my mother, she said my problem was that I was "trying to 'carry' my mother, and the weight is too heavy."

June, who was sitting beside me, and who was angry but not embarrassed by my tears, put her arms around me and said:

"But why shouldn't you carry your mother; she carried *you*, didn't she?"

That is perfection in a short response.

I had to giggle. And the giggle and the tears and the holding and the sanctioning of responsibility to those we love and those who have loved us is what I know will see us through.

1979

· · · · · · · · ·

TO THE BLACK SCHOLAR

[I wrote the following memo to the editors of the *Black Scholar* in response to an article that appeared in the 1979 March/April issue written by Dr. Robert Staples and titled "The Myth of Black Macho: A Response to Angry Black Feminists." The editors considered the memo both too "personal" and too "hysterical" to publish. They suggested change, and I withdrew it.]

· · ·

It will not do any good—and is a waste of time—to attack Ntozake Shangé and Michele Wallace, since they are not, in fact, attacking you. They are affirming themselves and remarking on the general condition of black life as they know it, which they are entitled to do, middle-class black women or not. Whatever flaws exist in their vision or in their works (and there are some), there is also a sizable element of truth that black women and men all over the country recognize. (Not simply us "angry black feminists" who are in the women's movement anyway, according to Staples, not because we are intelligent, sensitive, and self-respecting, but because we have been called to the aid of white feminists to put black males "in their place." A sad and scurrilous insult to black women liberationists the world over, and one designed, in this essay, to produce more heat than light.) That element of truth is that, because of sexism (as much as racism, generally, and capitalism, yes) black women and men (who, despite all "isms," own their own souls, I hope) are at a crisis in their relationship with each other. There *is* hatred, dislike, distrust between us. Should this continue, we can say good-bye to the black peoplehood our myths and legends, struggles and triumphs have promised us.

Instead of arguing, *at once*, about whether there is or is not sexism in the black community (and how could our community possibly be different from every other in that one respect), look around you. Look at the black men and women that you know. Look at your family. Look at your brothers—and their wives. Look at your sisters—and their husbands. Look at all those relatives you admire who are not tied up this way. Look at the children. "Strong black women are not perceived as feminine in this culture." Are your daughters weak? Do your sons think the color black itself too "strong" to be feminine? What does this mean? Look at what we are told: We are told, for example, that many black women are *in fact* alone and unhappy. Yet Shangé and Wallace are criticized for saying we should learn to enjoy it.

Look hard at yourself. Look hard at how you feel, really, about the people among whom fate so indifferently dropped you. Would you feel better as someone else? Look at what we actually *do* to each other. Look at what we actually *say*. Look about you as if there were no white people about, whom you have been wishing to impress. Know that if we fail to impress *each other*, we've lost something precious that we once had.

Now you are in good condition to see Ntozake Shangé's play.* Excellent shape to hoist a beer (you always need something, watching relatives) and read Michele Wallace's book. Try not to think how successful they are. Try to blot out how much money Shangé has made. Don't be pissed off at how beautifully she writes, or with what courage and vulnerability. Resist the temptation to blame her for all those audiences from Marin and Scarsdale. Remember if you can that she didn't know they were coming.

Think big.

We have been a People.
What are we now?
And for how long?

Having said this, and having, I hope, made it clear that I do not find the Staples article at all useful, except as a reminder of how far, still, we have to go (apparently the *whole* way), let me add to it.

One of my own great weaknesses, which I am beginning to recognize more clearly than ever around the Michele Wallace book, is a deep reluctance to criticize other black women. I am much more comfortable praising them. Surely there is no other group more praiseworthy, but on the other hand, no other group is more deserving of justice, and good criticism must be, I think, simple justice.

In Michele Wallace's book, there are many good things, things that (though not as original as she thinks) can be very helpful to us, if we will *hear* them. For example, it is really true that unless you are very old and fat, you risk being both insulted

For Colored Girls Who Have Considered Suicide, When the Rainbow Is Enuf

and assaulted in any black ghetto neighborhood in America. Black men speak to us like dogs: "Hey, Brown Coat!" "Come here, Black Jacket!" "Hey, girl! Cutie! Won't speak, huh?! What you need is a good fucking! Bitch." And these were all things addressed to me while attempting to get my shopping done in the past two days. Try respecting people who talk to you like that. Look at what we are laughing at on television: it is true, as Wallace points out, that black men made it painfully clear that, as Redd Foxx articulated it, they would rather have a Raquel Welch in the bedroom than a Shirley Chisholm in the White House. What could be more sexist and more pathetic? And look at the ignorance of black men about black women. Though black women have religiously read every black male writer that came down the pike (usually presenting black females as witches and warlocks), few black men have thought it of any interest at all to read black women. As far as they're concerned, they have the whole picture. In this respect, Michele Wallace is also guilty. She points to male ignorance throughout the book, yet for her own research she chose mainly white and black male writers. And though this was pointed out to her before the book was published, she considered the male version of reality enough. Though she tossed in Ntozake Shangé, Toni Morrison, Angela Davis, and Nikki Giovanni at the end, it is a puzzle to the reader what we are to make of them, since the stereotypes she attempts to apply to each woman cannot possibly fit creative, moving, thoughtful, and evolving human beings, not to mention human beings who have the added possibilities that come from being black women.

The line in Wallace's book that has given black women more cases of apoplexy than any other is this one: "I think that the black woman thinks of her history and her condition as a wound which makes her different and therefore special and therefore exempt from human responsibility." Like the majority of black women in America, I am delighted when another black woman speaks her mind and offers her own opinion, but this one —even in context—is a stunner. In what way have we not been responsible? How have we been exempt? This statement seems criticism taken to such extreme that there is nothing one can think of to which it actually applies.

The one statement in Wallace's book that I made an effort to suppress (beyond writing notes to the author herself: all ignored, as far as I can see in the book) is this one:

> From the intricate web of mythology which surrounds the black woman, a fundamental image emerges. It is of a woman of inordinate strength, with an ability for tolerating an unusual amount of misery and heavy, distasteful work. This woman does not have the same fears, weaknesses, and insecurities as other women, but believes herself to be and is, in fact, stronger emotionally than most men. Less of a woman in that she is less "feminine" and helpless, she is really *more* of a woman in that she is the embodiment of Mother Earth, the quintessential mother with infinite sexual, life-giving, and nurturing reserves. In other words, she is a superwoman.
>
> *Through the years this image has remained basically intact, unquestioned even by the occasional black woman writer or politician* [my italics].

Her editor requested an endorsement of the book. I agreed but only if this paragraph was removed. "It is a lie," I said. "I can't speak for politicians but I can certainly speak for myself. I've been hacking away at that stereotype for years, and so have a good many other black women writers." I thought, not simply of Meridian, but of Janie Crawford, of Pecola, Sula, and Nell, of Edith Jackson, even of Iola LeRoy and Megda, for God's sake.

(Characters by black women writers Ms. Wallace is unacquainted with; an ignorance that is acceptable only in someone not writing a book about black women.) "Fifty thousand black women will call you on this one," I ranted further.

I was too late. Nor was there any apparent attention paid to anything I'd said. My earlier "advice" had in no way been made use of. And perhaps the editor and Wallace were correct not to be swayed. Fifty thousand black women have so far not even managed to write letters of protest to *Ms.* (where an excerpt of the book appeared) with their objections, though I have received both letters and phone calls, as if it is my responsibility to make the bad parts of *Black Macho* go away.*

No one can do that now. Nor can we carp continually about the bad parts without facing the many truths of the good parts. And there *are* good parts. It is a book that, while not sound or visionary or even honest enough to "shape the eighties," can still help us shape our thinking. It is, in short, an expression of one black woman's reality. And I persist in believing all such expressions (preferably stopping short of self-contempt and contempt for others) are valuable and will, in the long run, do us more good than harm.

1979

*Presumably because I was an editor at *Ms.* at the time and held responsible for every black piece published, though I was not the editor for Wallace's piece.

. . . .

BROTHERS AND SISTERS

We lived on a farm in the South in the fifties, and my brothers, the four of them I knew (the fifth had left home when I was three years old), were allowed to watch animals being mated. This was not unusual; nor was it considered unusual that my older sister and I were frowned upon if we even asked, innocently, what was going on. One of my brothers explained the mating one day, using words my father had given him: "The bull is getting a little something on his stick," he said. And he laughed. "What stick?" I wanted to know. "Where did he get it? How did he pick it up? Where did he put it?" All my brothers laughed.

I believe my mother's theory about raising a large family of five boys and three girls was that the father should teach the boys and the mother teach the girls the facts, as one says, of life. So my father went around talking about bulls getting something on their sticks and she went around saying girls did not need to know about such things. They were "womanish" (a very bad way to be in those days) if they asked.

The thing was, watching the matings filled my brothers with an aimless sort of lust, as dangerous as it was unintentional. They knew enough to know that cows, months after mating, produced calves, but they were not bright enough to make the same connection between women and their offspring.

Sometimes, when I think of my childhood, it seems to me a particularly hard one. But in reality, everything awful that happened to me didn't seem to happen to *me* at all, but to my older sister. Through some incredible power to negate my presence around people I did not like, which produced invisibility (as well as an ability to appear mentally vacant when I was nothing of the kind), I was spared the humiliation she was subjected to, though at the same time, I felt every bit of it. It was as if she suffered for my benefit, and I vowed early in my life that none of the things that made existence so miserable for her would happen to me.

The fact that she was not allowed at official matings did not mean she never saw any. While my brothers followed my father to the mating pens on the other side of the road near the barn, she stationed herself near the pigpen, or followed our many dogs until they were in a mating mood, or, failing to witness something there, she watched the chickens. On a farm it is impossible *not* to be conscious of sex, to wonder about it, to dream . . . but to whom was she to speak of her feelings? Not to my father, who thought all young women perverse. Not to my mother, who pretended all her children grew out of stumps she magically found in the forest. Not to me, who never found anything wrong with this lie.

When my sister menstruated she wore a thick packet of clean rags between her legs. It stuck out in front like a penis.

The boys laughed at her as she served them at the table. Not knowing any better, and because our parents did not dream of actually *discussing* what was going on, she would giggle nervously at herself. I hated her for giggling, and it was at those times I would think of her as dim-witted. She never complained, but she began to have strange fainting fits whenever she had her period. Her head felt as if it were splitting, she said, and everything she ate came up again. And her cramps were so severe she could not stand. She was forced to spend several days of each month in bed.

My father expected all of his sons to have sex with women. "Like bulls," he said, "a man *needs* to get a little something on his stick." And so, on Saturday nights, into town they went, chasing the girls. My sister was rarely allowed into town alone, and if the dress she wore fit too snugly at the waist, or if her cleavage dipped too far below her collarbone, she was made to stay home.

"But why can't I go too," she would cry, her face screwed up with the effort not to wail.

"They're boys, your brothers, *that's* why they can go."

Naturally, when she got the chance, she responded eagerly to boys. But when this was discovered she was whipped and locked up in her room.

I would go in to visit her.

"Straight Pine,"* she would say, "you don't know what it *feels* like to want to be loved by a man."

"And if this is what you get for feeling like it I never will," I said, with—I hoped—the right combination of sympathy and disgust.

---

*A pseudonym.

"Men smell so good," she would whisper ecstatically. "And when they look into your eyes, you just melt."

Since they were so hard to catch, naturally she thought almost any of them terrific.

"Oh, that Alfred!" she would moon over some mediocre, square-headed boy, "he's so *sweet!*" And she would take his ugly picture out of her bosom and kiss it.

My father was always warning her not to come home if she ever found herself pregnant. My mother constantly reminded her that abortion was a sin. Later, although she never became pregnant, her period would not come for months at a time. The painful symptoms, however, never varied or ceased. She fell for the first man who loved her enough to beat her for looking at someone else, and when I was still in high school, she married him.

My fifth brother, the one I never knew, was said to be different from the rest. He had not liked matings. He would not watch them. He thought the cows should be given a choice. My father had disliked him because he was soft. My mother took up for him. "Jason is just tender-hearted," she would say in a way that made me know he was her favorite; "he takes after me." It was true that my mother cried about almost anything.

Who was this oldest brother? I wondered.

"Well," said my mother, "he was someone who always loved you. Of course he was a great big boy when you were born and out working on his own. He worked on a road gang building roads. Every morning before he left he would come in the room where you were and pick you up and give you the biggest kisses. He used to look at you and just smile. It's a pity you don't remember him."

I agreed.

At my father's funeral I finally "met" my oldest brother. He is tall and black with thick gray hair above a young-looking face. I watched my sister cry over my father until she blacked out from grief. I saw my brothers sobbing, reminding each other of what a great father he had been. My oldest brother and I did not shed a tear between us. When I left my father's grave he came up and introduced himself. "You don't ever have to walk alone," he said, and put his arms around me.

One out of five ain't *too* bad, I thought, snuggling up.

But I didn't discover until recently his true uniqueness: He is the only one of my brothers who assumes responsibility for all his children. The other four all fathered children during those Saturday-night chases of twenty years ago. Children—my nieces and nephews whom I will probably never know—they neither acknowledge as their own, provide for, or even see.

It was not until I became a student of women's liberation ideology that I could understand and forgive my father. I needed an ideology that would define his behavior in context. The black movement had given me an ideology that helped explain his colorism (he *did* fall in love with my mother partly because she was so light; he never denied it). Feminism helped explain his sexism. I was relieved to know his sexist behavior was not something uniquely his own, but, rather, an imitation of the behavior of the society around us.

All partisan movements add to the fullness of our understanding of society as a whole. They never detract; or, in any case, one must not allow them to do so. Experience adds to experience. "The more things the better," as O'Connor and Welty both have said, speaking, one of marriage, the other of Catholicism.

I desperately needed my father and brothers to give me male models I could respect, because white men (for example; being particularly handy in this sort of comparison)—whether in films or in person—offered man as dominator, as killer, and always as hypocrite.

My father failed because he copied the hypocrisy. And my brothers—except for one—never understood they must represent half the world to me, as I must represent the other half to them.*

1975

*Since this essay was written, my brothers have offered their name, acknowledgment, and some support to all their children.

PART
FOUR

Just east of the central African great jungle belt lies an open Savanna believed to have been the home of the first human beings—hunters and gatherers set apart from the great apes in part by their ability to walk upright, which enabled them to fashion tools. Now, studies being carried on . . . propose that the first implements crafted by these people were not designed by men to hunt animals, as has long been assumed, but by women, to gather plants for eating.

—"New Anthropological Finds:
   The Swords Started Out as Ploughshares,"
   MS. Gazette, August 1979

SILVER WRITES

It is true—
I've always loved
the daring
        ones
Like the black young
man
Who tried
to crash
All barriers
at once,
    wanted to
swim
At a white
beach (in Alabama)
Nude.

Of all the poems I wrote during the period of most intense struggle for Civil Rights* (the early sixties), this one (from *Once*) remains my favorite. I like it because it reveals a moment in which I recognized something important about myself, and my own motivations for joining a historic, profoundly revolutionary movement for human change. It also reveals why the term "Civil Rights" could never adequately express black people's revolutionary goals, because it could never adequately describe our longings and our dreams, or those of the non-black people who stood among us. And because, as a term, it is totally lacking in color.

In short, although I value the Civil Rights Movement *deeply*, I have never liked the term itself. It has no music, it has no poetry. It makes one think of bureaucrats rather than of sweaty faces, eyes bright and big for *Freedom!*, marching feet. No; one thinks instead of metal filing cabinets and boring paperwork.

This is because "Civil Rights" is a term that did not evolve out of black culture, but, rather, out of American law. As such, it is a term of limitation. It speaks only to physical possibilities —necessary and treasured, of course—but not of the spirit. Even as it promises assurance of greater freedoms it narrows the area in which people might expect to find them. No wonder "Black Power," "Black Panther Party," even "Mississippi Freedom Democratic Party" and "Umoja" always sounded so much better and *sui generis*, if in the end they accomplished (perhaps) less.

When one reads the poems, especially, of the period, this

---

*Older black country people did their best to instill what *accurate* poetry they could into this essentially white civil servants' term (acknowledging the ultimate power behind the formulation of the majority of America's laws) by saying the words with a comprehending passion, irony, and insight, so that what one *heard* was *"Silver writes."*

becomes very clear. The poems, like the songs of that time, reveal an entirely different *quality of imagination and spirit* than the term "Civil Rights" describes. The poems are full of protest and "civil disobedience," yes, but they are also full of playfulness and whimsicality, an attraction to world families and the cosmic sea—full of a lot of naked people longing to swim free.

1982

. . . .

ONLY JUSTICE CAN STOP A CURSE

To the Man God: O Great One, I have been sorely tried by my enemies and have been blasphemed and lied against. My good thoughts and my honest actions have been turned to bad actions and dishonest ideas. My home has been disrespected, my children have been cursed and ill-treated. My dear ones have been backbitten and their virtue questioned. O Man God, I beg that this that I ask for my enemies shall come to pass:

That the South wind shall scorch their bodies and make them wither and shall not be tempered to them. That the North wind shall freeze their blood and numb their muscles and that it shall not be tempered to them. That the West wind shall blow away their life's breath and will not leave their hair grow, and that their fingernails shall fall off and their bones shall crumble. That the East wind shall make their minds grow dark, their sight shall fail and their seed dry up so that they shall not multiply.

I ask that their fathers and mothers from their furthest generation will not intercede for them before the great throne, and the wombs of their women shall not bear fruit except for strangers, and that they shall become extinct. I pray that the children who may come shall be weak of mind and paralyzed of limb and that they themselves shall curse them in their turn for ever turning the breath of life into their bodies. I pray that disease and death shall be forever with them and that their worldly goods shall not prosper, and that their crops shall not multiply and that their cows, their sheep, and their hogs and all their living beasts shall die of starvation and thirst. I pray that their houses shall be unroofed and that the rain, the thunder and lightning shall find the innermost recesses of their home and that the foundation shall crumble and the floods tear it asunder. I pray that the sun shall not shed its rays on them in benevolence, but instead it shall beat down on them and burn them and destroy them. I pray that the moon shall not give them peace, but instead shall deride them and decry them and cause their minds to shrivel. I pray that their friends shall betray them and cause them loss of power, of gold and of silver, and that their enemies shall smite them until they beg for mercy which shall not be given them. I pray that their tongues shall forget how to speak in sweet words, and that it shall be paralyzed and that all about them will be desolation, pestilence and death. O Man God, I ask you for all these things because they have dragged me in the dust and destroyed my good name; broken my heart and caused me to curse the day that I was born. So be it.

This is a curse-prayer that Zora Neale Hurston collected in the 1920s. And by then it was already old. I have often marveled at it. At the precision of its anger, the absoluteness of its bitterness. Its utter hatred of the enemies it condemns. It is a curse-prayer by a person who would readily, almost happily, commit suicide, if it meant her enemies would also die. Horribly.

I am sure it was a woman who first prayed this curse. And I see her—black, yellow, brown or red, *"aboriginal"* as the Ancients are called in South Africa and Australia and other lands invaded, expropriated, and occupied by whites. And I think, with astonishment, that the curse-prayer of this colored woman —starved, enslaved, humiliated, and carelessly trampled to death—over centuries, is coming to pass. Indeed, like ancient peoples of color the world over, who have tried to tell the white man of the destruction that would inevitably follow from the uranium-mining plunder of their sacred lands, this woman— along with millions and billions of obliterated sisters, brothers, and children—seems to have put such enormous energy into her hope for revenge that her curse seems close to bringing it about. And it is this hope for revenge, finally, I think, that is at the heart of many People of Color's resistance to the present antinuclear movement.

In any case, this has been my own problem.

When I have considered the enormity of the white man's crimes against humanity. Against women. Against every living person of color. Against the poor. Against my mother and my father. Against me . . . When I consider that at this very moment he wishes to take away what little freedom I have died to achieve, through denial of my right to vote . . . Has already taken away education, medicine, housing, and food . . . That William Shockley is saying at this moment that he will run for the Senate of my country to push his theory that blacks are genetically inferior and should be sterilized . . . When I consider that he is, they are, a real and present threat to my life and the life of my daughter, my people, I think—in perfect harmony with my sister of long ago: *Let the earth marinate in poisons. Let the bombs cover the ground like rain. For nothing short of total destruction will ever teach them anything.*

And it would be good, perhaps, to put an end to the species in any case, rather than let white men continue to subjugate it, and continue their lust to dominate, exploit, and despoil not just our planet, but the rest of the universe, which is their clear and oft-stated intention; leaving their arrogance and litter not just on the moon, but on everything else they can reach.

If we have any true love for the stars, planets, the rest of Creation, we must do everything we can to keep white men away from them. They who have appointed themselves our representatives to the rest of the universe. They who have never met any new creature without exploiting, abusing, or destroying it. They who say we poor (white included) and colored and female and elderly blight neighborhoods, while they blight worlds.

What they have done to the Old, they will do to the New.

Under the white man every star would become a South Africa, every planet a Vietnam.

Fatally irradiating ourselves may in fact be the only way to save others from what Earth has already become. And this is a consideration that I believe requires serious thought from every one of us.

However, just as the sun shines on the godly and the ungodly alike, so does nuclear radiation. And with this knowledge it becomes increasingly difficult to embrace the thought of extinction purely for the assumed satisfaction of—from the grave —achieving revenge. Or even of accepting our demise as a planet as a simple and just preventive medicine administered to the universe. Life is better than death, I believe, if only because it is less boring, and because it has fresh peaches in it. In any case, Earth is my home—though for centuries white people have tried to convince me I have no right to exist, except in the dirtiest, darkest corners of the globe.

So let me tell you: I intend to protect my home. Praying —not a curse—only the hope that my courage will not fail my love. But if by some miracle, and all our struggle, the Earth is spared, only justice to every living thing (and everything is alive) will save humankind.

And we are not saved yet.

Only justice can stop a curse.

1982

NUCLEAR MADNESS:

WHAT YOU CAN DO

Nuclear Madness is a book you should read immediately. Before brushing your teeth. Before making love. Before lunch. Its author is Helen Caldicott (with the assistance of Nancy Herrington and Nahum Stiskin), a native Australian, pediatrician, and mother of three children. It is a short, serious book about the probability of nuclear catastrophe in our lifetime, eminently thoughtful, readable, and chilling, as a book written for nuclear nonexperts, as almost all Americans are, would have to be.

Caldicott was six years old when the atomic bomb was dropped on Hiroshima, and calls herself a child of the atomic age. She grew up, as many of us did, under the threat of nuclear war. She recalls the fifties, when students were taught to dive under their desks at the sound of the air-raid siren and Americans by the thousands built underground fallout shelters.

During the sixties, political assassinations, the Civil Rights Movement, and the Vietnam War turned many people away from concern about atomic weapons and toward problems they felt they could do something about. However, as Caldicott states, the Pentagon continued resolutely on its former course, making bigger and "better" bombs every year.

Sometime during the sixties Robert McNamara, then Secretary of Defense, said that between the United States and the Soviet Union there already existed some four hundred nuclear bombs, enough to kill millions of people on both sides, a viable "deterrent," in his opinion, to nuclear war. The Pentagon and the Kremlin, however, apparently assumed this was not enough, and so today between the two "superpowers" there are some *fifty thousand* bombs.

What this means is that the U.S. and the U.S.S.R. literally have more bombs than they know what to do with: so they have targeted every city in the Northern Hemisphere with a population of at least twenty-five thousand with the number of bombs formerly set aside to wipe out whole countries. So even as you squeeze out your toothpaste, kiss your lover's face, or bite into a turkey sandwich, you are on the superpowers' nuclear hit list, a hit list made up by people who have historically been unable to refrain from showing off every new and shameful horror that they make.

For several years Caldicott has been on leave from her work at the Harvard Medical Center, and spends all her time practicing what she calls "preventative medicine," traveling across the Earth attempting to make people aware of the dangers we face. Like most medicine, hers is bitter, but less bitter, she believes, than watching helplessly while her child patients suffer and die from cancer and genetic diseases that are directly caused by the chemical pollutants inevitably created in the production of nuclear energy.

The nuclear industry, powerful, profit-oriented, totally unconcerned about our health, aided and abetted by a government that is its twin, is murdering us and our children every day. And it is up to us, each one of us, to stop it. In the event of a nuclear war all life on the planet will face extinction, certainly human beings. But even if there is no war we will face the same end— unless we put an end to the nuclear-power industry itself—only it will be somewhat slower in coming, as the air, the water, and the soil become too poisoned from nuclear waste (for which there is no known safe disposal) to support life.

What can we do? Like Caldicott, but even more so, I do not believe we should waste any time looking for help from our legal system. Nor do I have faith in politicians, scientists, or "experts." I have great faith, however, in individual people: you with the toothbrush, you in the sack, and you there not letting any of this shit get between you and that turkey sandwich. If it comes down to it, I know one of us *individuals* (just think of Watergate) may have to tackle the killer who's running to push the catastrophe button, and I even hope said tackle will explain why so many of us are excellent football players. (Just as I hope *something* will soon illustrate for us what our brothers learned of protecting life in Vietnam.)

As individuals we must join others. No time to quibble about survival being "a white issue." No time to claim you don't live here, too. Massive demonstrations are vital. Massive civil disobedience. And, in fact, massive anything that's necessary to save our lives.

Talk with your family; organize your friends. Educate anybody you can get your mouth on. Raise money. Support those who go to jail. Write letters to those senators and congressmen who are making it easy for the nuclear-power industry to kill us: tell them if they don't change, "cullud" are going to invade their fallout shelters. In any case, this is the big one. We must save

Earth, and relieve those who would destroy it of the power to do so. Join up with folks you don't even like, if you have to, so that we may all live to fight each other again.

But first, read Caldicott's book, and remember: the good news may be that Nature is phasing out the white man, but the bad news is that's who She thinks we all are.

1982

TO THE EDITORS OF MS. MAGAZINE

[I wrote the following memo a few weeks prior to the Israeli invasion of Lebanon and a few months before the Beirut massacres, in response to an article, "Anti-Semitism in the Women's Movement," by Letty Cottin Pogrebin, which appeared in the June 1982 issue of *Ms.*]

There is a close, often unspoken bond between Jewish and black women that grows out of their awareness of oppression and injustice, an awareness many gentile women simply do not have. For example, last year at the height of publicity about the Atlanta child murders I visited a small college in middle Ohio to read poetry. Two women, a white Jew and a white gentile, met me at the airport and drove me to a restaurant for dinner. I was wearing two green ribbons,* one on my overcoat and

*In solidarity with the children and mothers of Atlanta.

another on my sweater. As soon as the four white people at the opposite table noticed this (and perhaps it was merely *my* color they noticed) they ordered the piano player at the front of the room to strike up "Mammy's Li'l Baby Loves Shortnin' Bread," which they sang at the top of their lungs (the two women—a visual obliteration of the possibility of interracial woman bonding—hanging onto the men like appendages) and at the end of each stanza, after "Called for the doctor, the doctor said . . ." they added, ". . . *and another one dead!*" with emphasis, foot-stomping, and hoots of hickish laughter. When they finished this, they clamored for a rendition of "Sweet Georgia Brown," which the piano player claimed (mercifully) not to know.

The Jewish woman and I froze the moment the singing began. The gentile woman placidly ate her meal. Eventually the singers left and the Jewish woman said: "We have to do something about this." "Yes," I said. The gentile woman said: "What's the matter?"

The Jewish woman explained it to her.

And *she* said: "Oh, I noticed they were singing loud, but *when I realized it wasn't anything against women*, I just ignored them."

As we made our objections to the restaurant manager ("Well, one of those women works here and that's just one of the songs we have in the songbook we hand out here") the gentile woman continued to look perplexed. Whereas the Jewish woman seemed about to start swinging with her pocketbook.

But this is only part of the story.

Several months ago, when Israel "annexed" the Golan Heights, a Jewish friend of mine visited that country. Upon his return he explained that Israel *needed* that land to protect itself from the possibility of enemy shells, apparently lobbed off its cliffs, into Israel.

"But doesn't that land belong to people?" I asked.

"They're not doing anything with it," he replied.

I thought: I have a backyard I'm not 'doing anything with.' Does that give you the right to take it?

He continued telling me the glories of Israel, but I found it hard to listen: Crazy Horse, Lame Deer, and Black Elk stoppered my ears. He sounded like a typical American *wasichu* (a Sioux word for white men, meaning fat-takers) to me. It seemed only incidental he was a Jew.

I think I am glad Letty Pogrebin has added her article to the necessary and continuing discussion of anti-Semitism in the women's movement. As a black gentile, encountering black anti-Semites is always distressing, because what history clearly shows, if nothing else, is that anti-Semites are never happy. But also because black people, to keep faith with their own ancestors, must struggle to resist all forms of oppression—and it is this necessity that so often brings them to the side of people like the Palestinians, *as well as to the side of Jewish Israelis.* And this middle ground is where most black people who think about the Middle East at all seem to me have been, until a few years ago. Before that—and perhaps I am merely tracing my own personal history—most black people sided emphatically with Israel.

I remember Egypt's attack on Israel in 1967 and how frightened my Jewish husband and I were that Israel would be —as Egypt threatened—"driven into the sea." When Israel won the Six-Day War we were happy and relieved. I had little consciousness of the Palestinian question at the time. All I considered was the Holocaust, the inhuman fact that Jews were turned away by virtually every country they sought to enter, that they had to live *somewhere* on the globe (there had been talk by the British during the forties of settling them in Uganda, where Britain had already "settled" thousands of its own citizens) and I had seen the movie *Exodus*, with its haunting sound track: "This land is mine, God gave this land to me." Over the next several years—thanks largely to a Jewish woman friend who visited Palestinian camps and came home with a Palestinian name—I became more aware. When I tried to talk to my husband about the Palestinians, however (*all* the Palestinians, not just those in camps or those in the PLO), he simply shut down. He considered my friend a traitor to Jews, and any discussion that questioned Israel's behavior seemed literally to paralyze his thoughts. I understood his fear, and shared it. But when he said, "Israel has to exist," I could only answer, "Yes, and so do those other folks."

One thing that troubles me greatly is how in Pogrebin's article the word "imperialism" is hardly used. It is like reading nineteenth-century European history and seeing the word "colonialism" once or twice.

"After the great outcry against Israel's annexation of the Golan Heights," she writes, "I heard a woman joke, 'Israel is Hitler's last laugh on the Jews'—as if Menachem Begin's *ultra-nationalism* [my italics: denoting Pogrebin's equation of an ideology with an act] would destroy the Jewish people better than Hitler could."

"Ultra-nationalism" in this case should read "imperialism." For what can you call Israel's establishment of colonies on other people's territories if not imperialism? Regardless of what other folks, like the Americans and Russians, are doing (imperialists both) I think it would help our dialogue if we could say, for instance: Yes, Israel must exist—because Jews, after heinous world maltreatment, deserve affirmative action (as Pogrebin describes it), but when it moves into other people's lands, when it establishes colonies in other people's territories, when it forces folks out of their kitchens, vineyards, and beds, then it must be opposed, just as Russia is or as America is. And, as with those countries, I think there has to be some distinction made between Jews per se and the Israeli government. (Many Americans will undoubtedly say that the settlement of Israel was itself an imperialistic act on the part of the British, and that on that basis it should not exist, but those Americans will have to concede the same thing about America, and answer the question Am I ready to leave and give it back to the Indians?)

I do not believe black people want Israel to "commit suicide," because so many of them still hope the war will slacken enough for them to visit, but any person who has experienced occupation or colonialization will have a hard time condoning Israel's establishment of "settlements" it controls in areas where indigenous people already live. Looking at Israel's "settlements," I think of all those forts that dot the American plains. Israel's "settlements" look chillingly familiar and American to me.

Andrea Dworkin's comment that "I resent the expectation that, having been oppressed, Jews should exercise a higher morality running their country than anyone else" makes me realize I have expected exactly that: I have an identical problem with African countries (and just as frequently face disappointment). That Israel would *not* be a little America or a little Russia (Idi Amin *not* be a black Andrew Jackson). That it would not seek to enlarge its empire through the acquisition of "satellites," "protectorates," "colonies," or "states." This was obviously foolish on my part, and I reluctantly accept that. But if Jews are going to behave exactly like other folks (and notably like white Christian men), what then is their Jewishness if not simply their belief in their right to occupy a chosen piece of land? Anybody can observe the Sabbath, but making it holy surely takes the rest of the week.

To many people in the Third World, Zionism doesn't equal racism so much as it equals Israeli imperialism. (Though when Pogrebin quotes someone as saying most Israelis are dark-skinned Jews—and Zionists—one does wonder why none of them seem to be in the Knesset or ever shown as the majority of Israelis when Israelis are presented to us on TV.) And they are against it not because they hate Jews (though some of them may) but because they recognize and condemn imperialistic behavior. When Third World people condemn American or Russian imperialism (and they do) I know perfectly well they are not talking about those millions of Americans or Russians who abhor virtually every political action our respective governments make. If I am appalled by Menachem Begin's policies (and I am, and many Israelis—including soldiers in the Israeli army—are, and many American Jews are) my response is not that Israel should cease to exist, but that Israelis should stop electing him to power.

I felt even closer to my Jewish friend after she went to visit the Palestinian camps. She did not assume Palestinian women "wished her dead," and she was happily surprised to discover they did not. She did discover she looked a lot like them (dark and Semitic: "Cousins my ass," she said, "*sisters,* or somebody's mirror is lying"), that they shared many historical and cultural similarities, and that Palestinian women were no more wedded to the notion of violence than she was. But this was during the sixties, and perhaps everything *has* changed since then. Unlike my husband, who considered her a traitor to Jews because she got all intimate with "the enemy," I thought (in my naïve, "positively stereotypical" way) that her action was very Jewish. It showed courage, a sense of humor, an incorrigible one-worldism, and a faith in her own perception of reality. It took —how you say—*chutzpah.* She knew something I, too, deeply believe: to find out any part of the truth, women must travel *themselves* where they hope to find it. In my opinion and experience, imperialists of all nations and races will tell us anything to keep us fighting. For them.

There is a brilliant essay by the writer June Jordan in her

book *Civil Wars* that black and Jewish feminists might consider using.as a consciousness-raising piece. In it she describes what happened when a Jewish woman friend of hers read an essay Jordan had written denouncing the murder of a young black man in Brooklyn by Hassidic Jews. Her friend gave her a book about anti-Semitism so Jordan could "recognize her problem." Anyone familiar with Jordan's work (as her friend must have been: they worked together for years) would know Jordan never hesitates to denounce *anyone* she feels deserves it; and just as she denounces all kinds of murder, she denounces murder by Jews. This does not make her anti-Semitic; it makes her impartial.

What her friend wanted from her, it seems to me, is *silent* and uncritical loyalty to Jews, no matter what they do. But many black women feel that silent, uncritical loyalty is something you don't even inflict on your child. In the sixties some black women swerved out of our historical path of challenging everything that looked wrong to us to keep mum while black men "ran the black nation." This was psychically crippling to a generation of black women (and black people in general) and we say, Never again. We deeply appreciate the value of alliances and coalitions, but we come complete with our mouths. It is when we are silent that there is cause to worry.

Every affront to human dignity necessarily affects me as a human being on the planet, because I know every single thing on earth is connected. It depresses me that Pogrebin imagines Jewish women's work for "civil rights, welfare rights, Appalachian relief" was work that did not "necessarily affect [their] own lives." Meaning, logically, that this work was charity, dispensed to the backward, the poor, and the benighted, and that Jewish feminists should now be able to expect "payment" in the form of support. Fortunately I have worked with too many Jewish women in social movements to believe many of them think this—rather than that any struggle against oppression lightens the load on all of us—but if they do, we are worse off than I thought.

Jewish feminists will have to try to understand people of color's hatred of imperialism and colonialism: we who have lost whole continents to the white man's arrogance and greed, and to his white female accomplice's inability to say no to stolen gold, diamonds, and furs. And yes, I suspect Jewish feminists *will* have to identify as Jews within feminism with as much discomfort as they identify as feminists within Judaism; every other woman of an oppressed group has always experienced this double bind. And people of color will have to try to understand Jewish fears of another Holocaust and of being left without a home at all. That is our story too. The black person who honestly believes "being anti-Semitic is one way blacks can buy into American life," has the perception of a flea, and a total ignorance of historically documented, white American behavior. As for those who think the Arab world promises freedom, the briefest study of its routine traditional treatment of blacks (slavery) and women (purdah) will provide relief from all illusion. If Malcolm X had been a black woman his last message to the world would have been entirely different. The brotherhood of Moslem men—all colors—may exist there, but part of the glue that holds it together is the thorough suppression of women.

1983

. . . .

WRITING THE COLOR PURPLE

I don't always know where the germ of a story comes from, but
with *The Color Purple* I knew right away. I was hiking through
the woods with my sister, Ruth, talking about a lovers' triangle
of which we both knew. She said: "And you know, one day The
Wife asked The Other Woman for a pair of her drawers."
Instantly the missing piece of the story I was mentally writing
—about two women who felt married to the same man—fell
into place. And for months—through illnesses, divorce, several
moves, travel abroad, all kinds of heartaches and revelations—
I carried my sister's comment delicately balanced in the center
of the novel's construction I was building in my head.

I also knew *The Color Purple* would be a historical novel,
and thinking of this made me chuckle. In an interview, discussing my work, a black male critic said he'd heard I might write
a historical novel someday, and went on to say, in effect: Heaven

protect us from it. The chuckle was because, womanlike (he would say), my "history" starts not with the taking of lands, or the births, battles, and deaths of Great Men, but with one woman asking another for her underwear. Oh, well, I thought, one function of critics is to be appalled by such behavior. But what woman (or sensuous man) could avoid being intrigued? As for me, I thought of little else for a year.

When I was sure the characters of my new novel were trying to form (or, as I invariably thought of it, trying to contact me, to speak *through* me), I began to make plans to leave New York. Three months earlier I had bought a tiny house on a quiet Brooklyn street, assuming—because my desk overlooked the street and a maple tree in the yard, representing garden and view —I would be able to write. I was not.

New York, whose people I love for their grace under almost continual unpredictable adversity, was a place the people in *The Color Purple* refused even to visit. The moment any of them started to form—on the subway, a dark street, and especially in the shadow of very tall buildings—they would start to complain.

"What is all this tall shit anyway?" they would say.

I disposed of the house, stored my furniture, packed my suitcases, and flew alone to San Francisco (it was my daughter's year to be with her father), where all the people in the novel promptly fell silent—I think, in awe. Not merely of the city's beauty, but of what they picked up about earthquakes.

"It's pretty," they muttered, "but us ain't lost nothing in no place that has earthquakes."

They also didn't like seeing buses, cars, or other people whenever they attempted to look out. "Us don't want to be seeing none of this," they said. "It make us can't think."

That was when I knew for sure these were country people.

So my lover* and I started driving around the state looking for a country house to rent. Luckily I had found (with the help of friends) a fairly inexpensive place in the city. This too had been a decision forced by my characters. As long as there was any question about whether I could support them in the fashion they desired (basically in undisturbed silence) they declined to come out. Eventually we found a place in northern California we could afford and that my characters liked. And no wonder: it looked a lot like the town in Georgia most of them were from, only it was more beautiful and the local swimming hole was not segregated. It also bore a slight resemblance to the African village in which one of them, Nettie, was a missionary.

Seeing the sheep, the cattle, and the goats, smelling the apples and the hay, one of my characters, Celie, began, haltingly, to speak.

But there was still a problem.

Since I had quit my editing job at *Ms.* and my Guggenheim Fellowship was running out, and my royalties did not quite cover expenses, and—let's face it—because it gives me a charge to see people who appreciate my work, historical novels or not, I was accepting invitations to speak. Sometimes on the long plane rides Celie or Shug would break through with a wonderful line or two (for instance, Celie said once that a self-pitying sick person she went to visit was "laying up in the bed trying to look dead"). But even these vanished—if I didn't jot them down—by the time my contact with the audience was done.

What to do?

Celie and Shug answered without hesitation: Give up all

---

*Ironically and unfortunately, "lover" is considered a pejorative by some people. In its original meaning, "someone who loves" (could be a lover of music, a lover of dance, a lover of a person . . .), it is useful, strong and accurate—and the meaning I intend here.

this travel. Give up all this talk. What is all this travel and talk shit anyway? So, I gave it up for a year. Whenever I was invited to speak I explained I was taking a year off for Silence. (I also wore an imaginary bracelet on my left arm that spelled the word.) Everyone said, Sure, they understood.

I was terrified.

Where was the money for our support coming from? My only steady income was a three-hundred-dollar-a-month retainer from *Ms.* for being a long-distance editor. But even that was too much distraction for my characters.

Tell them you can't do anything for the magazine, said Celie and Shug. (You guessed it, the women of the drawers.) Tell them you'll have to think about them later. So, I did. *Ms.* was unperturbed. Supportive as ever (they continued the retainer). Which was nice.

Then I sold a book of stories. After taxes, inflation, and my agent's fee of ten percent, I would still have enough for a frugal, no-frills year. And so, I bought some beautiful blue-and-red-and-purple fabric, and some funky old secondhand furniture (and accepted donations of old odds and ends from friends), and a quilt pattern my mama swore was easy, and I headed for the hills.

There were days and weeks and even months when nothing happened. Nothing whatsoever. I worked on my quilt, took long walks with my lover, lay on an island we discovered in the middle of the river and dabbled my fingers in the water. I swam, explored the redwood forests all around us, lay out in the meadow, picked apples, talked (yes, of course) to trees. My quilt began to grow. And, of course, everything was happening. Celie and Shug and Albert were getting to know each other, coming to trust my determination to serve their entry (sometimes I felt *re*-entry) into the world to the best of my ability, and what is more—and felt so wonderful—we began to love one another. And, what is even more, to feel immense thankfulness for our mutual good luck.

Just as summer was ending, one or more of my characters —Celie, Shug, Albert, Sofia, or Harpo—would come for a visit. We would sit wherever I was sitting, and talk. They were very obliging, engaging, and jolly. They were, of course, at the end of their story but were telling it to me from the beginning. Things that made me sad often made them laugh. Oh, we got through that; don't pull such a long face, they'd say. Or, You think Reagan's bad, you ought've seen some of the rednecks us come up under. The days passed in a blaze of happiness.

Then school started, and it was time for my daughter to stay with me—for two years.

Could I handle it?

Shug said, right out, that she didn't know. (Well, her mother raised *her* children.) Nobody else said anything. (At this point in the novel, Celie didn't even know where *her* children were.) They just quieted down, didn't visit as much, and took a firm Well, let's us wait and see attitude.

My daughter arrived. Smart, sensitive, cheerful, at school most of the day, but quick with tea and sympathy on her return. My characters adored her. They saw she spoke her mind in no uncertain terms and would fight back when attacked. When she came home from school one day with bruises but said, You should see the other guy, Celie (raped by her stepfather as a child and somewhat fearful of life) began to reappraise her own condition. Rebecca gave her courage (which she *always* gives me)—and Celie grew to like her so much she would wait until three-thirty to visit me. So, just when Rebecca would arrive home needing her mother and a hug, there'd be Celie, trying to give her both. Fortunately I was able to bring Celie's own children back to her (a unique power of novelists), though it took thirty years and a good bit of foreign travel. But this proved to be the largest single problem in writing the exact novel I wanted to write between about ten-thirty and three.

I had planned to give myself five years to write *The Color Purple* (teaching, speaking, or selling apples, as I ran out of money). But, on the very day my daughter left for camp, less than a year after I started writing, I wrote the last page.

And what did I do that for?

It was like losing everybody I loved at once. First Rebecca (to whom everyone surged forth on the last page to say good-bye), then Celie, Shug, Nettie, and Albert. Mary Agnes, Harpo, and Sofia. Eleanor Jane. Adam and Tashi Omatangu. Olivia. Mercifully, my quilt and my lover remained.

I threw myself in his arms and cried.

1982

. . . .

ONE *CHILD OF ONE'S OWN:*

A MEANINGFUL DIGRESSION WITHIN

THE WORK(S)

It is an honor for me to speak on a day that honors Muriel Rukeyser.* And the creation of the address I am about to give is especially indebted to Muriel—after all these years since I was her student—because it is about something always dear to her; something she did not teach from texts, but with her own life . . . that is, not merely the necessity of confirming one's *self* in a time of confrontation, but the confirmation of the child, the Life of One's Child, against the odds, always.

I think Muriel was the only teacher I ever had who brought the fundamentally important, joyous reality of The Child into the classroom. There to exist at ease among

---

*Muriel Rukeyser Day, Sarah Lawrence College, December 9, 1979. In the work of this essay, and beyond this essay, I am indebted to the courageous and generous spirits of Tillie Olsen, Barbara Smith, and Gloria Steinem.—A.W.

Wordsworth's daffodils, Whitman's Leaves of Grass, Hopkins's Pied Beauties . . . She taught no separations where there are, in fact, none—which so much of the instruction in the world is expressly for. If the world contains War, it also contains The Child. If the world contains Hunger, Nuclear Reactors, Fascists, it nevertheless contains The Child.

To some of us—artists, writers, poets, jugglers—The Child is perceived as threat, as danger, as enemy. In truth, society is badly arranged for children to be taken into happy account. How many of us can say we have never forgotten The Child? I cannot say this.

But I can say I am learning not to forget.

Muriel viewed The Child as, I think, she viewed herself: as teacher, student, poet, and friend. And to The Child, she held herself, her life, accountable. I do not know what struggles brought Muriel to her belief in the centrality of The Child. For me, there has been conflict, struggle, occasional defeat—not only in affirming the life of my own child (children) at all costs, but also in seeing in that affirmation a fond acceptance and confirmation of myself in a world that would deny me the untrampled blossoming of my own existence.

Not surprisingly, I have found this to be political in the deepest sense.

For those of us who both love and fear The Child— because of the work we do—but who would be lovers only, if we could, I propose and defend a plan of life that encourages *one* child of one's own, which I consider a meaningful —some might say *necessary*—digression within the work(s).

It is perfectly true that I, like many other women who work, especially as writers, was terrified of having children.

I feared being fractured by the experience if not over-whelmed. I thought the quality of my writing would be considerably diminished by motherhood—that nothing that was good for my writing could come out of having children.

My first mistake was in thinking "children" instead of "child." My second was in seeing The Child as my enemy rather than the racism and sexism of an oppressive capital-ist society. My third was in believing none of the benefits of having a child would accrue to my writing.

In fact, I had bought the prevailing sexist directive: you have to have balls (be a man) to write. In my opinion, having a child is easily the equivalent of having balls. In truth, it is more than equivalent: ballsdom is surpassed.

Someone asked me once whether I thought women artists should have children, and, since we were beyond discussing why this question is never asked artists who are men, I gave my answer promptly.

"Yes," I said, somewhat to my surprise. And, as if to amend my rashness, I added: "They should have children—*assuming this is of interest to them*—but only one."

"Why only one?" this Someone wanted to know.

"Because with one you can move," I said. "With more than one you're a sitting duck."

The year after my only child, Rebecca, was born, my mother offered me uncharacteristically bad advice: "You should have another one soon," said she, "so that Rebecca will have someone to play with, and so you can get it all over with faster."

Such advice does not come from what a woman recalls of her own experience. It comes from a pool of such misguidance women have collected over the millennia to help themselves feel less foolish for having more than one child. This pool is called, desperately, pitiably, "Women's Wisdom." In fact, it should be called "Women's Folly."

The rebellious, generally pithy advice that comes from a woman's own experience more often resembles my mother's automatic response to any woman she meets who pines for children but has been serenely blessed with none: "If the Lord sets you free, be free indeed." *This crafty justification of both nonconformity and a shameless reveling in the resultant freedom is what women and slaves everywhere and in every age since the Old Testament have appropriated from the Bible.*

"No thank you," I replied. "I will never have another child out of this body, again."

"But why do you say that?" she asked breathlessly, perhaps stunned by my redundancy. "You married a man who's a wonderful fatherly type. He has so much love in him he should have fifty children running around his feet."

I saw myself sweeping them out from around his feet like so many ants. If they're running around his feet for the two hours between the time he comes home from the office and the time we put them to bed, I thought, they'd be underneath my desk all day. Sweep. Sweep.

My mother continued. "Why," she said, "until my fifth child I was like a young girl. I could pick up and go anywhere I wanted to." She *was* a young girl. She was still under twenty-five when her fifth child was born, my age when I became pregnant with Rebecca. Besides, since I am the last child in a family of eight, this image of nimble flight is not the one lodged forever in my mind. I remember a woman struggling to get everyone else dressed for church on Sunday and only with the greatest effort being able to get ready on time herself. But, since I am not easily seduced by the charms of painful past experience, recalled in present tranquillity, I did not bring this up.

At the time my mother could "pick up and go" with five children, she and my father traveled, usually, by wagon. I can see how that would have been pleasant: it is pleasant still in some countries—in parts of China, Cuba, Jamaica, Mexico, Greece, and other places. A couple of slow mules, ambling along a bright Southern road, the smell of pine and honeysuckle, absence of smog, birds chirping. Those five, dear little voices piping up in back of the wagon seat, healthy from natural foods: Plums! Bird! Tree! Flowers! Scuppernongs! Enchanting.

"The other reason I will never have another child out of this body is because having a child *hurts*, even more than toothache (and I am sure no one who has had toothache but not childbirth can imagine this), and it changes the body."

Well, there are several responses from the general supply of Women's Folly my mother could have chosen to answer this. She chose them all.

"*That* little pain," she scoffed (*although, caught in a moment of weakness, she has let slip that during my very own birth the pain was so severe she could not speak, not even to tell the midwife I had been born, and that because of the pain she was sure she would die—a thought that no doubt, under the circumstances, afforded relief. Instead, she blacked out, causing me to be almost smothered by the bedclothes*). "That pain is over before you know it." That is response number one. Number two is, "The thing about that *kind* of pain is that it does a funny thing to a woman [*Uh-oh, I thought, this is going to be the Women's Folly companion to the women-sure-are-funny-creatures stuff*]; looks like the more it hurts you to give birth, the more you love the child." (Is *that* why she loves me so much, I wonder. Naturally, I had wanted to be loved for myself, not for her pain.) Number three: "Sometimes the pain, *they say*, isn't even real. Well, not as real as it feels at the time." (This one deserves comment made only with blows, and is one of the reasons women sometimes experience muscle spasms around their mothers.) And then, number four, the one that angers me most of all: "Another thing about the pain, *you soon forget it.*"

Am I mistaken in thinking I have never forgotten a pain in my life? Even those at parties, I remember.

"I remember every moment of it perfectly," I said. "Furthermore, I don't like stretch marks. I hate them, especially on my thighs" (which are otherwise gorgeous, and of which I am vain). Nobody had told me that my body, after bearing a child, would not be the same. I had heard things like: "Oh, your figure, and especially your breasts [of which I am also vain] will be better than ever." They sagged.

Well, why did I have a child in the first place?

Curiosity. Boredom. Avoiding the draft. Of these three reasons, I am redeemed only by the first. Curiosity is my natural state and has led me headlong into every worthwhile experience (never mind the others) I have ever had. It justifies itself. Boredom, in my case, means a lull in my writing, emotional distance from whatever political movement I am involved in, inability to garden, read, or daydream—easily borne if there are at least a dozen good movies around to attract me. Alas, in Jackson, Mississippi, where my husband, Mel, and I were living in 1968, there were few. About the draft we had three choices: the first, conscientious objector status for Mel, was immediately denied us, as was "alternative service to one's country," which meant, in his case, desegregating Mississippi; the second was to move to Canada, which did not thrill me but which I would gladly have done rather than have Mel go to prison (Vietnam was never one of our choices); the third was, if Mel could not become twenty-six years old in time, to make of him "a family man."

From my journal, July 1968:

And now we own our house. For a brief time, surely. And if the draft calls before I am certified pregnant, what will we do? Go to Canada? Mel hates running as much as I do, which is why we're in Mississippi. I hate this country, but that includes being made to leave it. . . .

January 2, 1969 (two months before I became pregnant):

Only two and a half months until Mel is 26. If we can make it without having to "flee" the country, we will be thankful. I still think his draft board has a nerve asking him to join the Army. He's already in the Army.

My bad days were spent in depression, anxiety, rage against the war, and a state of apprehension over the amount of annual rainfall in Vancouver, and the slow rate of racial "progress" in Mississippi. (Politicians were considered "progressive" if they announced they were running for a certain office as candidates "for *all* the people"; this was a subtle, they thought, announcement to blacks that their existence was acknowledged.) I was also trying to become pregnant.

My good days were spent teaching, writing a simple history book for use in black child-care centers in Jackson, recording black women's autobiographies, making a quilt (African fabrics, Mississippi string pattern), completing my second book, a novel —and trying to become pregnant.

Three days after I finished the novel, Rebecca was born. The pregnancy: The first three months I vomited. The middle three I felt fine and flew off to look at ruins in Mexico. The last three I was so big at 170 pounds I looked like someone else, which did not please me.

What is true about giving birth is . . . that it is miraculous. It might even be the one genuine miracle in life (which is, by the way, the basic belief of many "primitive" religions). The "miracle" of nonbeing, death, certainly pales, I would think, beside it. So to speak.

For one thing, though my stomach was huge and the baby (?!) constantly causing turbulence within it, I did not believe a baby, a person, would come out of me. I mean, look what had gone *in*. (Men have every right to be envious of the womb. I'm envious of it myself, and I have one.) But there she was, coming out, a long black curling lock of hair the first part to be seen, followed by nearly ten pounds of—a human being! Reader, I *stared*.

But this hymn of praise I, anyhow, have heard before, and will not permit myself to repeat, since there are, in fact, very few variations, and these have become boring and shopworn. They were boring and shopworn even at the birth of Christ, which is no doubt why "Virgin Birth" and "Immaculate Conception" were all the rage.

The point was, I was changed forever. From a woman whose "womb" had been, in a sense, her head—that is to say, certain small seeds had gone in, and rather different if not larger or better "creations" had come out—to a woman who . . . had two wombs! No. To a woman who had written books, conceived in her head, and who had also engendered at least one human being in her body. In the vast general store of *"literary* Women's Folly" I discovered these warnings: "Most women who wrote in the past were childless"—Tillie Olsen. Childless and *white*, I mentally added. "Those Lady Poets must not have babies, man," John Berryman, a Suicide Poet himself, is alleged to have said. Then, from "Anonymous," so often a woman who discourages you, "Women have not created as fully as men because once she has a child a woman cannot give herself to her work the way a man can. . . ."

Well, I wondered, with great fear (and resentment against all this bad news), where is the split in me now? What is the damage? *Am I done for?* So much of "Women's Folly," literary and otherwise, makes us feel constricted by experience rather than enlarged by it. Curled around my baby, feeling more anger and protectiveness than love, I thought of at least two sources of Folly Resistance "Women's Folly" lacks. It lacks all conviction that women have the ability to plan their lives for periods longer than nine months, and it lacks the courage to believe that experience, and the expression of that experience, may simply be different, unique even, rather than "greater" or "lesser." The art or literature that saves our lives *is great to us,* in any case; more than that, as a Grace Paley character might say, we do not need to know.

It helped tremendously that by the time Rebecca was born I had no doubts about being a writer. (Doubts about making a *living* by writing, always.) Write I did, night and day, *something,* and it was not even a choice, as having a baby was a choice, but a necessity. When I didn't write I thought of making bombs and throwing them. Of shooting racists. Of doing away—as painlessly and neatly as possible (except when I indulged in Kamikaze tactics of rebellion in my daydreams)—with myself. Writing saved me from the sin and *inconvenience* of violence—as it saves most writers who live in "interesting" oppressive times and are not afflicted by personal immunity.

I began to see, during a period when Rebecca and I were both ill—we had moved to New England for a year and a half because I needed a change from Mississippi—that her birth, and the difficulties it provided us, joined me to a body of experience and a depth of commitment to my own life hard to comprehend otherwise. Her birth was the incomparable gift of seeing the world at quite a different angle than before, and judging it by standards that would apply far beyond my natural life. It also forced me to understand, viscerally, women's need for a store of "Women's Folly," and yet feel on firm ground in my rejection of it. But rejection also has its pain.

Distance is required, even now.

Of a ghastly yet useful joint illness, which teacheth our pilgrim that her child might be called in this world of trouble the least of her myriad obstacles—

Illness has always been of enormous benefit to me. It might even be said that I have learned little from anything that did not in some way make me sick.

The picture is not an unusual one: a mother and small child, new to the harshness of the New England winter in the worst flu wave of the century. The mother, flat on her back with flu, the child, burning with fever and whooping cough. The mother calls a name someone has given her, a famous pediatrician—whose popular writings reveal him to be sympathetic, witty, something of a feminist, even—to be told curtly that she should not call him at his home at any hour. Furthermore, he does not make house calls of any kind, and all of this is delivered in the coldest possible tone.

Still, since he is the only pediatrician she knows of in this weird place, she drags herself up next morning, when temperatures are below zero and a strong wind is blasting off the river, and takes the child to see him. He is scarcely less chilly in person, but, seeing she is black, makes a couple of liberal comments to put her at her ease. She hates it when his white fingers touch her child.

A not unusual story. But it places mother and child forever on whichever side of society is opposite this man. She, the mother, begins to comprehend on deeper levels a story she wrote years before she had a child, of a black mother, very poor, who, worried to distraction that her child is dying and no doctor will come to save him, turns to an old folk remedy, "strong horse tea." Which is to say, horse urine. The child dies, of course.

Now too the mother begins to see new levels in the stories she is at that moment—dizzy with fever—constructing: Why, she says, slapping her forehead, all History is current; all injustice continues on some level, somewhere in the world. "Progress" affects few. Only revolution can affect many.

It was during this same period that, risen from her bed of pain, her child well again and adapting to the cold, the mother understood that her child, a victim of society as much as she herself—and more of one because as yet she was unable to cross the street without a guiding hand—was in fact the very least of her obstacles in her chosen work. This was brought home to her by the following experience, which, sickening as it was, yet produced in her several desired and ultimately healthful results. One of which was the easy ability to dismiss all people who thought and wrote as if she, herself, did not exist. By "herself" she of course meant multitudes, of which she was at any given time in history a mere representative.

Our young mother had designed a course in black women writers which she proceeded to teach at an upper-class, largely white, women's college (her students were racially mixed). There she shared an office with a white woman feminist scholar who taught poetry and literature. This woman thought black literature consisted predominantly of Nikki Giovanni, whom she had, apparently, once seen inadvertently on TV. Our young mother was appalled. She made a habit of leaving books by Gwendolyn Brooks, Margaret Walker, Toni Morrison, Nella Larsen, Paule Marshall, and Zora Neale Hurston face up on her own desk, which was just behind the white feminist scholar's. For the truly scholarly feminist, she thought, subtlety is enough. She had heard that this scholar was writing a massive study of women's imagination throughout the centuries, and what women's imaginations were better than those displayed on her desk, our mother wondered, what woman's imagination better than her own, for that matter; but she was modest and, as I have said, trusted to subtlety.

Time passed. The scholarly tome was published. Dozens of

imaginative women paraded across its pages. They were all white. Papers of the status quo, like the *Times*, and liberal inquirers like the *New York Review of Books* and the *Village Voice*, and even feminist magazines such as *Ms.* (for which our young mother was later to work) actually reviewed this work with varying degrees of seriousness. Yet to our young mother, the index alone was sufficient proof that the work could not be really serious scholarship, only serious white female chauvinism. And for this she had little time and less patience.

In the prologue to her book, *The Female Imagination*, Patricia Meyer Spacks attempts to explain why her book deals solely with women in the "Anglo-American literary tradition." (She means, of course, *white* women in the Anglo-American literary tradition.) Speaking of the books she has chosen to study, she writes: "Almost all delineate the lives of white middle-class women. Phyllis Chesler has remarked, 'I have no theory to offer of Third World female psychology in America. . . . As a white woman, I'm reluctant and unable to construct theories about experiences I haven't had.' So am I: the books I talk about *describe familiar experience, belong to a familiar cultural setting;* their particular immediacy depends partly on these facts. My bibliography *balances works everyone knows (Jane Eyre, Mid-dlemarch)* with works that should be better known *(The Story of Mary MacLane).* Still, the question remains: Why only these?" (my italics).

Why only these? Because they are white, and middle class, and because, to Spacks, female imagination is only that. Perhaps, however, this *is* the white female imagination, one that is "reluctant *and unable* to construct theories about experiences I haven't had." (Yet Spacks never lived in nineteenth-century Yorkshire, so why theorize about the Brontës?)

It took viewing "The Dinner Party," a feminist statement in art by Judy Chicago, to illuminate the problem. In 1975 when her book, *Through the Flower*, was published, I was astonished, after reading it, to realize she knew nothing of black women painters. Not even that they exist. I was gratified therefore to learn that in "The Dinner Party" there was a place "set," as it were, for black women. The illumination came when I stood in front of it.

All the other plates are creatively imagined vaginas (even the one that looks like a piano and the one that bears a striking resemblance to a head of lettuce: and of course the museum guide flutters about talking of "butterflies"!). The Sojourner Truth plate is the only one in the collection that shows—instead of a vagina—a face. In fact, *three* faces. One, weeping (a truly cliché tear), which "personifies" the black woman's "oppression," and another, screaming (a no less cliché scream), with little ugly pointed teeth, "her heroism," and a third, in gimcracky "African" design, smiling; as if the African woman, pre-American slavery, or even today, had no woes.* (There is of course a case to be made for being "personified" by a face rather than a vagina, but that is not what this show is about.)

It occurred to me that perhaps white women feminists, no less than white women generally, cannot imagine black women have vaginas. Or if they can, where imagination leads them is too far to go.

However, to think of black women as women is impossible if you cannot imagine them with vaginas. Sojourner Truth certainly had a vagina, as note her lament about her children, born of her body, but sold into slavery. Note her comment (straightforward, not bathetic) that when she cried out with a mother's grief, none but Jesus heard her. Surely a vagina has to be ac-

---

*Except for this plate and the choice of Sacajawea (who led Lewis and Clark on their Western expedition) as the subject of the Native American plate, I loved Chicago's art and audacity.

knowledged when one reads these words. (A vagina the color of raspberries and blackberries—or scuppernongs and muscadines —and of that strong, silvery sweetness, with, as well, a sharp flavor of salt.)

And through that vagina, Children.

Perhaps it is the black woman's children, whom the white woman—having more to offer her own children, and certainly not having to offer them slavery or a slave heritage or poverty or hatred, generally speaking: segregated schools, slum neighborhoods, the worst of everything—resents. For they must always make her feel guilty. She fears knowing that black women want the best for their children just as she does. But she also knows black children are to have less in this world so that her children, white children, will have more (in some countries, all).

Better then to deny that the black woman has a vagina. Is capable of motherhood. Is a woman.

So, our mother thought, cradling her baby with one hand, while grading student papers with the other (she found teaching extremely compatible with child care), the forces of the opposition are in focus. Fortunately, she had not once believed that all white women who called themselves feminists were any the less racist, because work after ambitious work issued from the country's presses and, with but a few shining examples (and our mother considered Tillie Olsen's *Silences* the *most* shining), white women feminists revealed themselves as incapable as white and black men of comprehending blackness and feminism in the same body, not to mention within the same imagination. By the time Ellen Moers's book *Literary Women: The Great Writers* was published in 1976—with Lorraine Hansberry used as a token of what was not to be included, even in the future, in women's literature—our mother was well again. Exchanges like the following, which occurred wherever she was invited to lecture, she handled with aplomb:

WHITE STUDENT FEMINIST: "Do you think black women artists should work in the black community?"

OUR MOTHER: "At least for a period in their lives. Perhaps a couple of years, just to give back some of what has been received."

WHITE STUDENT FEMINIST: "But if you say that black women should work in the black community, you are saying that race comes before sex. What about black *feminists?* Should *they* be expected to work in the black community? And if so, isn't this a betrayal of their feminism? Shouldn't they work with women?"

OUR MOTHER: "But of course black people come in both sexes."

(Pause, while largely white audience, with sprinkle of perplexed blacks, ponders this possibility.)

In the preface to Ellen Moers's book, she writes: "Just as we are now trying to make sense of women's literature in the great feminist decade of the 1790s, when Mary Wollstonecraft blazed and died, and when, also, Mme. de Staël came to England and Jane Austen came of age, so the historians of the future will try to order women's literature of the 1960s and 1970s. They will have to consider Sylvia Plath as a woman writer and as a poet; but what will they make of her contemporary compatriot, the playwright Lorraine Hansberry? Born two years before Plath, and dead two years after her in her early thirties, Hansberry was not a suicide but a victim of cancer; she eloquently affirmed life, as Plath brilliantly wooed death. *Historians of the future will undoubtedly be satisfied with the title of Lorraine Hansberry's posthumous volume* (named not by Hansberry, but by her former husband who became executor of her estate), *To Be Young, Gifted, and Black;* and they will talk of her admiration for Thomas Wolfe; but of Sylvia Plath they will have to say "young, gifted, *and a woman*" (my italics).

It is, apparently, inconvenient, if not downright mind straining, for white women scholars to think of black women *as women*, perhaps because "woman" (like "man" among white males) is a name they are claiming for themselves, and themselves alone. Racism decrees that if *they* are now women (years ago they were ladies, but fashions change) then black women must, perforce, be something else. (While they were "ladies," black women could be "women," and so on.)

In any case, Moers expects "historians of the future" to be as dense as those in the past, and at least as white. It doesn't *occur* to her that they might be white women with a revolutionary rather than a reactionary or liberal approach to literature, let alone *black* women. Yet many are bound to be. Those future historians, working-class black and white women, should have no difficulty comprehending: "Lorraine Hansberry—Young, Gifted, Black, Activist, Woman, Eloquent Affirmer of Life"; and "Sylvia Plath—Young, Gifted, White, Nonactivist Woman (in fact, fatally self-centered), Brilliant Wooer of Death."

Of Our Mother's Continued Pilgrimage Toward Truth at the Expense of Vain Pride, or: One More River to Cross

It was a river she did not even know was there. Hence her difficulty in crossing it.

Our mother was glad, during the period of the above revelations—all eventually salutary to her mental health—to have occasion to address a large group of educated and successful black women. She had adequate respect for both education and success, since both were often needed, she thought, to comprehend the pains and anxieties of women who have neither. She spoke praisingly of black herstory; she spoke as she often did, deliberately, of her mother (formerly missing from both literature and history); she spoke of the alarming rise in the suicide rate of young black women all over America. She asked that these black women address themselves to this crisis. Address themselves, in effect, to themselves.

Our mother was halted in mid-speech. She was told she made too much of black herstory. That she should not assume her mother represented poor mothers all over the world (which she did assume) and she was told that those to address were black men; that, though it appeared more black women than men were committing suicide, still everyone knew black women to be the stronger of these two. Those women who committed suicide were merely sick, apparently with an imaginary or in any case a causeless disease. Furthermore, our mother was told: "Our men must be supported in every way, *whatever they do.*" Since so many of "our men" were doing little at the time but denigrating black women (and especially such educated and "successful" black women as those assembled), when they deigned to recognize them at all, and since this denigration and abandonment were direct causes of at least some of the suicides, our mother was alarmed.

However, our mother did not for one moment consider becoming something other than black and female. She was in the condition of twin "afflictions" for life. And, to tell the truth, she rather enjoyed being more difficult things in one lifetime than anybody else. She was, in her own obstacle-crazed way, a snob.

But it was while recuperating from this blow to her complete trust in *all* black women (which was foolish, as all categorical trust is, of course) that she began to understand a simple principle: People do not wish to appear foolish; to avoid the appearance of foolishness, they were willing actually to remain fools. This led directly to a clearer grasp of many black women's attitudes about the women's movement.

They had seen, perhaps earlier than she (she was notorious for her optimism regarding any progressive group effort), that white "feminists" are very often indistinguishable in their behavior from any other white persons in America. She did not blame white *feminists* for the overturned buses of schoolchildren from Baton Rouge to Boston, as many black women did, or for the black schoolchildren beaten and spat upon. But look, just look, at the recent exhibit of women painters at the Brooklyn Museum!

("Are there no black women painters represented here?" one asked a white woman feminist.

"It's a *women's* exhibit!" she replied.)

Of the need for internationalism, alignment with non-Americans, non-Europeans, and nonchauvinists and against male supremacists or white supremacists wherever they exist on the globe, with an appreciation of all white American feminists who know more of nonwhite women's herstory than "And Ain't I a Woman?" by Sojourner Truth

There was never a time when someone spoke of "the women's movement" that our mother thought this referred only to the women's movement in America. When she thought of women moving, she automatically thought of women all over the world. She recognized that to contemplate the women's movement in isolation from the rest of the world would be— given the racism, sexism, elitism, and ignorance of so many American feminists—extremely defeating of solidarity among women, as well as depressing to the most optimistic spirit. Our mother had traveled and had every reason to understand that women's freedom was an idea whose time had come, and that it was an idea sweeping the world.

The women of China "hold up half the sky." They, who once had feet the size of pickles. The women of Cuba, fighting the combined oppression of African and Spanish macho, know that their revolution will be "shit" if they are the ones to do the laundry, dishes, and floors after working all day, side by side in factory and field with their men, "making the revolution." The women of Angola, Mozambique, and Eritrea have picked up the gun and, propped against it, demand their right to fight the enemy within as well as the enemy without. The enemy within is the patriarchal system that has kept women virtual slaves throughout memory.

Our mother understood that in America white women who are truly feminist—for whom racism is inherently an impossibility—are largely outnumbered by *average* American white women for whom racism, inasmuch as it assures white privilege, is an accepted way of life. Naturally, many of these women, to be trendy, will leap to the feminist banner because it is now the place to be seen. What was required of women of color was to learn to distinguish between who was the real feminist and who was not, and to exert energy in feminist collaborations only when there is little risk of wasting it. The rigors of this discernment will inevitably keep throwing women of color back upon themselves, where there is, indeed, so much work, of a feminist nature, to be done. From the stopping of clitoridectomy and "female circumcision" in large parts of Arabia and Africa to the heating of freezing urban tenements in which poor mothers and children are trapped alone to freeze to death. From the encouragement of women artists in Latin America to the founding of feminist publications for women of color in North America. From the stopping of pornography, child slavery, forced prostitution, and molestation of minors in the home and in Times Square to the defense of women beaten and raped each Saturday night the world over, by their husbands.

To the extent that black women dissociate themselves from the women's movement, they abandon their responsibilities to women throughout the world. This is a serious abdication from and misuse of radical black herstorical tradition: Harriet Tubman, Sojourner Truth, Ida B. Wells, and Fannie Lou Hamer would not have liked it. Nor do I.

Before the coming of the Europeans, for hundreds—perhaps thousands—of years, the Ohlones rose before dawn, stood in front of their tule houses, and facing the east shouted words of greeting and encouragement to the rising sun. They shouted and talked to the sun because they believed that the sun was listening to them, that it would heed their advice and pleas. They shouted to the sun because . . . they felt that the sun had "a nature very much like their own."

The Ohlones were very different from us. They had different values, technologies, and ways of seeing the world. These differences are striking and instructive. Yet there is something that lies beyond differences. For as we stretch and strain to look through the various windows into the past, we do not merely see a bygone people hunting, fishing, painting their bodies, and dancing their dances. If we look long enough, if we dwell on their joy, fear, and reverence, we may in the end catch glimpses of almost forgotten aspects of our own selves.
—*Malcolm Margolin,*
THE OHLONE WAY: INDIAN LIFE IN THE SAN
FRANCISCO–MONTEREY BAY AREA

Only you and I can help the sun rise each coming morning
If we don't it may drench itself out in sorrow.
—*Joan Baez,*
album notes to "Farewell Angelina"

From my journal, Jackson, Mississippi, June 15, 1972:
If one lives long enough, nothing will seem very important,

*or the past very painful. (This will seem truer on some days than
on others.)*

*Rebecca said today: "I can cook soup, and eggs, and
windows!"*

*She also said, while drawing letters on the kitchen table: "A,
Ɔ, and O." Then, "Oh-oh, the O is upside down!"*

I feel very little guilt about the amount of time "taken from
my daughter" by my work. I was amazed that she could exist and
I could read a book at the same time. And that she easily learned
that there are other things to enjoy besides myself. Between an
abstracted, harassed adult and an affectionate sitter or neighbor's child who can be encouraged to return a ball, there is no
contest.

There *was* a day when, finally, after five years of writing
Meridian (a book "about" the Civil Rights Movement, feminism, socialism, the shakiness of revolutionaries, and the radical-
ization of saints—the kind of book out of the political sixties that
white feminist scholar Francine du Plessix Gray declared recently in the *New York Times Book Review* did not exist), I felt
a pang.

I wrote this self-pitying poem:

> Now that the book is finished,
> now that I know my characters will live,
> I can love my child again.
> She need sit no longer
> at the back of my mind
> the lonely sucking of her thumb
> a giant stopper in my throat.

But this was as much celebration as anything. After all, the
book *was* finished, the characters *would* live, and of course I'd
loved my daughter all along. As for "a giant stopper in my

throat," perhaps it is the fear of falling silent, *mute*, that writers have from time to time. This fear is a hazard of the work itself, which requires a *severity* toward the self that is often overwhelming in its discomfort, more than it is the existence of one's child, who, anyway, by the age of seven, at the latest, is one's friend, and can be told of the fears one has, that she can, by listening to one, showing one a new dance step, perhaps, sharing a coloring book, or giving one a hug, help allay.

In any case, it is not my child who tells me: I have no femaleness white women must affirm. Not my child who says: I have no rights black men must respect.

It is not my child who has purged my face from history and herstory and left mystory just that, a mystery; my child loves my face and would have it on every page, if she could, as I have loved my own parents' faces above all others, and have refused to let them be denied, or myself to let them go.

Not my child, who in a way *beyond* all this, but really of a piece with it, destroys the planet daily, and has begun on the universe.

We are together, my child and I. Mother and child, yes, but *sisters* really, against whatever denies us all that we are.

For a long time I had this sign, which I constructed myself, deliberately, out of false glitter, over my desk:

> Dear Alice,
> Virginia Woolf had madness;
> George Eliot had ostracism,
> somebody else's husband,
> and did not dare to use
> her own name.
> Jane Austen had no privacy
> and no love life.
> The Brontë sisters never went anywhere

and died young
and dependent on their father.
Zora Hurston (ah!) had no money
and poor health.

You have Rebecca—who is
much more delightful
and less distracting
than any of the calamities
above.

1979

. . . .

BEAUTY: WHEN THE OTHER DANCER

IS THE SELF

It is a bright summer day in 1947. My father, a fat, funny man with beautiful eyes and a subversive wit, is trying to decide which of his eight children he will take with him to the county fair. My mother, of course, will not go. She is knocked out from getting most of us ready: I hold my neck stiff against the pressure of her knuckles as she hastily completes the braiding and then beribboning of my hair.

My father is the driver for the rich old white lady up the road. Her name is Miss Mey. She owns all the land for miles around, as well as the house in which we live. All I remember about her is that she once offered to pay my mother thirty-five cents for cleaning her house, raking up piles of her magnolia leaves, and washing her family's clothes, and that my mother—she of no money, eight children, and a chronic earache—refused it. But I do not think of this in 1947. I am two and a half years old. I want to go everywhere my daddy goes. I am excited at the prospect of riding in a car. Someone has told me fairs are fun. That there is room in the car for only three of us doesn't faze me at all. Whirling happily in my starchy frock, showing off my biscuit-polished patent-leather shoes and lavender socks, tossing my head in a way that makes my ribbons bounce, I stand, hands on hips, before my father. "Take me, Daddy," I say with assurance; "I'm the prettiest!"

Later, it does not surprise me to find myself in Miss Mey's shiny black car, sharing the back seat with the other lucky ones. Does not surprise me that I thoroughly enjoy the fair. At home that night I tell the unlucky ones all I can remember about the merry-go-round, the man who eats live chickens, and the teddy bears, until they say: that's enough, baby Alice. Shut up now, and go to sleep.

It is Easter Sunday, 1950. I am dressed in a green, flocked, scalloped-hem dress (handmade by my adoring sister, Ruth) that has its own smooth satin petticoat and tiny hot-pink roses tucked into each scallop. My shoes, new T-strap patent leather, again highly biscuit-polished. I am six years old and have learned one of the longest Easter speeches to be heard that day, totally unlike the speech I said when I was two: "Easter lilies / pure and white / blossom in / the morning light." When I rise to give my speech I do so on a great wave of love and pride and expectation. People in the church stop rustling their new crinolines. They seem to hold their breath. I can tell they admire my dress, but it is my spirit, bordering on sassiness (womanishness), they secretly applaud.

"That girl's a little *mess*," they whisper to each other, pleased.

Naturally I say my speech without stammer or pause, unlike those who stutter, stammer, or, worst of all, forget. This is before the word "beautiful" exists in people's vocabulary, but "Oh,

isn't she the *cutest* thing!" frequently floats my way. "And got
so much sense!" they gratefully add . . . for which thoughtful
addition I thank them to this day.

It was great fun being cute. But then, one day, it ended.

I am eight years old and a tomboy. I have a cowboy hat, cowboy
boots, checkered shirt and pants, all red. My playmates are my
brothers, two and four years older than I. Their colors are black
and green, the only difference in the way we are dressed. On
Saturday nights we all go to the picture show, even my mother;
Westerns are her favorite kind of movie. Back home, "on the
ranch," we pretend we are Tom Mix, Hopalong Cassidy, Lash
LaRue (we've even named one of our dogs Lash LaRue); we
chase each other for hours rustling cattle, being outlaws, deliver-
ing damsels from distress. Then my parents decide to buy my
brothers guns. These are not "real" guns. They shoot "BBs,"
copper pellets my brothers say will kill birds. Because I am a girl,
I do not get a gun. Instantly I am relegated to the position of
Indian. Now there appears a great distance between us. They
shoot and shoot at everything with their new guns. I try to keep
up with my bow and arrows.

One day while I am standing on top of our makeshift
"garage"—pieces of tin nailed across some poles—holding my
bow and arrow and looking out toward the fields, I feel an
incredible blow in my right eye. I look down just in time to see
my brother lower his gun.

Both brothers rush to my side. My eye stings, and I cover
it with my hand. "If you tell," they say, "we will get a whipping.
You don't want that to happen, do you?" I do not. "Here is a
piece of wire," says the older brother, picking it up from the
roof; "say you stepped on one end of it and the other flew up
and hit you." The pain is beginning to start. "Yes," I say. "Yes,

I will say that is what happened." If I do not say this is what happened, I know my brothers will find ways to make me wish I had. But now I will say anything that gets me to my mother.

Confronted by our parents we stick to the lie agreed upon. They place me on a bench on the porch and I close my left eye while they examine the right. There is a tree growing from underneath the porch that climbs past the railing to the roof. It is the last thing my right eye sees. I watch as its trunk, its branches, and then its leaves are blotted out by the rising blood.

I am in shock. First there is intense fever, which my father tries to break using lily leaves bound around my head. Then there are chills: my mother tries to get me to eat soup. Eventually, I do not know how, my parents learn what has happened. A week after the "accident" they take me to see a doctor. "Why did you wait so long to come?" he asks, looking into my eye and shaking his head. "Eyes are sympathetic," he says. "If one is blind, the other will likely become blind too."

This comment of the doctor's terrifies me. But it is really how I look that bothers me most. Where the BB pellet struck there is a glob of whitish scar tissue, a hideous cataract, on my eye. Now when I stare at people—a favorite pastime, up to now—they will stare back. Not at the "cute" little girl, but at her scar. For six years I do not stare at anyone, because I do not raise my head.

Years later, in the throes of a mid-life crisis, I ask my mother and sister whether I changed after the "accident." "No," they say, puzzled. "What do you mean?"

What do I mean?

I am eight, and, for the first time, doing poorly in school, where I have been something of a whiz since I was four. We have just moved to the place where the "accident" occurred.

We do not know any of the people around us because this is a different county. The only time I see the friends I knew is when we go back to our old church. The new school is the former state penitentiary. It is a large stone building, cold and drafty, crammed to overflowing with boisterous, ill-disciplined children. On the third floor there is a huge circular imprint of some partition that has been torn out.

"What used to be here?" I ask a sullen girl next to me on our way past it to lunch.

"The electric chair," says she.

At night I have nightmares about the electric chair, and about all the people reputedly "fried" in it. I am afraid of the school, where all the students seem to be budding criminals.

"What's the matter with your eye?" they ask, critically.

When I don't answer (I cannot decide whether it was an "accident" or not), they shove me, insist on a fight.

My brother, the one who created the story about the wire, comes to my rescue. But then brags so much about "protecting" me, I become sick.

After months of torture at the school, my parents decide to send me back to our old community, to my old school. I live with my grandparents and the teacher they board. But there is no room for Phoebe, my cat. By the time my grandparents decide there *is* room, and I ask for my cat, she cannot be found. Miss Yarborough, the boarding teacher, takes me under her wing, and begins to teach me to play the piano. But soon she marries an African—a "prince," she says—and is whisked away to his continent.

At my old school there is at least one teacher who loves me. She is the teacher who "knew me before I was born" and bought my first baby clothes. It is she who makes life bearable. It is her presence that finally helps me turn on the one child at the school who continually calls me "one-eyed bitch." One day I simply grab him by his coat and beat him until I am satisfied. It is my teacher who tells me my mother is ill.

My mother is lying in bed in the middle of the day, something I have never seen. She is in too much pain to speak. She has an abscess in her ear. I stand looking down on her, knowing that if she dies, I cannot live. She is being treated with warm oils and hot bricks held against her cheek. Finally a doctor comes. But I must go back to my grandparents' house. The weeks pass but I am hardly aware of it. All I know is that my mother might die, my father is not so jolly, my brothers still have their guns, and I am the one sent away from home.

"You did not change," they say.

Did I imagine the anguish of never looking up?

I am twelve. When relatives come to visit I hide in my room. My cousin Brenda, just my age, whose father works in the post office and whose mother is a nurse, comes to find me. "Hello," she says. And then she asks, looking at my recent school picture, which I did not want taken, and on which the "glob," as I think of it, is clearly visible, "You still can't see out of that eye?"

"No," I say, and flop back on the bed over my book.

That night, as I do almost every night, I abuse my eye. I rant and rave at it, in front of the mirror. I plead with it to clear up before morning. I tell it I hate and despise it. I do not pray for sight. I pray for beauty.

"You did not change," they say.

I am fourteen and baby-sitting for my brother Bill, who lives in Boston. He is my favorite brother and there is a strong bond between us. Understanding my feelings of shame and ugliness he and his wife take me to a local hospital, where the "glob" is removed by a doctor named O. Henry. There is still a small bluish crater where the scar tissue was, but the ugly white stuff is gone. Almost immediately I become a different person from the girl who does not raise her head. Or so I think. Now that I've raised my head I win the boyfriend of my dreams. Now that I've raised my head I have plenty of friends. Now that I've raised my head classwork comes from my lips as faultlessly as Easter speeches did, and I leave high school as valedictorian, most popular student, and *queen*, hardly believing my luck. Ironically, the girl who was voted most beautiful in our class (and was) was later shot twice through the chest by a male companion, using a "real" gun, while she was pregnant. But that's another story in itself. Or is it?

"You did not change," they say.

It is now thirty years since the "accident." A beautiful journalist comes to visit and to interview me. She is going to write a cover story for her magazine that focuses on my latest book. "Decide how you want to look on the cover," she says. "Glamorous, or whatever."

Never mind "glamorous," it is the "whatever" that I hear. Suddenly all I can think of is whether I will get enough sleep the night before the photography session: if I don't, my eye will be tired and wander, as blind eyes will.

At night in bed with my lover I think up reasons why I should not appear on the cover of a magazine. "My meanest critics will say I've sold out," I say. "My family will now realize I write scandalous books."

"But what's the real reason you don't want to do this?" he asks.

"Because in all probability," I say in a rush, "my eye won't be straight."

"It will be straight enough," he says. Then, "Besides, I thought you'd made your peace with that."

And I suddenly remember that I have.

I remember:

I am talking to my brother Jimmy, asking if he remembers anything unusual about the day I was shot. He does not know I consider that day the last time my father, with his sweet home remedy of cool lily leaves, chose me, and that I suffered and raged inside because of this. "Well," he says, "all I remember is standing by the side of the highway with Daddy, trying to flag down a car. A white man stopped, but when Daddy said he needed somebody to take his little girl to the doctor, he drove off."

I remember:

I am in the desert for the first time. I fall totally in love with it. I am so overwhelmed by its beauty, I confront for the first time, consciously, the meaning of the doctor's words years ago: "Eyes are sympathetic. If one is blind, the other will likely become blind too." I realize I have dashed about the world madly, looking at this, looking at that, storing up images against the fading of the light. *But I might have missed seeing the desert!* The shock of that possibility—and gratitude for over twenty-five years of sight—sends me literally to my knees. Poem after poem comes—which is perhaps how poets pray.

ON SIGHT

I am so thankful I have seen
The Desert
And the creatures in the desert
And the desert Itself.

The desert has its own moon
Which I have seen
With my own eye.

There is no flag on it.

Trees of the desert have arms
All of which are always up
That is because the moon is up
The sun is up
Also the sky
The stars
Clouds
None with flags.

If there *were* flags, I doubt
the trees would point.
Would you?

But mostly, I remember this:

I am twenty-seven, and my baby daughter is almost three. Since her birth I have worried about her discovery that her mother's eyes are different from other people's. Will she be embarrassed? I think. What will she say? Every day she watches a television program called "Big Blue Marble." It begins with a picture of the earth as it appears from the moon. It is bluish, a little battered-looking, but full of light, with whitish clouds swirling around it. Every time I see it I weep with love, as if it is a picture of Grandma's house. One day when I am putting Rebecca down for her nap, she suddenly focuses on my eye. Something inside me cringes, gets ready to try to protect myself. All children are cruel about physical differences, I know from experience, and that they don't always mean to be is another matter. I assume Rebecca will be the same.

But no-o-o-o. She studies my face intently as we stand, her inside and me outside her crib. She even holds my face maternally between her dimpled little hands. Then, looking every bit as serious and lawyerlike as her father, she says, as if it may just possibly have slipped my attention: "Mommy, there's a *world* in your eye." (As in, "Don't be alarmed, or do anything crazy.") And then, gently, but with great interest: "Mommy, where did you *get* that world in your eye?"

For the most part, the pain left then. (So what, if my brothers grew up to buy even more powerful pellet guns for their sons and to carry real guns themselves. So what, if a young "Morehouse man" once nearly fell off the steps of Trevor Arnett Library because he thought my eyes were blue.) Crying and laughing I ran to the bathroom, while Rebecca mumbled and sang herself off to sleep. Yes indeed, I realized, looking into the mirror. There *was* a world in my eye. And I saw that it was possible to love it: that in fact, for all it had taught me of shame and anger and inner vision, I *did* love it. Even to see it drifting out of orbit in boredom, or rolling up out of fatigue, not to mention floating back at attention in excitement (bearing witness, a friend has called it), deeply suitable to my personality, and even characteristic of me.

That night I dream I am dancing to Stevie Wonder's song "Always" (the name of the song is really "As," but I hear it as "Always"). As I dance, whirling and joyous, happier than I've ever been in my life, another bright-faced dancer joins me. We dance and kiss each other and hold each other through the night. The other dancer has obviously come through all right, as I have done. She is beautiful, whole and free. And she is also me.

1983

PUBLICATION

ACKNOWLEDGMENTS

(Prepared by Susan Kirschner)

.   .   .   .

"Saving the Life That Is Your Own: The Importance of Models in the Artist's Life": A speech given at the Modern Language Association, San Francisco, 1975. *Women's Center Reid Lectureship: Papers by Alice Walker and June Jordan.* New York: Barnard College Women's Center, 1976.

"The Black Writer and the Southern Experience": *New South,* Fall 1970.

" 'But Yet and Still the Cotton Gin Kept on Working . . .' ": *Black Scholar,* January–February 1970.

"A Talk: Convocation 1972": *Sarah Lawrence Alumni Magazine* (as "A Talk by Alice Walker '65: Convocation 1972"), Summer 1972.

"Beyond the Peacock: The Reconstruction of Flannery O'Connor": *Ms.,* December 1975.

"The Divided Life of Jean Toomer": Review of *The Wayward and the Seeking: A Collection of Writings by Jean Toomer,* edited with an introduction by Darwin T. Turner. *New York Times,* July 13, 1980.

"A Writer Because of, Not in Spite of, Her Children": Review of *Second Class Citizen,* by Buchi Emecheta. *Ms.,* January 1976.

"Gifts of Power: The Writings of Rebecca Jackson": Review of *Gifts of Power: The Writings of Rebecca Jackson (1795–1871), Black Visionary, Shaker Eldress,* edited with an introduction by Jean McMahon Humez. *Black Scholar,* November–December 1981.

"Zora Neale Hurston: A Cautionary Tale and a Partisan View": Foreword to *Zora Neale Hurston: A Literary Biography,* by Robert Hemenway. Urbana: University of Illinois Press, 1977.

"Looking for Zora": *Ms.* (as "In Search of Zora Neale Hurston"), March 1975.

"The Civil Rights Movement: What Good Was It?": *American Scholar,* Autumn 1967.

"The Unglamorous but Worthwhile Duties of the Black Revolutionary Artist, or of the Black Writer Who Simply Works and Writes": *Black Collegian,* 1971.

"The Almost Year": Review of *The Almost Year,* by Florence Engel Randall. *New York Times,* April 11, 1971.

"Choice: A Tribute to Dr. Martin Luther King, Jr.": *South Today* (as "View from Rosehill Cemetery: A Tribute to Dr. Martin Luther King, Jr."), 1973.

"Coretta King: Revisited": *Redbook* (as "The Growing Strength of Coretta King"), September 1971.

"Choosing to Stay at Home: Ten Years after the March on Washington": *New York Times Magazine* (as "Staying Home in Mississippi: Ten Years After the March on Washington"), August 26, 1973.

"Good Morning, Revolution": Review of *Good Morning, Revolution: Uncollected Writings of Social Protest,* by Langston Hughes, edited by Faith Berry. *Black Scholar,* July–August 1976.

"Making the Moves and the Movies We Want": Review of *Countdown at Kusini,* produced by Delta Sigma Theta, directed by Ossie Davis. *Ms.* (as "Black Sorority Bankrolls Action Film"), July 1976.

"Lulls": *Ms.,* January 1977.

"My Father's Country Is the Poor": *New York Times,* March 21, 1977, and *Ms.* ("Secrets of the New Cuba"), September 1977.

"In Search of Our Mothers' Gardens": *Ms.,* May 1974.

"From an Interview": "Alice Walker," in *Interviews with Black Writers,* edited by John O'Brien. New York: Liveright, 1973.

"A Letter to the Editor of *Ms.*": On the founding of the National Black Feminist Organization. *Ms.,* August 1974.

"Breaking Chains and Encouraging Life": Review of *Conditions: Five, the Black Women's Issue,* edited by Lorraine Bethel and Barbara Smith. *Ms.,* April 1980.

"If the Present Looks Like the Past, What Does the Future Look Like?": *Essence Magazine* (as "Embracing the Dark and the Light"), July 1982.

"Looking to the Side, and Back": *Ms.* (as "Other Voices, Other Moods"), February 1979.

Publication Acknowledgments

"Brothers and Sisters": *Ms.* (as "Can I Be My Brother's Sister?" by Straight Pine), October 1975.

"Silver Writes": U.S. Commission on Civil Rights, *Perspectives: The Civil Rights Quarterly,* 1982.

"Only Justice Can Stop a Curse": A speech given at an anti-Nuke rally, Grace Cathedral, San Francisco, 1982. *Mother Jones* (as "Nuclear Exorcism: Beyond Cursing the Day We Were Born"), September–October 1982.

"Nuclear Madness: What You Can Do": Review of *Nuclear Madness: What You Can Do,* by Dr. Helen Caldicott, with the assistance of Nancy Herrington and Nahum Stiskin. *Black Scholar,* Spring 1982.

"Writing *The Color Purple":* San Francisco Chronicle Book Review (as "The Color Purple Didn't Come Easy"), October 10, 1982.

"One Child of One's Own: A Meaningful Digression within the Work(s)": *Ms.,* August 1979.

"Beauty: When the Other Dancer Is the Self": *Ms.,* May 1983.